The Armies of Angkor

BIBLIOTHECA ASIATICA

THE ARMIES OF ANGKOR

Military Structure and Weaponry of the Khmers

Michel Jacq-Hergoualc'h

translated by
Michael Smithies

preface by
Jean Boisselier

Orchid Press

Michel Jacq-Hergoualc'h
THE ARMIES OF ANGKOR: Military Structure and Weaponry of the Khmers

Originally published as: *L'Armament et l'organisation de l'armée Khmère aux XIIe et XIIIe siècles, d'après les bas-reliefs d'Angkor Vat, du Bàyon et de Banteay Chamar*, Presses Universitaires de France, Paris, 1979, in association with the publications of the Musée Guimet, Collection Recherches et Documents d'Art et d'Archéologie, vol. XII.

First English edition, 2007.

ORCHID PRESS
P.O. Box 19,
Yuttitham Post Office,
Bangkok 10907 Thailand
www.orchidbooks.com

ISBN 978-974-524-154-1

Contents

List of Illustrations

Preface

It is well known, thanks to the publication in 1863 of the account of the naturalist Herni Mouhot in the *Tour du Monde*, and, in 1868 of the volume by the anthropologist Adolf Bastian, *Bei den Ruinen von Ancor in Cambodia,* translated into English the following year, that the importance and abundance of early architecture in Cambodia was revealed to the West. The interest of research workers being aroused, the desire to study the monuments to attempt a reconstruction of a history that was almost entirely forgotten was soon translated into a scientific undertaking, the scope of which is often underestimated. In this enterprise the study of the narrative bas-reliefs, able to provide important information, could not be overlooked. All the authors were quick to describe at greater or lesser length the reliefs at Angkor Wat, while the huge ensembles of the Bayon and Banteay Chmar were to remain for many years difficult to study.

General de Beylié only indicated, in 1907, 'the amusing precision' with which 'the bas-reliefs of the Bayon and Angkor Wat' showed festivals and retinues, but Lunet de Lajonquière, four years later, indicated a new research objective. Describing the bas-reliefs of the galleries of Angkor Wat in the third volume of his *Inventaire descriptif des monuments du Cambodge*, and leaving to specialists—particularly Georges Coedès—the task of pinpointing the various identifications, he mapped out what was in effect a complete work programme: 'To summarize,…[the reliefs], from the artistic viewpoint, have an indisputable decorative value rather than a real command of draughtsmanship. They constitute all the same a veritable mine of information concerning dress and armaments, and help in the reconstitution of a past which has completely disappeared, when they are studied as meticulously as they deserve from this particular viewpoint.' Though with undoubted excessive severity in discussing Khmer statuary, which he continually berated at 'mediocre', he appreciated the exceptional interest of this huge narrative ensemble. His comments, though, found little immediate resonance. Ten years later Georges Groslier, in his *Recherches sur les Cambodgiens*, followed up the programme outlined by Lunet de Lajonquière, in a first and only response. In his encyclopedic work, which (in spite of the imperfections noted by Louis Finot in his review in *BEFEO*, XXII and which is inevitably dated) has not been overtaken, the subject studied here by Michel Jacq-Hergoualc'h was approached for the first time. The whole of chapter 9 in the *Recherches* was given over to arms, and the Khmer army is considered at great or lesser length in chapters 5, on dress, 6, on hair styles, 8, on the honorific symbols, and 10, on vehicles and harnesses.

Although in his conclusion Finot emphasized 'the *Recherches sur les Cambodgiens* constitutes one of the most important works to have appeared about Khmer archaeology, and future work needed to note carefully the facts assembled and the ingenious ideas pullullating therein', G. Groslier has hardly any rival up to now. The long-withheld consideration of the Khmer armies is a fact all the more surprising since there are few arts anywhere in the world which portrayed their armies in such vast and complex ensembles, going into the smallest details with great precision. This rich and clearly defined theme has, though, over more than fifty years, inspired only a few studies of limited scope. Without attempting a real inventory, we should mention 'The ballistae of the Bayon' by Paul Mus (*BEFEO*, XXIX), and 'Boats in Khmer bas-reliefs' by Paul Paris (*BEFEO*, XLI). Add to this the *Etude Cambodigenne* XXVII of G. Coedès, 'Some suggestions about how to interpret the bas-reliefs at Banteay Chmar, and the outer gallery of the Bayon' (*BEFEO*, XXXII), of only indirect interest to the subject, and with these we have covered all the works hitherto devoted to a theme which undoubtedly deserved closer attention.

The records used only come from three temples and deal with a relatively brief period of roughly a century. But these records are so plentiful and constitute such a coherent whole, in spite of the changes occurring between the reign of Sūryavarman II (1113–*c*.1150), to which Angkor Wat belongs, and that of Jayavarman VII (1181–*c*.1218), during which the Bayon and Banteay Chmar were built, that they fully justify the overview given them by Michel Jacq-Hergoualc'h. The introduction states the scope: a study deliberately limited to iconographic research and to temples illustrating armies. This was the wisest course. It would have been dangerous to attempt to integrate into a homogenous whole the descriptive information which this pediment or that lintel might at long intervals provide. It would have been still more dangerous to extend the conclusions reached here to the entire history of ancient Cambodia; moreover the changes which took place between the reigns of Sūryavarman II and Jayavarman VII point to the foolhardiness of any extrapolation. But precisely defined aims do not imply a denial of relevant information, and Jacq-Hergoualc'h has sought in local epigraphy and non-local sources useful precisions, while spurning risky hypotheses which might have resulted from interpretative initiatives. If we do not give to the infantry as important a role as does the author, because the chronicles, over many centuries, constantly emphasize the role played by war elephants, and if we believe that the crowds accompanying the soldiers were very different from those who, over long periods and in Europe too, camped alongside the troops, we still concur with his restrained conclusions and the importance of his observation that the Khmer army was not merely organized following an Indian model.

Some will be surprised that Jacq-Hergoualc'h limited himself to the analysis of the figures and apparently overlooked the suggestions of Georges Coedès. But, apart from the fact that the proposed method only concerned Banteay Chmar and the Bayon and served no purpose for Angkor Wat, it would have run the risk of pushing the study into the realm of conjecture. The problem of identification of certain scenes which Coedès had in mind does not exist just in the terms of an illustrated chronicle. The illustrations of the legends of the gods and the epics draw on everyday reality, and these bas-reliefs were certainly conceived from the same viewpoint as the Bayeux tapestry. The contrast apparently pitting Khmers against Chams are rather the struggles between the Gods and the Asuras—as epigraphic records indicate—where the land of Kambu is 'similar to the Heavens' and the Chams become the Asuras. Such considerations would inevitably have led Jacq-Hergoualc'h far from his subject and he was right to exclude them.

As it was conceived, this study required extensive illustrations. The scenes selected, entirely drawn by the author himself, are certainly those corresponding best to his intentions. The best photographs could not replace linear representations for this type of work. The very complete documentation assembled here is not just an indispensable adjunct to Jacq-Hergoualc'h's research, it also constitutes a source of intrinsic interest. The clarity of line and the elimination of superfluous details make the figures stand out. The way in which essential themes are pinpointed on the often confusing photographic documents assists the reader without giving way to any personal interpretation. The didactic intentions and probity that have guided Jacq-Hergoualc'h in this conception and realization result in a work of superior standard and constitute an indisputable research tool. It will undoubtedly occupy an important position in the Musée Guimet's collection of research documents covering art and archaeology.

Jean Boisselier

Abbreviations relating to the drawings

gal.: gallery	N: north	Doc.: document
ext.: external	S: south	pl.: plate
int.: internal	E: east	
	W: west	

Bibliographic abbreviations

BEFEO	*Bulletin de l'Ecole Française d'Extrême Orient*
BCAI	*Bulletin de la Commission Archéologique de l'Indochine*
JA	*Journal Asiatque*
Zhou	*Zhou Daguan*

We would like to express our sincere thanks to the EFEO which kindly agreed to the reproduction of a number of documents in its possession.

Notice concerning the captions to the drawings

All the drawings illustrate scenes or specific details in the bas-reliefs, but when the scenes or details are found in many identical or similar examples, no precise location is indicated other than the monument and incidentally the gallery.

However, when the scenes or details are unusual, unique, or rarely met with, a precise location is given with references to the photographs of the only complete series to date [1979] illustrating the ensemble of the bas-reliefs of each of the three monuments. These are:

G. Coedès, *Le temple d'Angkor Vat*, 3ᵉ part, *La galérie des bas-reliefs*, Paris, 1932.
> The numbers are found at the bottom of the photographs. The references take the form 'Coedes 540'.

H. Dufour and G. Carpeaux, *Le Bayon d'Angkor Thom*, Paris, 1913.
> The photograph numbers to note are those at the top right of each plate. The photographs of the bas-reliefs of the outer gallery have an additional number placed immediately beneath these (one plate is formed by joining several photographs). The plates of the bas-reliefs of the two galleries form a separate series. The references take the form 'Dufour pl.78'.

General de Beylié, Photographs of bas-reliefs of Banteay Chmar, 1913.
> Deposited in the photographic library of the Musée Guimet. The numbers of the photographs are found on the reverse. The references take the form 'Beylié 34'.

Introduction

Our intention in this study is to shed some light on what was the royal army and its weapons in the reigns of two great Khmer kings, Sūryavarman II (1113-1150?), and Jayavarman VII (1181-1218?), that is, over a period of roughly one hundred years, covering most of the twelfth and the beginning of the thirteenth centuries.

These limits, which are only approximate, are prescribed by the source materials used as the basis of this study, the bas-reliefs of three temples: Angkor Wat, the bas-reliefs of which are justly famous, the Bayon, and Banteay Chmar, also amply decorated with narrative scenes. These two last monuments have been treated in the same individual style and illustrate similar or identical subjects which can be attributed to the reign of Jayavarman VII.

The study we are embarking on will therefore be essentially iconographic. We shall not overlook the information found in various foreign written sources and Khmer epigraphic texts dealing with the army, but these sources and texts are rather meager.

We also wish to react against an excessive tendency among authors who have considered the matter of wanting the scenes found in the bas-reliefs essentially to illustrate the state of the Khmer army as they wished to reconstitute it from these sources and texts, howsoever limited they are.

The problem is more critical, as will be seen when we analyse the bas-reliefs and note that there are many dissimilarities between the organization of the Khmer army and the Indian army which has traditionally been held to be its model.

In the first part, we shall examine, analyse and select bas-reliefs of the three monuments. After this selection, we shall study the weapons of the different constituents of the army which we propose to identify.

In the second part, we shall study in turn these different elements, trying to establish their importance in the army in relation to each other.

Lastly, in the third part, we shall examine the crowds of people surrounding the army proper and which make it all the more picturesque.

PART I

1. The documents

Jean Filliozat, in an article in *Arts Asiatiques*[1] defines the Khmer temple-mountain in these terms: 'The Khmer temples, or at least the "temple mountains", are above all an earthly representation in physical form of the residence of the sovereign of the gods, of whom the human king is likewise a terrestrial representation. They are cosmic-political monuments, so to say, rather than merely religious.'

In this respect, Angkor Wat is the temple-mountain of Sūryavarman II, the monument through which, after his difficult accession to the throne, he sought to affirm his authority, as some of his predecessors had done, like Yaśovarman I, the founder of Angkor with Phnom Bakheng, Rājendravarman II with Pre Rup, Jāyaviravarman with Ta Keo, or Udāyadityavarman with the Baphuon. But this ambitious new ruler wanted a mountain, namely Angkor Wat, surpassing in splendour all previous examples.[2]

We cite Groslier's description. The temple measures 187 x 215 m at the base and the central tower rises more than 65 m above the causeway. Structurally it forms a pyramid with three superimposed terraces. Each level is girded by a gallery, marked by towers at the corners and pavilions on the axial stairways. The central tower of the third level is linked to these pavilions by galleries on pillars and is divided into a cloister with four courtyards. On the western side of the first level the three stairways give onto as many galleries with pillars leading to the corresponding steps of the second level, which is thus reached under cover. The flights of stairs are also protected by interlocking superimposed vaults whose successive pediments are admirably outlined against the sky.[3]

B-P. Groslier considered that the temple was begun about 1122 and was almost complete when the king died about 1150. Unlike the earlier temple-mountains, which were all Śaivite, it is unusually consecrated to Viṣṇu. Equally unusually, it faces west, a distinction probably linked to the fact that the god Viṣṇu governs this cardinal point. But the west is also the cardinal point of the dead, and there are valid reasons for thinking that the monument served as the funerary temple of Sūryavarman II whose posthumous name is Paramaviṣṇuloka.[4]

The decoration of the temple is entirely given over to glorifying Viṣṇu. The principal element of this decoration is the ensemble of bas-reliefs covering the base wall of the surrounding gallery of the first level. This gallery marked the limit of the area open to the public; the bas-reliefs 2 m high show legendary and historic scenes. Eight cover the portions of the walls between the axial stairways and the corner pavilions. As the monument is rectangular and the north-south axis is shifted to the east, the sections

---

[1] J. Filliozat, 'Le temple de Hari dans le Harivarṣa', *Art Asiatiques*, Paris, 1961, VIII/3, p. 196.

[2] B-P. Groslier, *Indochine, carrefour des arts*, Paris (A. Michel), 1960, pp. 156-7.

[3] Op. cit., p. 153.

[4] G. Coedès, *Pour mieux comprendre Angkor*, Paris (A. Maisonneuve), 2nd ed. 1947, ch. IV, and M. Giteau, *Histoire d'Angkor*, Paris, 1974.

of the walls are of unequal length. Given this, the longest are those corresponding to the west wings of the north and south galleries; they measure no less than 98 m.

The scenes with figures, though mostly military, could not also be used in our study, as will be seen by a rapid overview of their subjects.

For this, we shall follow the path suggested by the temple facing west, and by the disposition of the subjects: we shall pass through the monument keeping it to our left side. This is the *prasavya*, the circumambulation used in funeral rites.[5]

(a) W gal., S wing, the battle of Kurukṣetra, in which the god Viṣṇu is shown in the form of his avatar Kṛiṣṇa acting as an equerry to Pāṇḍava Arjuna, and possessing four arms. The two armies march to confront each other, the Kaurava on the north, and they meet in the middle of the panel. Space is used to the best effect, and the frays are chaotic. But, above all, this is an illustration of an episode in the Indian epic, the *Mahābhārata*, which was known in Cambodia, though less so than its counterpart, the *Rāmāyaṇa*. In this the sculptors tried to be faithful to the text, which gives precise details about the arms used in the battle, particularly by the leaders. Constrained by this text, details are shown which may not correspond to anything in Cambodia at the time the carvings were made. Some other things, like details concerning clothes, were exaggerated and enriched. This bas-relief needs to be studied with reservations.

(b) In the S gal., W wing appears a bas-relief entirely relevant to our study. It consists of a procession taken to be 'historic' according to stone inscriptions which identify the principal participants in the scene. The most important person in the bas-relief is none other than the king, indicated by his posthumous name, Paramaviṣṇuloka. At first he is seen seated in the middle of armed officials, while on the level immediately below passes a procession of court ladies reclining in their palanquins or litters, surrounded by their attendants.

But the scene changes very quickly and, from two levels one above the other, a single level shows a military procession in which Paramaviṣṇuloka appears seated on his elephant, the quintessential royal mount. Other elephants precede and follow him, surrounded by the infantry and preceded by cavalry.

No doubt this shows a march past of the royal armies going into battle. The presence of the holy fire, the royal high priest and other priests indicates that a religious ceremony is taking place, the importance of which is not revealed, but which must have been particularly important and solemn during the king's reign.

The troops shown cannot be considered to compromise the entire army; only its most important elements are to be seen; the leaders, of course, mounted on elephants, officers on horseback, and the elite corps of the infantry.

In spite of these reservations, which we made *a priori*, the bas-relief is of exceptional interest as indicating a certain state of the Khmer army in the reign of Sūryavarman II.

---

[5] For a description of the bas-reliefs, see G. Coedès, 'Les bas-reliefs d'Angkor Vat', BCAI, Paris, 1911, p. 170 and L. Finot, *Le temple d'Angkor Vat*, pt 3, *La galerie des bas-reliefs*, Bangkok 1995 (Paris, 1932).

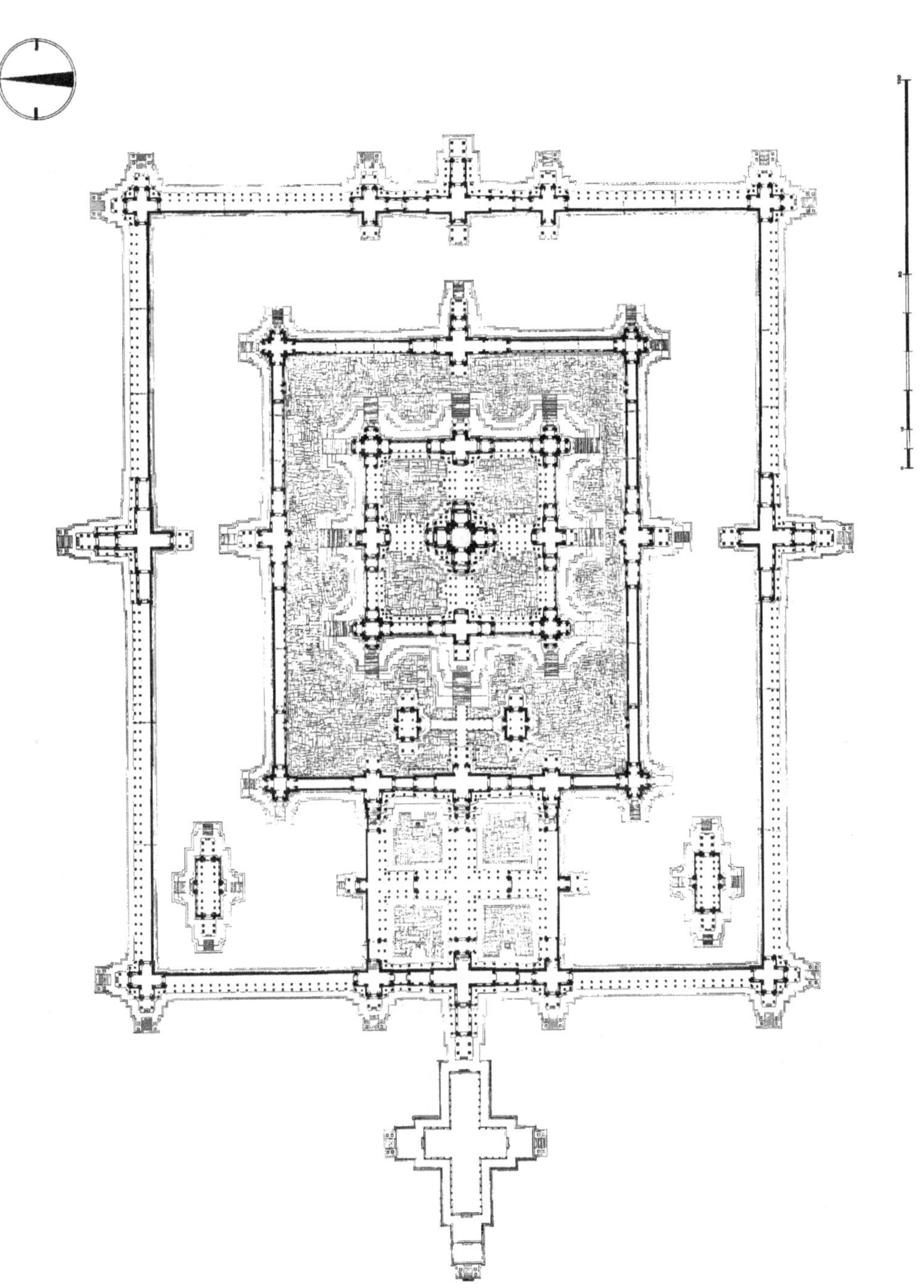

Fig. 1. Angkor Wat. Plan of the whole temple.
Pl. III in G. Nafilyan, Angkor Vat, Description graphique du temple.

(c)   Also in the S gallery, but the E wing, are scenes of no interest to this study, the bas-reliefs of the 'Heavens and Hells' also called the 'Judgment of the Dead': Yama, assisted by Dharma and Citragupta, secure this judgment which distributes humans among the 32 hells and 37 heavens shown.

(d)   The S wing of the E gallery is given over to illustrating the 'Churning of the Sea of Milk' by the Deva and the Asura.

This bas-relief is exceptional but is only of interest in this study in examining, with some difficulty, the vehicles of the Deva and the Asura, shown at either end.

(e)   The following bas-relief shows in the E gal., N wing 'Viṣṇu Caturbhuja mounted on the Garuḍa fighting the Dānava' and next N gal., E wing, the 'Victory of Kṛiṣṇa over Bāṇa'.

These are martial scenes, but, for the same reasons already given concerning the battle of Kurukṣetra, we could only have considered them with the same reservations, and in fact have to disregard them completely, since they are very late works. G. Coedès, pinpointed the date[6] they were carved very precisely, since they were produced between 8 September 1546 and 27 February 1564. Apart from being late works, they are also extremely clumsy.

(f)   The last two bas-reliefs form part of the ensemble produced in the twelfth century. One is in the N gal., W wing, of the 'Battle between the Deva and the Daitya' in which Viṣṇu mounted on the Garuḍa occupies pride of place in the centre, with the Asura Kālanemi as antagonist. The other, in the W gal., N wing, evokes one of the most famous episodes in the *Rāmāyaṇa*, the battle for Laṅkā, in which Rāma, an incarnation of Viṣṇu, overcomes the *rākṣaṣa* Rāvaṇa in combat.

We shall use these two bas-reliefs with the same reservations as those indicated for the battle of Kurukṣetra.

It therefore seems, in this rapid survey of the bas-reliefs of Angkor Wat, that our study will be centred around the so-called 'historic' bas-reliefs of the S gal., W wing. The others, of the same period, show non-military subjects, or illustrate epic scenes in conditions and with details which must have been far removed from twelfth century Cambodian military reality.

The other two ensembles of bas-reliefs we shall investigate are in the temples of the Bayon and Banteay Chmar, both dating from the reign of Jayavarman VII.

The Bayon occupies the geometric centre of the city of Angkor Thom which this king ordered to be built. We shall use the description of J. Commaille.[7]

Overall, the temple comprises two concentric galleries separated by a surrounding courtyard and a terrace surmounted by a conical tower, 40 m high (Fig. 2).

'The first gallery, called the outer gallery, measures rather more than 600 m in circumference. The N and S sides are 161 m long and the E and W sides 142 m. It is raised on a foundation some 2 m high, with a veranda all around, and a solid wall

---

[6] G. Coedès, 'La date d'exécution des deux bas-reliefs tardifs d'Angkor Vat', *JA*, 1962, pp. 235-43.

[7] H. Dufour, *Le Bayon d'Angkor Thom, Notice archéologique* (description by J. Commaille), Paris, 1913.

6

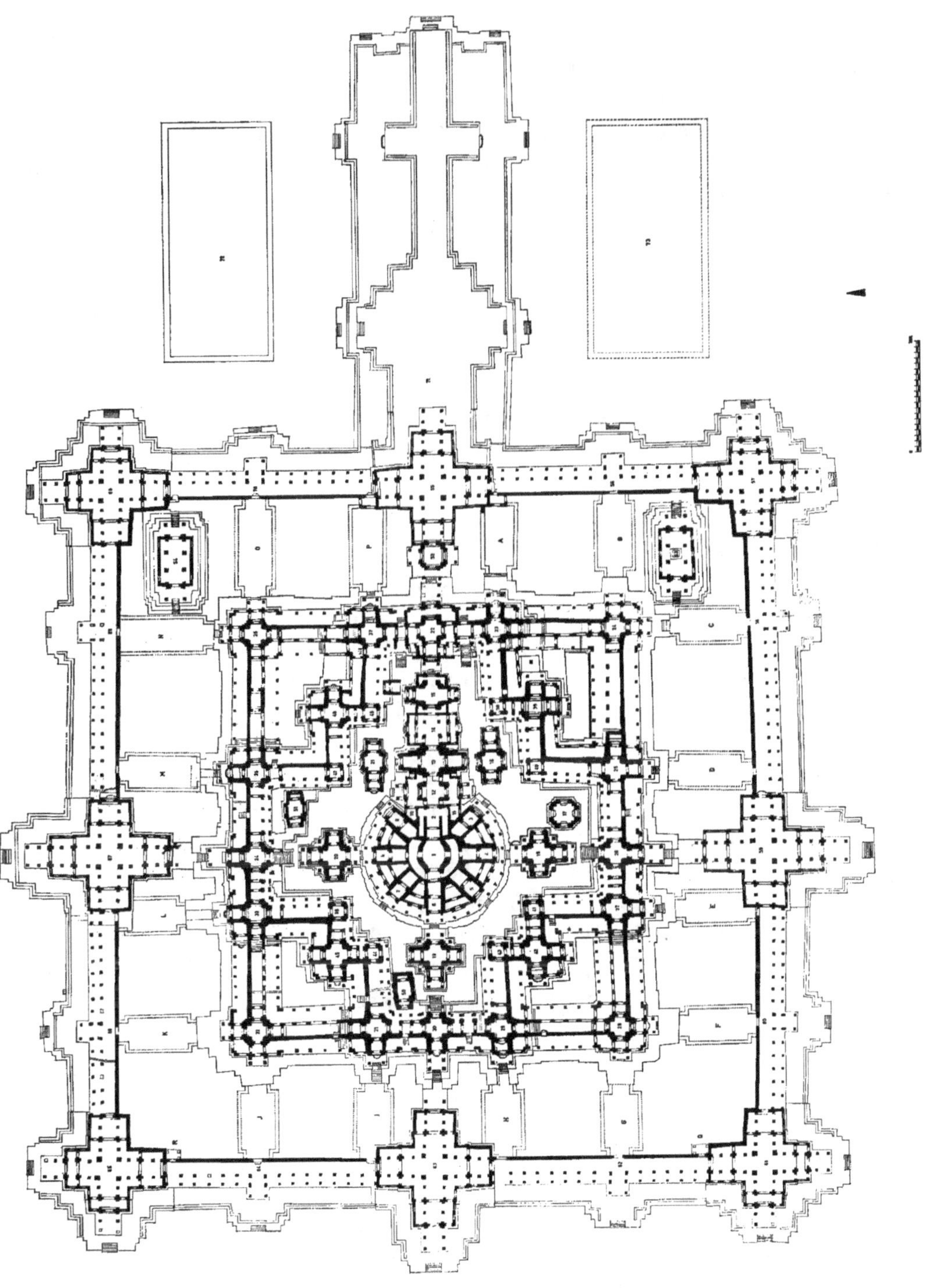

Fig. 2. The Bayon. General plan of the temple.
Pl. III in J. Dumarçay and B-P. Groslier, Le Bayon, Histoire architecturale du temple.

(carved with bas-reliefs), a row of tall pillars and another row of smaller pillars', which upheld, in the Cambodian fashion, a corbelled vault and half-vault. Both of these have collapsed, exposing the walls with the bas-reliefs.

In the middle of each side of the outer gallery are porticoes leading to cruciform vestibules and the surrounding courtyard. Secondary doorways led to the wall with the bas-reliefs; they were walled up later.

The corners of the outer gallery are occupied by pavilions without any access to the interior of the temple.

The surrounding courtyard is paved. It is almost completely broken in the middle of each side by the extension of access vestibules from the outer gallery and the projection of the entrances of the first level. Two symmetrical structures are located in the NE and SE corners of the courtyard.

The second gallery measures 87 m E-W and 76 m N-S, and is more complicated than the first. It is cut into two lengthwise: one part gives on to the surrounding courtyard, and the part of the wall facing this direction is decorated with bas-reliefs. The other part, comprising the gallery proper and the internal veranda, faces four courtyards introduced into the inner corners of the second level.

Communication between the two parts is effected by means of small doorways at the level of the vestibules and at the level of the wings of the E and W facades.

The central mass has a cruciform foundation (64 m E-W, 53 m N-S) with numerous redentations forming the terrace which is reached by five stairways (two being on the E side). The circular mass of the central shrine is built on the upper terrace, and has twelve radiating cells.

The holiest shrine, the chapels, the secondary structures, and the pavilions were all topped by a tower in which four colossal faces were carved, each facing one of the cardinal points.

The ensemble, which is confusing to the uninitiated, is perfectly comprehensible as a symbol, but of what, specialists remain divided.

J. Boisselier, in an unpublished document, sees here the material form on earth of one of the 'Assemblies of Good Order' (*Sudhammā Sabhā*) formed by the gods, and mentioned by J. Filliozat as appearing in Pali texts, in an article on the symbolism of Phnom Bakheng.[8]

These assemblies are held once a year. The thirty-three gods examine the good and just among men, and all the gods coming under Indra, Śiva and Viṣṇu included. They are assembled in the presence of Indra, seated in a position of total reflection. Then Brahmā appears, and seeing them completely calm, gets up and proclaims the excellence of the Buddha in a voice with eight characteristics which correspond to the eight faces probably topping the central tower, the summit of which has disappeared. Then he subdivides himself into thirty-three shapes to give the impression to each god that that he is there for him alone. Then he regains his single form and sits on the same seat as Indra, presiding jointly with him over the assembly to glorify the Buddha and his Law.

---

[8] J. Filliozat, 'Le symbolism du Phnom Bakheng', *BEFEO*, XLIV, 1954, pt 2, pp. 527-54.

From this viewpoint, the significance of the bas-reliefs has to be reconsidered. Coedès[9] considered those in the outer gallery scenes from daily life, compositions illustrating historic events. According to Boisselier, they evoke the struggle of the Asura against the heaven of the thirty-three gods paralleled by contemporary events in the reign of Jayavarman VII and represented with the means then available, like artists of the Middle Ages representing the Holy Family in costumes of the artists' period.

One can also consider the battle scenes occurring all though the gallery as evidence concerning the army and weapons at the end of the twelfth and the beginning of the thirteenth centuries. This testimony is essential with its scenes of figures which, even when barely outlined, are full of vitality and realism.

The bas-reliefs of the inner gallery are comparatively mediocre and uneven. They illustrate legends of the gods (Viṣṇu, Śiva, etc) invited to the meeting of the thirty-three gods, but as a lower level. Given this reference to the world of the gods, we need, as at Angkor Wat, to study them with reservations, because here too the excesses are numerous in the evocation of the military achievements of these divinities.

The temple of Banteay Chmar,[10] the bas-reliefs of which will also be examined, is a long way from Angkor, being in the NW of Cambodia in a completely deprived area which is also very difficult to reach (Fig. 3).

---

[9] G. Coedès, Le Bayon d'Angkor Thom, op. cit. (Notice archéologique, les bas-reliefs.)

[10] We use here the elements of his description in the article by G. Groslier which appeared in *L'Illustration* on 3 April 1937.

Fig. 3. Location of Banteay Chmar in relation to Angkor.

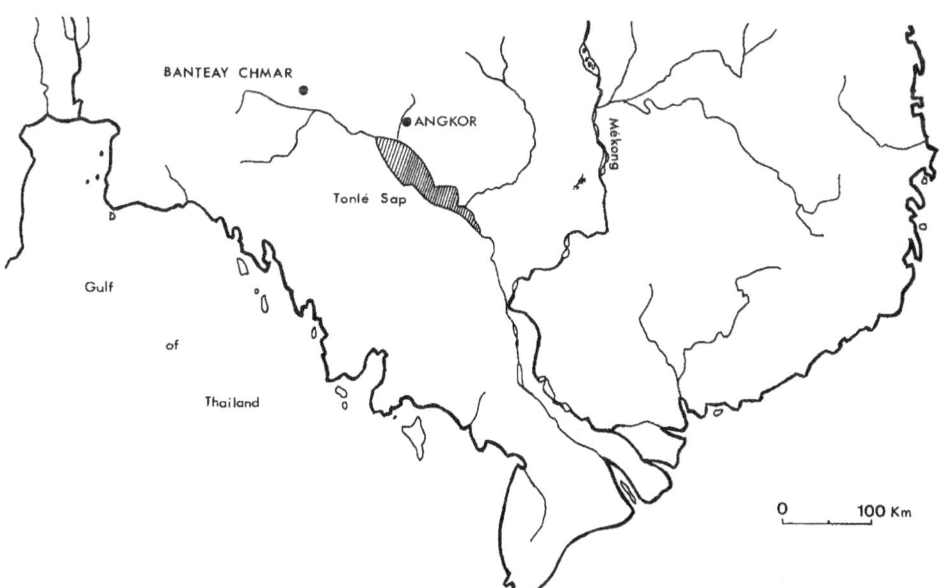

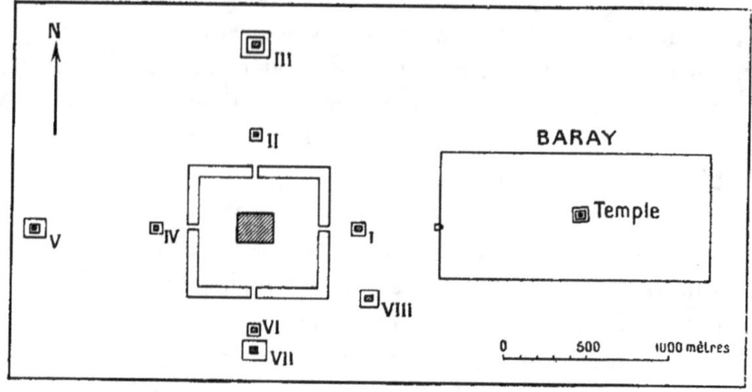

Fig. 4. Banteay Chmar and its region.
Plan taken from the article by G. Groslier, 'Banteay Chmar, ville
ancienne du Cambodge', L'Illustration, 3 April 1937.

In its period of glory, it was integrated, like many Khmer constructions, in a complex ensemble (Fig. 4).

To the E of the monument, which is indicated by a hatched rectangle in Fig. 4, was a huge reservoir (*baray*) with a temple in the middle; around the temple proper moats 65 m long and 3.6 m deep were constructed with four axial approach paths lined with guardians upholding, as at Angkor Thom, a *nāga* forming a parapet. Lastly eight satellite shrines aligned on the N-S and E-W axes, with one exception, were constructed around the main temple.

The monument has an extremely complex plan (Fig. 5).

The reconstitution and description given by G. Groslier are sullied by errors but few other descriptions concerning the little-known temple exist.

'A surrounding gallery completely encloses the temple in a rectangle 250 X 190 m from each axis. It comprises a vault raised on the walls and pillars, flanked by a half vault. On the outer side of the wall are found bas-reliefs showing, over a total surface of 1,090 sq m, historic and legendary scenes... the elucidation of which is not yet complete... The workmanship and the mostly war-like subjects link the bas-reliefs directly to those at the Bayon. Each façade is interrupted on the axes by a monumental triple entrance with three towers...

A rectangular gallery surrounds a courtyard having itself a cross-shaped gallery. This well-proportioned structure was originally detached from the temple proper. To the N and S are two pools, with steps leading down to the water, and two annexes raised to 4 m high foundations...

The main temple structure, the grid-iron of galleries, is subdivided into three complexes from E to W, like three complete temples strung together. Each has its central sanctuary tower preceded by its own antechamber, its corner towers and its monumental N and S doorways. They are both joined and independent. As one proceeds W, the composition becomes more compact, the towers and the antechambers are multiplied until the main shrine is reached. Then comes an open courtyard containing

10

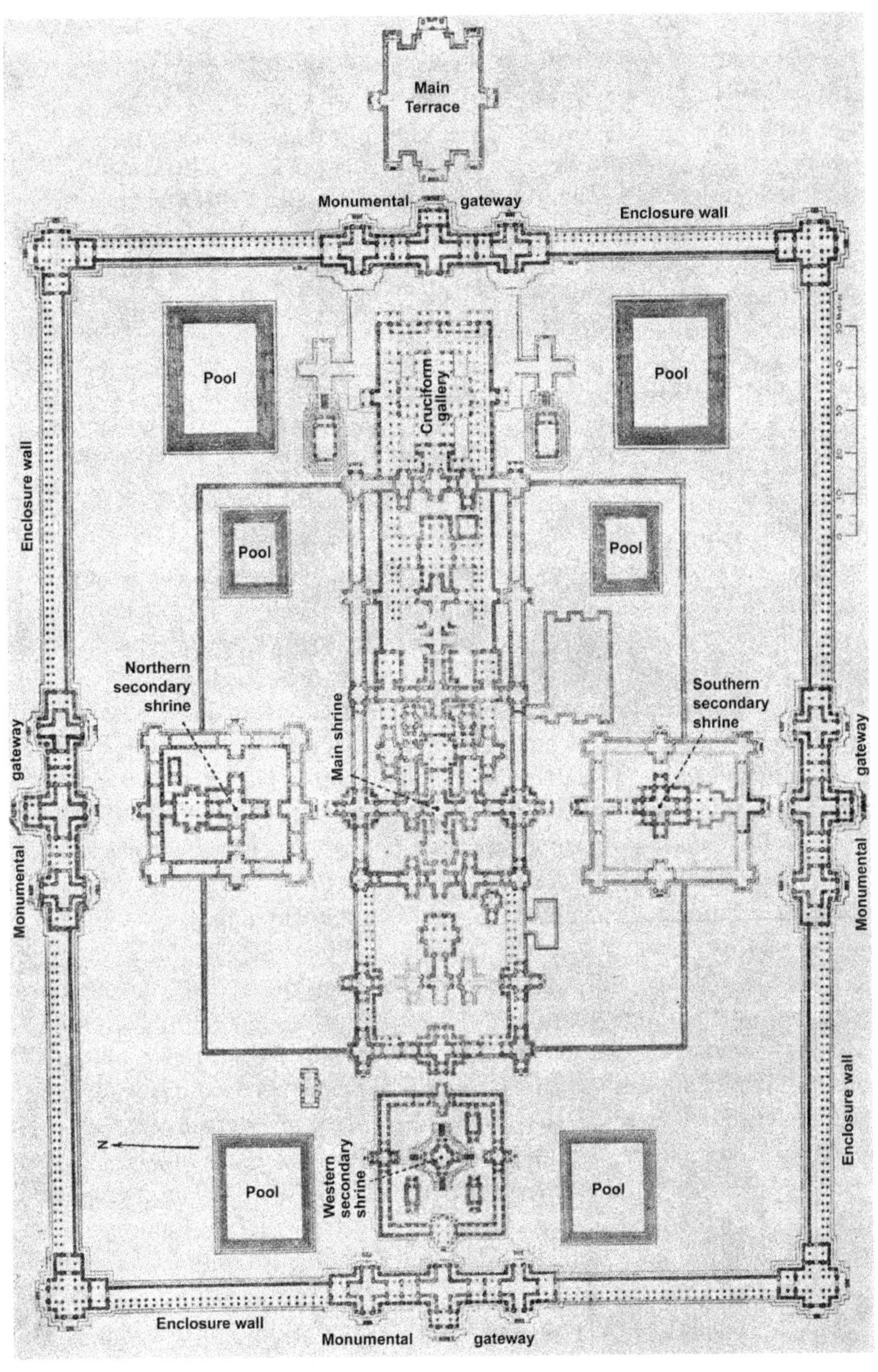

Fig. 5. Banteay Chmar. Overall plan of the temple.
Taken from the article by G. Groslier, 'Banteay Chmar, ville ancienne du Cambodge',
L'Illustration, *3 April 1937.*

just three isolated towers…'; the towers decorated with four faces and comprise four successive levels.

The main building is 170 m long E-W and some 40 m N-S. It is flanked on the N and the S by 'two symmetrical groups similar to each other and independent of the rest. These are two shrines topped with towers with faces surrounded by a rectangular gallery.

Lastly, on the W side, is an ensemble like the two others [to the E]. But the central shrine here is raised on a 3.7 m high foundation, with mouldings and redentations, flanked by four stairways…'

The plan is thus unusual and the meaning of the monument poses problems we shall not begin to discuss here. We have only given this brief description to situate the bas-reliefs in the overall schema of the temple. To see them it is not necessary to go inside the temple.

The basis of this study, then, is these three ensembles of bas-reliefs in their architectural setting. We have indicated some of their limitations concerning our subject, essentially the descriptive excesses of some groupings, the late period of some others, or their irrelevance to this study, like the 'Judgment of the Dead' and the 'Churning of the Sea of Milk' at Angkor Wat, to which can be added many scenes on the bas-reliefs at the Bayon and Banteay Chmar dealing with civil or religious life.

But before beginning this study proper, we need to draw attention to other difficulties inherent in these bas-reliefs. Khmer sculptors had a feeling for relating an anecdote and for mordant details. There were also able sometimes to create very harmonious compositions. But they were never concerned about a need to provide, for example, completely faithful details of harnesses or weapons. Often one is astonished at the lack of comprehension they showed over an insignificant details which seems obvious to us Westerners but which apparently was not so important in their eyes.

It was also very difficult for us to constitute all the equipment of a war elephant or a chariot. As for the uniforms sported by the warriors, we have not attempted to explain the way they were worn.

The last difficulty presented by this study lies in the mediocre nature of the photographic documentation available to us. The most recent complete publication of the bas-reliefs of Angkor Wat dates from 1932 and the photographs are very unclear. The only edition of the bas-reliefs of the Bayon date from 1913, and the photographs of them by C. Carpeaux were taken between 1901 and 1904. They are, though, clearer than those of Angkor Wat. The photographs of the bas-reliefs of Banteay Chmar are those of General de Beylié and his assistant, who took them in 1913. They are found in the photographic library of the Musée Guimet and are very difficult to study.

This photographic library, which has several advantages, only has recent photographs of fragments of the bas-reliefs, so it as often impossible to specify in the detail one would have liked this particular weapon or that piece of military equipment.

With these reservations, we shall begin our study, which will be conducted in the spirit which governed our earlier research.

2. The army and its technological sophistication

When viewing the series of photographs of these bas-reliefs, focusing on the martial aspect, one gains at first sight an impression of considerable confusion: armies march past, others confront each other in heated battles, and one wonders how to set about organizing these combatants into a coherent whole.

The complete or partial elimination of certain bas-reliefs, for reasons already given, makes the task a little easier. Then, after following the warriors in their marches and interminable conflicts, one can realize that they did not go into battle without some organization.

The fact that most of them were on foot suggests at first that the infantry in the Khmer army was very important. Furthermore, one is struck by the number of elephants guided by mahouts on the backs of which are combatants. The elephants and the infantry form such a cohesive block that when they are on the march, the elephants' feet cannot be seen.

The cavalry can be seen too, as a group or isolated, along with chariots drawn by horses and filled with armed warriors.

Given the cultural ties linking Cambodia with India, it is tempting, given these initial observations, to see the Khmer army as a model of the Indian army such as is presented traditionally on the strength of Indian texts, the most famous of which is the *Arthaśāstra*,[1] an ancient Indian political treatise, attributed diverse dates, but which is traditionally attributed to Kauṭilya, a famous minister who helped Candragupta, the first Maurya ruler, to gain power.

One of the fifteen 'books' of this work, the tenth, is devoted to war, and allusions are found in the others. It is stated that the army consists of four types of fighting units: the infantry, the cavalry, the chariots, and the elephants.

All the authors who have considered the matter in relation to India refer to this work, the more readily as allusions to these four corps in the army are often found in other texts, notably in the two great Indian epics, the *Rāmāyaṇa* and the *Mahābhārata*.

Let us consider, too, *a priori*, that the Khmer army comprised four corps. It will be possible to modify this affirmation by the detailed study we shall make based on the evidence of the bas-reliefs.

But before doing this, to avoid repetition, we shall consider what was the technological level of this army, that is, what were the weapons it used, for, of course, contrary to what Zhou Daguan[2] affirms, namely that the use of bows, arrows, ballistae, and breastplates was unknown to the Khmer army, it did in fact have these arms.

It is true that, in the bas-reliefs of the three monuments, they are not found in great variety. Those reliefs showing the least, and also chronologically the earliest, at Angkor

---

[1] R.P. Kangle, *The Kauṭilya Arthaśāstra*, Bombay, 1960-1965, 3 vols.

[2] Zhou (Tcheou Ta-kouan), *Mémoires sur les coutumes du Cambodge au XIIIe siècle*, translated by P. Pelliot, *BEFEO*, 1902, p. 175, and a new version with an unfinished commentary, Paris, Maisonneuve, 1951 (*Oeuvres posthumes*, vol. III).

Wat, only show the most banal hand-held weapons, namely:
a)   lances and bucklers, which go together
b)   bows and arrows, sometimes with quivers
c)   sabres of various sizes
d)   typical axes, or *phkā'ks*
e)   knives and cutlasses of all sizes

This is not a great number. One should add a defensive weapon frequently found in this monument, the breastplate.

On the reliefs of the Bayon and Banteay Chmar, the same range of hand-held weapons can be found, except that swords make their appearance and bows become more infrequent, especially among the infantry. Moreover breastplates are extremely rare and knives and cutlasses are also seen less frequently.

On the other hand, new arms appear: ballista, war weapons of various kinds mounted on the backs of elephants or on wheels, to which can be added a curious machine to be found at the Bayon.

In the intervening period separating the construction of these three monuments, a minor revolution seems to have occurred in armaments, with the appearance of war weapons hitherto unknown, and showing a certain evolution in ordinary types of arms. But let us examine things more closely to understand the matter better.

Let us begin with the bucklers, which, with lances, are the most common arms.

The buckler is above all a defensive weapon. At Angkor Wat it is mostly the infantry bearing lances which have bucklers, but some commanders on elephants or horseback also sometimes sport them.

They come in two kinds (Fig. 6): round (roundels), or in an elongated form like the shields of our horsemen in the Middle Ages. Most, though, are round, and these will be described first.

They have little decoration. They generally have (Fig. 6.1 & 2) an edge apparently made of stiff hairs (but perhaps this is a guide of the carvers). The outer edge may be set off with beading. The surface is decorated with concentric circles, marked in the centre, or arranged on the circumference; sometimes both motifs are combined.

More unusual, though rarer, are the bucklers entirely covered with the grimacing face of an imaginary animal (Fig. 6.3).

The infantry in general hold the bucklers close to their chests; only the cavalry and the combatants mounted on elephants brandish them, and when this occurs we can see the inner side of the bucklers (Fig. 6.4), with a double strap or haft fixed between two parallel transversal battens. The foot soldier, after placing his forearm under the first strap, grasps the second with his clenched fingers. The buckler was thus securely kept in position. The inner side was decorated at the edges in the same fashion as the outer side, the rest of the surface often sporting small flowers.

These bucklers were easy to handle because they were small (their diameter could not have been more than 0.40 or 0.50 m), but they could only have given modest protection in battle.

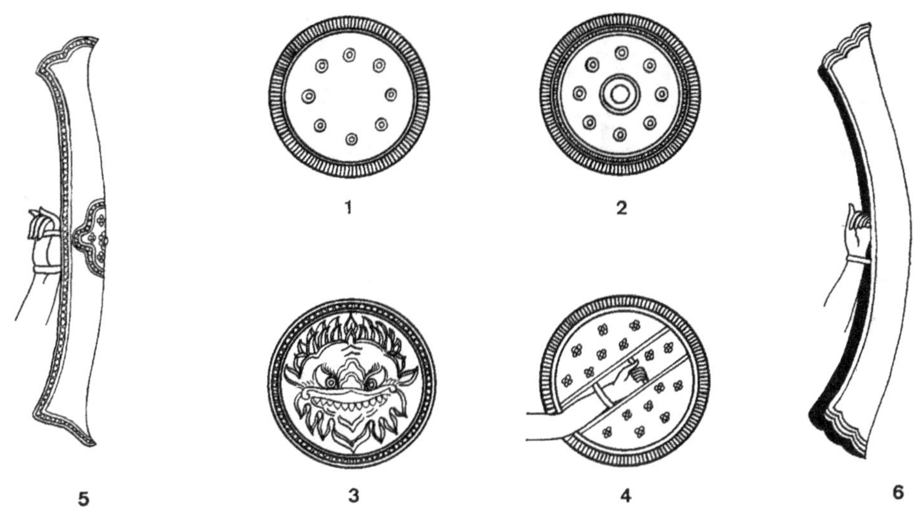

Fig. 6. Bucklers at Angkor Wat, S gal., W wing.

Some foot soldiers have long bucklers, but given the tight marching order shown in the so-called 'historic' bas-relief, these bucklers are always hidden by the backs of warriors coming after them, and only the tips can be seen. But these appear to be very similar to the long bucklers sported by some soldiers mounted on elephants. They are shown in profile (Fig. 6.5 & 6); this profile is curved, sometimes markedly so, and the ends are slightly tipped outwards.

The edges are decorated with beading or grooves; the centre sometimes had a decorative motif. Several examples show the means by which the long bucklers are attached to the warrior's arm, similar to the round bucklers. We could find no example of a long buckler viewed from the front.

Their size appears variable, from 80 cm to 1 m, to a height close to two-thirds of the warrior carrying it. They probably offered fairly efficient protection to the warrior given their size and enveloping shape. This can best be seen at the Bayon and Banteay Chmar.

In the two monuments, the buckler is very common, carried by all the infantry except the few who carry a bow. The cavalry also frequently have one. Only the officers mounted on elephants do not have them, though their mahouts sometimes sport one.

As at Angkor Wat, they are round or long, both forms being found. Depending on the panels of the bas-reliefs, one shape or the other may predominate, but very often they are mixed.

The round bucklers are completely identical to those at Angkor Wat in their structure and dimensions, but their decoration seems possibly more varied. Some examples are shown here (Fig. 7).

(a) Type 1 has no ornamentation, but a kind of flange at the edge and concentric circles at the centre, perhaps representing a boss. This is the most frequently represented

15

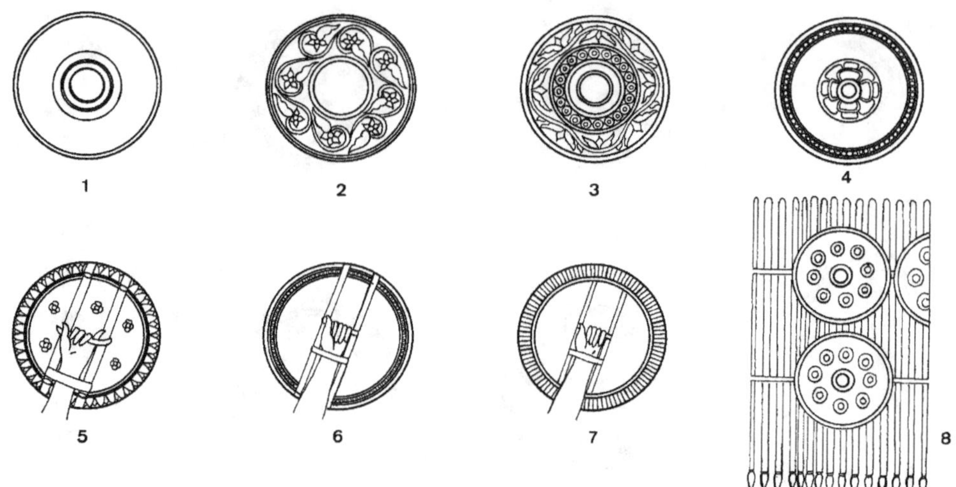

Fig. 7. Round bucklers, Bayon, Banteay Chmar.
S gal., W wing of Banteay Chmar. Beylié 43 for drawing #8.

type on the two monuments. Unusually, though, the outer surface can be more richly decorated.

(b) Type 2 shows a garland and flowers forming a rosette.

(c) Type 3 links the garland to a line of beading.

(d) Type 4 is decorated at the edge with beading and a rosette of the lotus flower.

(e) Types 5, 6, and 7 show that the bucklers were held and decorated on the inside in the same way as at Angkor Wat.

At Banteay Chmar (Fig. 7.8) can be seen the curious details of a line of lances stuck in the ground, the shafts linked by two parallel straps, to which roundels are fixed, decorated in a similar way to some bucklers at Angkor Wat (Fig. 6.2). This is an example of the striking details to be found in the bas-reliefs of these two monuments.

The long bucklers (Fig. 8), unlike those at Angkor Wat, are extremely varied in shape, though these differences only concern the extremities. They are almost always shown in profile but, most unusually, they are illustrated twice from the front, once at the Bayon (Fig. 8.11) and once at Banteay Chmar (Fig. 8.12), in scenes of similar inspiration, to the right of two naval battles. They are lined up in a row, and behind them only the heads of the warriors who are holding them can be seen. Their shape seems distinctly triangular; only the upper end assumes a vaguely triangular shape in which there is a head of a grimacing monster. The marked convexity evident in all the bucklers shown in profile is not suggested here. Perhaps these are unusual variations.

Let us return to the bucklers shown in profile (Fig. 8.1-10)

The simplest shapes (1, 2, and 3) have no special decoration, except for beading or a border on the circumference; in all cases there is a slight curve outwards at the ends. The central part of these three types is also slightly outwardly curved.

With types 4, 5, and 6 the form evolves somewhat. The central part of the buckler, from being convex, tends to become concave. The top and bottom become more

16

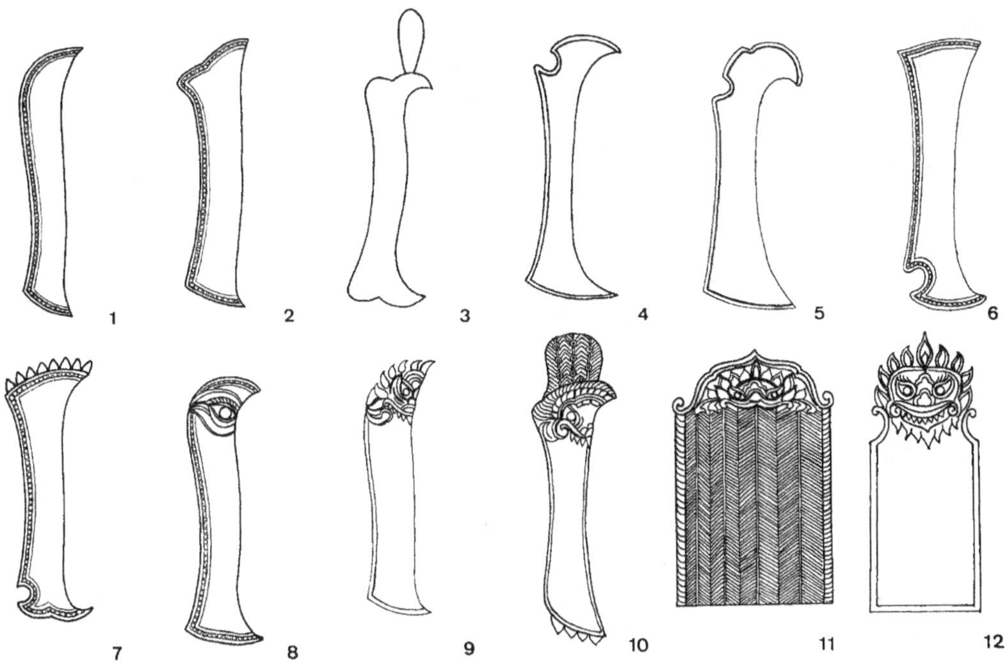

Fig. 8. Round bucklers, Bayon, Banteay Chmar.
Ext. gal., S side, E wing of Bayon. Dufour 43 for drawing #11; E gal.,S wing of Banteay Chmar. Beylié 65 for drawing #12.

pointed, and one of them has a deep notch at the bottom (type 6). The decoration is plain and limited to beading or a border as in the previous examples.

These six types of bucklers are mostly found in the hands of the foot soldiers. Sometimes, but rarely, the same types have some decoration. These are

(a) scalloping on the upper edge of the type of buckler 7, similar to type 6.

(b) a motif of a menacing eye on type 8 which is similar to type 1.

(c) a monster's head on the upper part of type 9 which in profile is similar in general form to type 1.

(d) a monster's head is also found on the upper edge, and scalloping on the lower edge found in type 10, similar in general form to type 1.

Overall, the bucklers are generally similar, apart from some details concerning the decoration, the notches, and the relative convexity or concavity.

Their size, as at Angkor Wat, is extremely varied. They are often very long and almost as high as the person carrying them. Some, though, either in reality or because of faulty draughtsmanship, are smaller and not half the height of the foot soldier. The average seems to be two-thirds of his height. The warrior could always extend his buckler with an addition (Fig. 8.3) which might have been made of finely-woven rattan, as is clearly seen in type 10.

The bucklers with these extensions, all in one line, constitute for the warriors at Banteay Chmar a kind of rampart behind which they defend themselves from assaults of the enemy. In this scene they appear to be quite tall, but one has to take into consideration the sculptor's limitations. We have simplified the illustration in our sketch (Fig. 9.1) for greater clarity, but the battle seems ferocious. The bowmen are lined up in two rows on each side, and the dead are numerous.

The straps of the bucklers on the foot soldiers' arms never appear in the examples found in the bas-reliefs of these two monuments.

They should, though, be the same in their design as those shown at Angkor Wat. Though lacking this detail, a foot soldier at the Bayon, taking part in a march which was probably tiring, can be seen carrying this type of buckler in a non-combatant position (Fig. 9.2); while drinking from his gourd, he holds his buckler horizontally under his arm with the help of a long strap passing over his shoulder.

To complete this study of bucklers, we need to ask a few questions about the materials used in their making. Type 11 at the Bayon, seen from the front, seems for the most part made of woven rattan, but this material can only be seen elsewhere in the extensions sometimes found on the long bucklers. Perhaps this is only an oversight of the sculptors, and some bucklers were probably made of rattan coated with resin, like 'some contemporary Moi bucklers'.[3] However, the decoration of the upper part of the model was certainly made of some other material; it might be anything—carved wood, thin leaves of pressed metal, or something else.

Before describing the whole range of Khmer arms, it would seem logical, after examining the bucklers, to speak about another defensive arm, the breastplate. This underwent some evolution in the period being considered.

At Angkor Wat, breastplates were mostly worn by soldiers of higher rank riding elephants or horses rather than by the foot soldiers. The breastplates have a special wrap-around form which encloses the chest, leaving the arms and the neck free.

---

[3] G. Groslier, *Recherches sur les Cambodgiens*, Paris, 1921, p. 93.

Fig. 9.1. Long bucklers forming a rampart.
Banteay Chamr, S gal., W wing, lower level. Beylié 41.

Fig. 9.2. Special way of carrying a buckler.
Bayon, ext. gal., S side, E wing, lower level. Dufour 38.

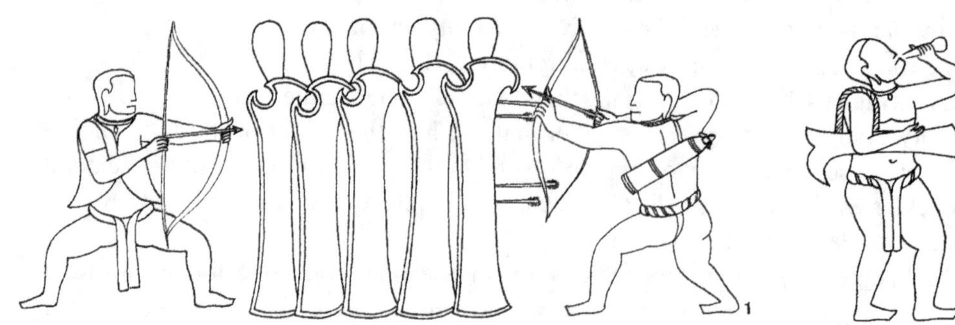

At the Bayon and Banteay Chmar, breastplates are very rarely seen (at the Bayon it would be difficult to find as many as a dozen). From the few examples worn by the foot soldiers or warriors on elephants, they consist of two quadrangular plates, one at the front and one at the back, kept in position by straps and epaulettes, while other types seem to continue the forms found at Angkor Wat with some modifications. Let us examine them now in detail.

At Angkor Wat, the breastplate is like a cylinder that the soldier slips on (Fig. 10.4: two cut-out parts are introduced for the arms). The whole seems to be held in position by straps which pass over the shoulders and are crossed over in front, but it is not very easy to understand how, with this arrangements, the straps could keep anything in position (Figs 10.1-3).

At the height of the left shoulder, the edge of the breastplate has a slit, which in most examples is filled with a strap, allowing one or two cutlasses to be held there (Fig. 10.1). Some soldiers (Fig. 10.1) supplement one or two further cutlasses, held in position at the crossing of the straps in front.

Most of the breastplates show on their lower edge a flounce which is not, in spite of its appearance, to be confused with the end of the short jacket the soldiers wear underneath: this is always confirmed by its short sleeves. The flounce must correspond to a kind of internal padding to the breastplate, which is decorated with beading, rows of leaves and lotus flower motifs on the upper, middle, and lower parts (Fig. 10.1-4).

The nature of the small free-standing piece of cloth sometimes shown at the level of the right shoulder and which was probably attached at the back is not readily explicable (Fig. 10.1). It could be nothing more than a decorative element introduced and tied to the breastplate.

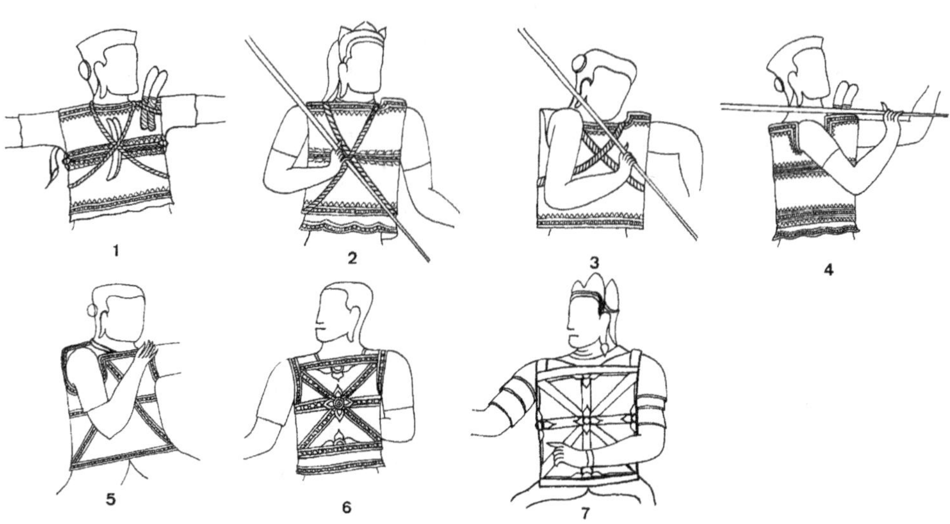

Fig. 10. Breastplates.
Angkor Wat, S gal., W wing, 1-4. Bayon, Banteay Chmar, 5-7,
ext. gal., E side, N wing, Dufour 118 for #6, and ext. gal. W side, N wing. Dufour 62 for #7.

At the Bayon and Banteay Chmar some types, almost unique, seem to be inspired by the breastplates of Angkor Wat and cover the entire chest (Fig. 10.5 & 6), but there is no trace of the slit or cutlass on the left shoulder, and the straps have given way to decorative bands crossing at diagonals, adding to the decoration of the edged and the middle part. There is a new and significant detail: the epaulettes seem to hold the breastplate in position better than the straps as Angkor Wat.

Other types (Fig. 10.7), equally unusual, seem to be formed, as we have said, by two quadrangular plaques, one at the front and the other at the back, and held in position by epaulettes. Here too the straps found at Angkor Wat are replaced by decorative diagonal bands. But distinguishing these types at the Bayon and Banteay Chmar is often difficult and we cannot be dogmatic. What may appear as a new type may perhaps be no more than sculptors' clumsiness.

We need to emphasize in particular their greater rarity in those two monuments in comparison to Angkor Wat. Lastly we need to consider the materials used in their making.

In an article on the 'art and military constructions of the Vietnamese', Louis Besacier,[4] investigating the origins of the Annamese army, became interested in the excavations at the site of Dongson. The results of this work were published by V. Goloubew[5] and in particular dealt with an important collection of arms dated to the Bronze Age, from the middle or the second half of the first century BC (the most recent research on the Dongson culture[6] dates it much earlier, to about 500–258 BC). Bezacier hypothesizes, without foundation in our opinion, that (1941, 324) 'the men in this army probably wore a skin breastplate—buffalo skin no doubt—of Chinese origin, whose method of fabrication is given by the *Zhou-li*, a Chinese work of the twelfth century before our era. This breastplate consisted of two parts, corresponding to the two parts of the body above and below the loins…' Besides this Chinese-influenced breastplate, Bezacier adds that 'another probably existed, made of tree bark similar to those used by the Dyak in Borneo' which he links rather too readily to the types seen in Angkor Wat and the Bayon. 'This tree-bark breastplate is also found among the Lolo in North Tonkin and especially in Yunnan,' he adds. Stressing the more tangible discoveries of Dongson, he then invokes (1941, 325) the remains of bronze breastplates found there: small square plaques which when put together must have formed a kind of armour for the officers. He adds 'This kind of protection cannot date from before the Han, as it is not mentioned in *Zhou-li*.'

From all this, we can bear in mind that Khmer breastplates, as we have described them, possibly used the materials cited by Bezacier: buffalo skins, tree bark, and bronze, even if this metal was replaced by iron at the period we are discussing, if indeed metal was used in making this armour. This was the case of the king, if we can

---

[4] L. Bezacier, 'L'art et les constructions militaires annamites', *Bulletin des Amis du Vieux Hué*, 28th year, no. 4, Oct-Dec 1941, pp.323-49.

[5] V. Goloubew, 'L'Age du Bronze au Tonkin et dans le Nord-Annam', *BEFEO*, XXIX, 1929, pp. 1-46.

[6] Nguyen Phuc Long , 'Les nouvelles recherches archéologiques au Vietnam', *Arts Asiatiques*, XXXI, Paris, 1975.

believe Zhou Daguan,[7] who in the thirteenth century AD indicates that the sovereign 'had his body clad in iron, so that even knives and arrows, striking his body, could not harm him'.

After having considered defensive weapons, we can now turn to offensive arms. The most common was without doubt the lance. It can be seen in the hands of warriors of all ranks, but mostly it was used by the foot soldiers. When on the move, it was carried on the right shoulder, with the tip facing down, and the left hand holding a buckler.

The types varied little during the period which interests us. At Angkor Wat (Fig. 11.1-3) the lances generally have a very long shaft which, in the upper part, is sometimes decorated with a piece of material tied to it, which perhaps improved its trajectory when thrown (Fig. 11.1). The pommel ends in a kind of bulb, with the tip more or less emphasized. The shape of the lance head varies little. It is most often round, pointed, and tapering, or of a flattened triangular form.

At the Bayon and Banteay Chmar, the lances seem very rough. They have generally no pommel and their lance heads, of variable length, are oval, pointed or even triangular (Fig. 11.4 & 5).

Given the height of the warriors, the length of these lances is remarkable. They are clearly longer at Angkor Wat, where they often come to two metres; in the other two monuments their length is almost always less than the height of the foot soldier, and probably measured about 1.25 m.

After the lance, the bow, at least at Angkor Wat, is the most common weapon. At the Bayon and Banteay Chmar, the pre-eminence of the lance is such that all other arms become curiosities, but the warriors on elephants use the bow fairly frequently.

---

[7] Zhou, *Mémoires…* op. cit., p. 176.

Fig. 11. Lances.
Angkor Wat 1, 2, 3. Bayon, Banteay Chmar 4, 5.

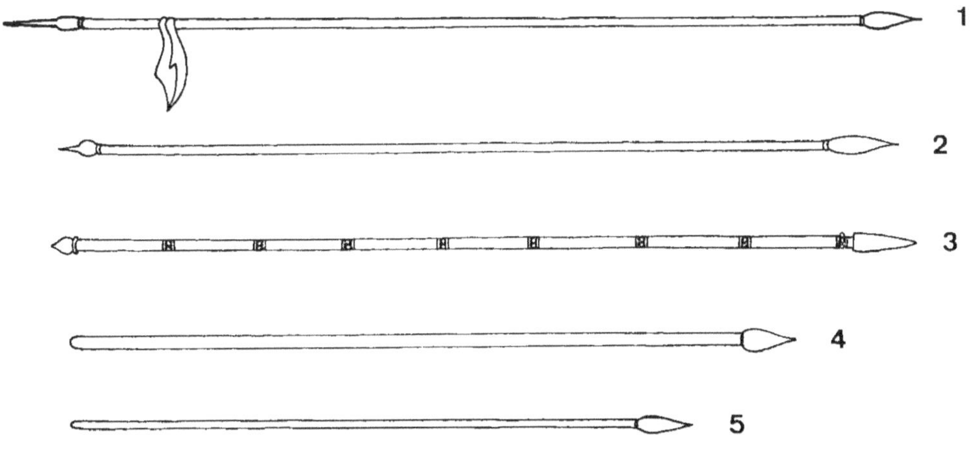

At Angkor Wat then, the bow alternates among the infantry with the lance, without assuming the importance of the latter. In addition, a certain number of warriors on elephants also have a bow (Fig. 12.1-3).

These bows seem to be very big since, in the 'historic march past' of the S gallery, W wing, their upper end considerably extends above the heads of the foot soldiers.

The bows are simple in form, with a single curve, and the ends are turned up. The ends can be entirely plain, or decorated with stylized or realistic motifs.

The way the bow string is held in position is not clearly shown. The foot soldiers hold the bow in the left hand, vertically, and carry a bundle of arrows in their right hand (Fig. 62E, F)

None of them is shown with a quiver. The arrows (Fig. 12.6), as far as one can tell, seem to have a separate lozenge-shaped iron tip and most have, at the other end, symmetrically arranged vanes.

None of the foot soldiers is shown using his bow; only those on elephants can so be seen. They hold their bows almost vertically, the left arm taut, the thumb on the inside of the flexed bow, the end of the arrow being upheld by the hand, with the right hand drawing back the bowstring as far as the chin, and holding the base of the arrow. Their bows seem to be not so big as those of the foot soldiers.

On the howdahs of these warriors one sometimes sees quivers full of arrows, their arrow heads being inside the cylindrical quivers which are often decorated with beaded bands (Fig. 12.8 & 9).

At the Bayon and Banteay Chmar the bow becomes, as we have said, much rarer (Fig. 12.4) The shape is always simple and it lacks decoration at the ends. The bows are also smaller than at Angkor Wat. At the Bayon some quivers can be seen in the elephant howdahs, or hung on the outside as at Banteay Chmar (Fig. 12.10). They are

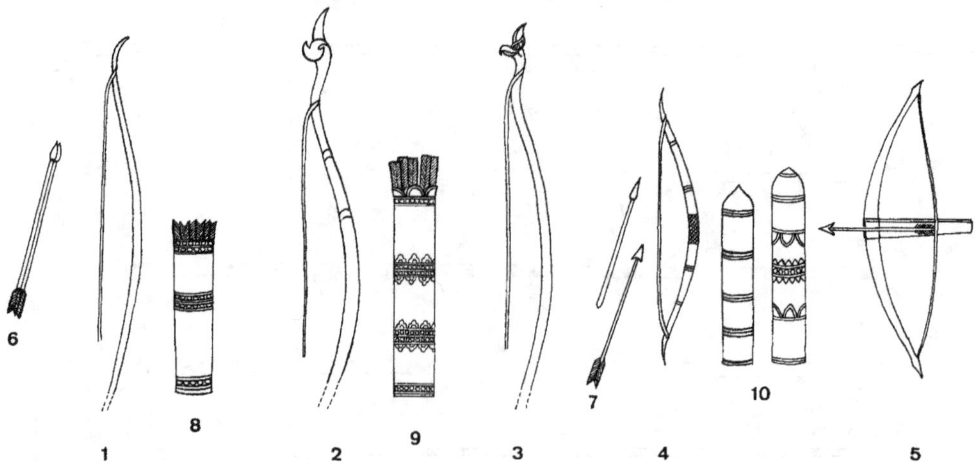

Fig. 12. Bows, arbalests, arrows, and quivers.
Angkor Wat 1, 2, 3, 6, 8, 9. Bayon, Banteay Chmar 4, 5, 7, 10.
Ext. gal. W side, N wing. Dufour 59 for #5.

cylindrical in shape, decorated with beading, and nearly always with a semi-spherical cover. The arrows are poorly reproduced and often seem very primitive (Fig. 12.7).

A very few foot soldiers with a bow also carry a quiver on their backs; we have already seen one example (Fig. 9.1). Others, equally rare, carry an arbalest. This weapon (Fig. 12.5), very poorly reproduced, seems to consist of a bow and a grooved guide. G. Groslier[8] suggests it is a wooden trigger holding taught the bowstring; this seems possible but we have found nothing like it.

Other offensive weapons are sabres and swords. At Angkor Wat the sabres are fairly often found in the hands of the warriors mounted on elephants, and especially among the cavalry (Fig. 13.1-4). They have a curved or straight blade; if curved it is but slightly so. It widens to the end which terminates obliquely. The hilt can be seen in the 'historic' march past.

At the Bayon and Banteay Chmar swords are, however, to be found, but never in use in battle, and only very rarely on the hands of important chiefs, like that on a chariot at Banteay Chmar, for example, who carries one, the blade unsheathed and brandished (Fig. 37). Usually they are seen on military parades, in the howdahs of some elephants, occasionally close by a bow and quiver, while the warrior brandishes a lance.

The swords (Fig. 13.5 & 6) seem short and pointed, with diversely decorated hilts. On howdahs they are sheathed; the sheaths are decorated, and bare blades are only seen in the hands of heroes or the gods. The sword, therefore, seems to mark rank rather than be an arm used in combat.

In these two monuments one can also see some sabres (Fig. 13.7-9) but they are rare, whereas they were common in Angkor Wat. It is difficult to study them as they belong to foot soldiers seen from the rear or to figures that are barely outlined (Ext. Gal, W side, N wing, and N side, W wing in the Bayon). The hilt is never visible, but one sees just the top of the blade; the forms appear less developed than at Angkor Wat.Before

---

[8] G. Groslier, *Recherches…*, op. cit., p. 89.

Fig. 13. Sabres and swords.
Angkor Wat 11-4, Bayon, Banteay Chmar 5-9

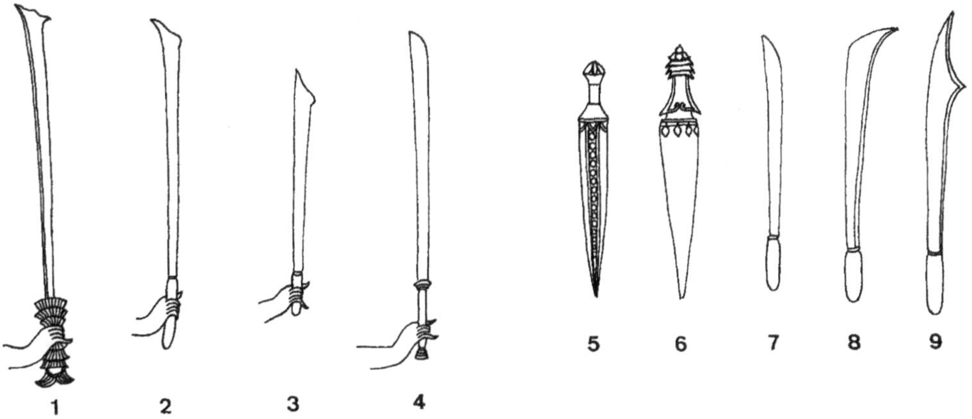

considering the last offensive Khmer weapon, the *phkā'k*, we should mention the knives, cutlasses or daggers so often seen at Angkor Wat when examining breastplates. They are always shown in their sheaths, and, apart from the breastplates, still at Angkor Wat, they can be seen stuck in the belts of sarongs or else, very frequently, and with all types of combatants, hung around their necks. Some examples will be found of the infantry we shall study later (Fig. 62.B, E, F).

It is clear this is only a supplementary weapon, serving as a simple tool in daily life. It is strange that they virtually disappear in the Bayon and at Banteay Chmar, and G. Groslier[9] notes that 'knives and cutlasses in wooden sheaths tied with rattan or bands of cloth have not varied in form since classic times', and that 'every Khmer who goes on a journey tucks one into his belt' (he was of course speaking of the Khmers at the beginning of the twentieth century).

Remaining to be studied is a weapon, the *phkā'k*, a kind of axe (which in this translation will be termed the Khmer axe) which, like the knives and cutlasses, remains the same in form from generation to generation until the present. Again, G. Groslier[10] notes this, saying that the Khmers have faithfully retained this weapon which 'is used in all domestic tasks in the forest and when hunting, with a long or short handle'. Boisselier however considers that the form of the *phkā'k* is only found, with its bent-back handle by the blade, in the north-west of the Tonle Sap and especially near Siem Reap.

At Angkor Wat (Fig. 14.1 & 2) this weapon can be found in the hands of high-ranking warriors on elephants or horseback. This is not a weapon for the infantry. The design is carefully observed: the bent handle, ending in a kind of bulb, has a splayed blade, cut obliquely at the end. The way the handle and blade are attached is unclear.

---

[9] G. Groslier, *Recherches…*, op. cit., p. 91.
[10] idem.

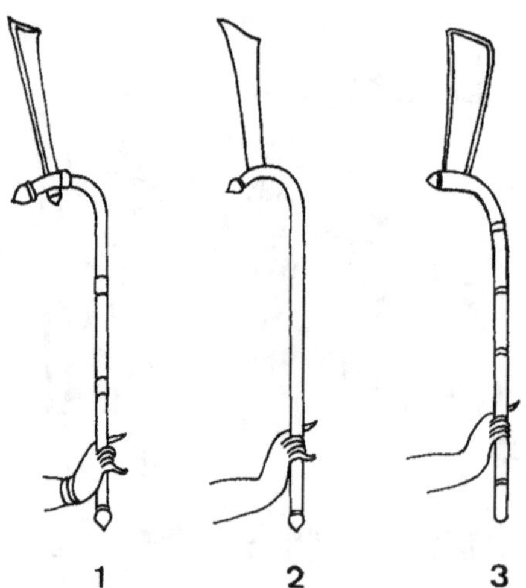

*Fig. 14. Phkā'k (Khmer axes).
Angkor Wat 1, 2; Bayon, Banteay Chmar 3.*

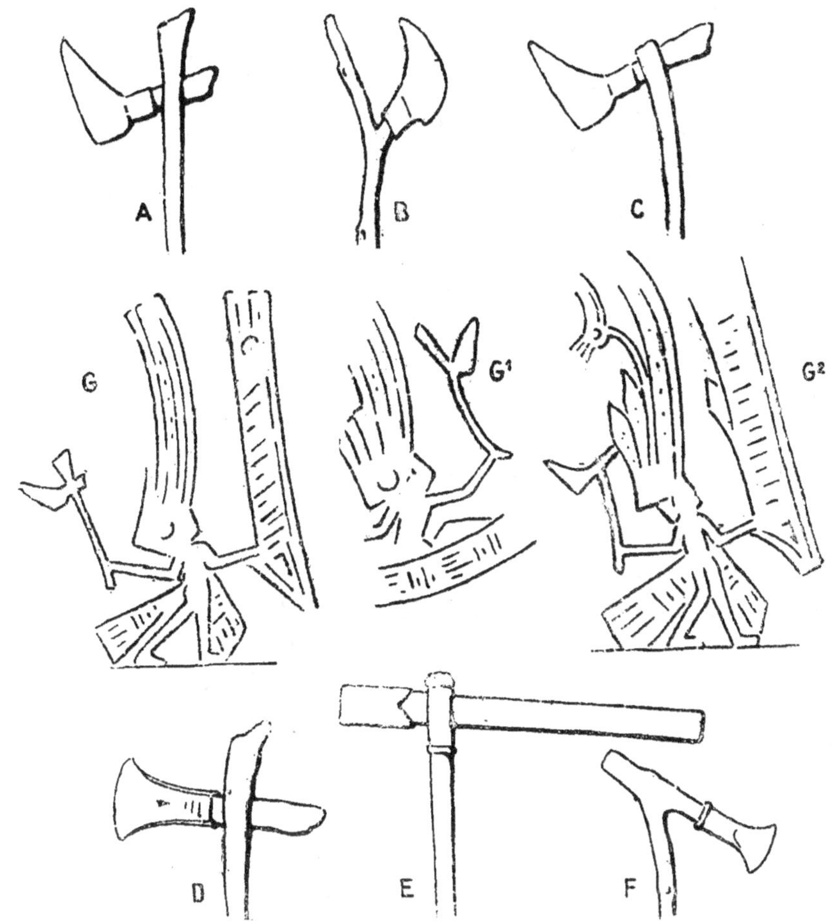

Fig. 15. A, B, C, D Fixing handles to Dongson axes. Reconstitution taken from designs on the Hanoi drum (G, G1, G2). E. Vietnamese cai riu. *F. A Lao axe socket. Figure taken from the article by V. Goloubew, 1929, p.15.*

At the Bayon and Banteay Chmar (Fig. 14.3) this is also the arm of the warriors of a certain rank, but some foot soldiers carry it too. It is always summarily represented and on the whole is found less often than at Angkor Wat.

An examination of the axes or *phkā'k* completes the hand-held weapons, defensive or offensive, in the Khmer armies. Before considering what we can pretentiously call 'war machines', this seems a good place to make some comparisons. They are suggested by the study of V. Goloubew which appeared in *BEFEO* which we have already mentioned when dealing with breastplates.[11]

The site of Dongson, apart from those fragments of bronze plaques which might have been parts of breastplates, revealed, among other objects, an important hoard of bronze

---

[11] V. Goloubew, 'L'âge de bronze...', op. cit.

weapons. Among these were axes which particularly interested Goloubew (Fig.15). Some had a symmetrical cutting edge, others irregular outlines. He compared them to scenes appearing on a famous bronze drum, known as the Hanoi drum. 'These scenes shown on the Hanoi drum provide us with precious information about how these axes were put together. When the cutting edge was asymmetrical and pointed, it was fixed to a bent and forked or Y-shaped handle, one end of which was inserted into the socket… It is to be wondered if this kind of mounting was not limited to axes used as missiles.'[12]

It seems to us that there is indeed a link between the Khmer axe and these Dongson weapons, as Goloubew has reconstituted them with the insertion of handles following the designs of the Hanoi drum.

We can also link the swords at the Bayon and Banteay Chmar with what Goloubew calls, at Don Son, daggers (Fig.16). He says (op. cit., 1929, p. 17) that 'they belong to the large family of Sino-Scythian daggers. Some examples are as long as 0.25 m and could pass for short swords.'

We have seen that the examples of swords on these two monuments were rather short (Fig. 13.5 & 6). There may also be a link here.

But perhaps it is not necessary to look for such distant links to these weapons. In Cambodia, at the site of Phnom Bayan, excavations unearthed a sword which recalls, in its form, those found in the bas-reliefs and which could be dated to the twelfth or thirteenth centuries. Another, of similar shape, was definitely dated to the eleventh century, thanks to its inscription, by Claude Jacques.[13]

---

[12] V. Goloubew, op. cit., p. 15.

[13] Claude Jacques, 'Supplément au tome VIII des inscriptions du Cambodge', *BEFEO*, LVIII, Paris, 1971, p. 183.

Fig. 16. Bronze Sino-Scythian daggers.
A. Siberia from N. Toll, Eurasia Septentrionalis Antique, *IV, p. 184. B. China, valley of the Huai (collection O. Siren,* Ars Asiatica, *VII, pl . 11). C. Dongson. (Fig. taken from the article by V. Goloubew,* BEFEO, *XXIX 1929, p. 6.)*

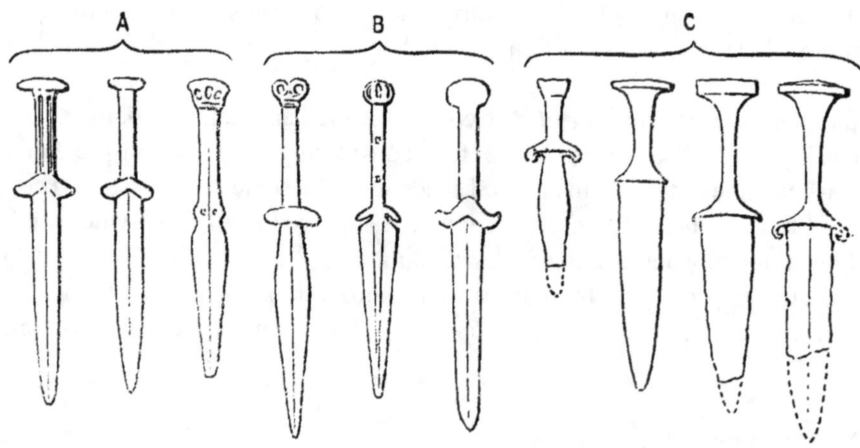

We shall complete this overview of Khmer weapons by examining the war machines which Paul Mus in an article in *BEFEO*[14] considered under the rubric of 'ballistae'.

One only sees these machines at the Bayon and Banteay Chmar where they appear in columns on the march, mounted on elephants or on wheels. Their reconstitution is far from easy because of the clumsiness of the workmanship of the bas-reliefs. In spite of that, Mus discerned four different types, the efficiency of which he considered in turn.

We shall begin with the ballistae on the backs of elephants, but it seems appropriate, before going into details, to examine the beast's harnessing, which was always the same, whatever it was transporting.

The elephant was harnessed very simply, to judge by the few models found in the outer gallery of the Bayon (Fig. 17). It had a breast strap, a saddle girth, and a crupper of a special type, these three ropes being interlinked. To these should be added a headpiece and a small bell round the neck, attached to the breast strap.

There was a stand on which the machine the animal carried was placed. The stand was not always detailed, and the way it was secured is never shown, but we think the

---

[14] Paul Mus, 'Les balistes du Bayon', *BEFEO*, XXIX, Paris, 1929, pp. 331-41.

Fig. 17. Harnessing of an elephant for carrying a ballista. Bayon, ext. gal, S side, W wing, lower level. Dufour 42

Fig. 18. Ballista on an elephant, Type I. Bayon, ext. gal., S side, W wing, lower level. Dufour 35

frame was part and parcel of this kind of equipment and with the harnessing which, we should emphasize, is rarely shown in all its details.

Now let us turn to the different machines.

One of the types of ballistae considered by Mus (Fig. 18) was described by G. Groslier.[15] 'The grooved guide (m) is positioned on a small stand placed on the elephant's saddle. Two bows placed back to back are simultaneously armed by sliding a string fixed to the rear and linking their two strings. I presume the horizontal apparatus, given the impossibility of showing this in perspective, is shown as vertical.'

Mus, considering this description of the contraption, the mechanism of which he does not *a priori* refute, namely that the string was made taut without any device, nevertheless considers that 'its ballistic superiority was limited and its effect would hardly have been greater than an ordinary bow because of the friction implied by slipping the string; this in spite of the fact that as the bending was the same as with an ordinary bow, the propulsive trajectory given to the arrow by this mechanism was not increased.' He demonstrates his assertions with a sketch which appears to support his remarks (Fig. 19).

The presence of the assistant next to the warrior who arms the ballista and who seems to hold the rear bow, appears suspect to Mus. He notes that he appears to release the bow which is therefore not fixed. According to Mus, the function of the assistant is superfluous. But it is impossible to decide what his role was, because the rear bow was perhaps fixed to the arbalest and the assistant helped to stabilize the ballista.

---

[15] G. Groslier, *Recherches…*, op. cit., p. 90.

28

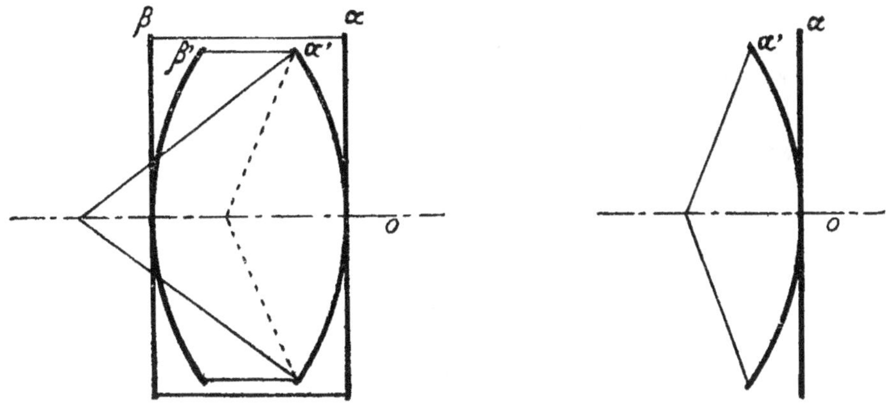

Fig. 19. Simple and double bow. Schema of propulsive trajectory.
Fig. taken from the article by P. Mus, BEFEO, *XXIX, 1929, p. 332.*

Mus resolves the problem he raised by supposing that the two bows are linked at their ends by two small strings independent of the string putting the front bow in tension. If this were so, the assistant would help in bending the first bow to bring the string attached to it to the next. It is difficult to settle the matter because of the poor quality of the bas-reliefs with this scene.

Fig. 20. Ballista on an elephant. Type 2.
Bayon, ext. gal., S side,
W wing lower level. Dufour 34.

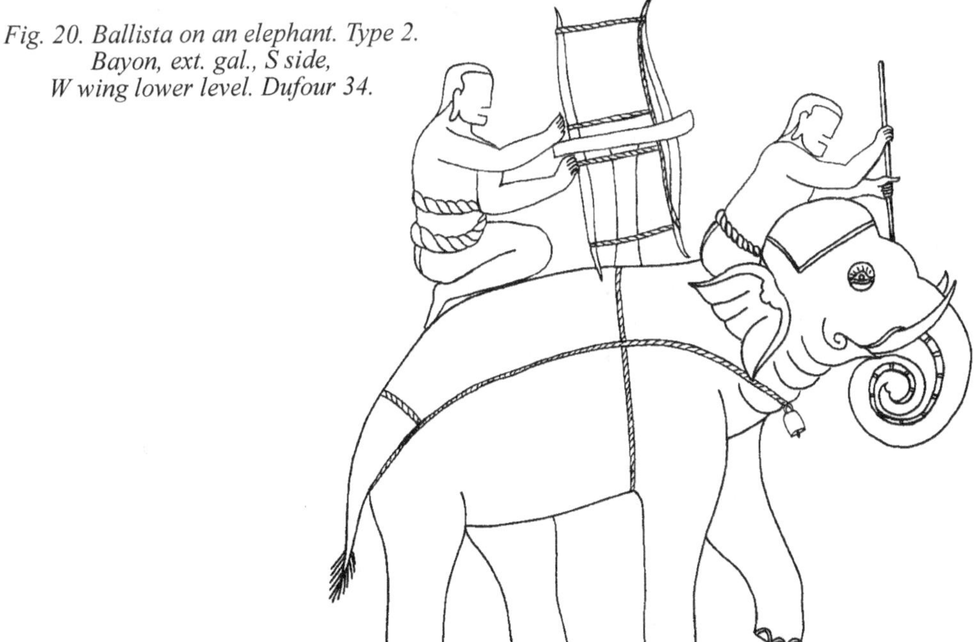

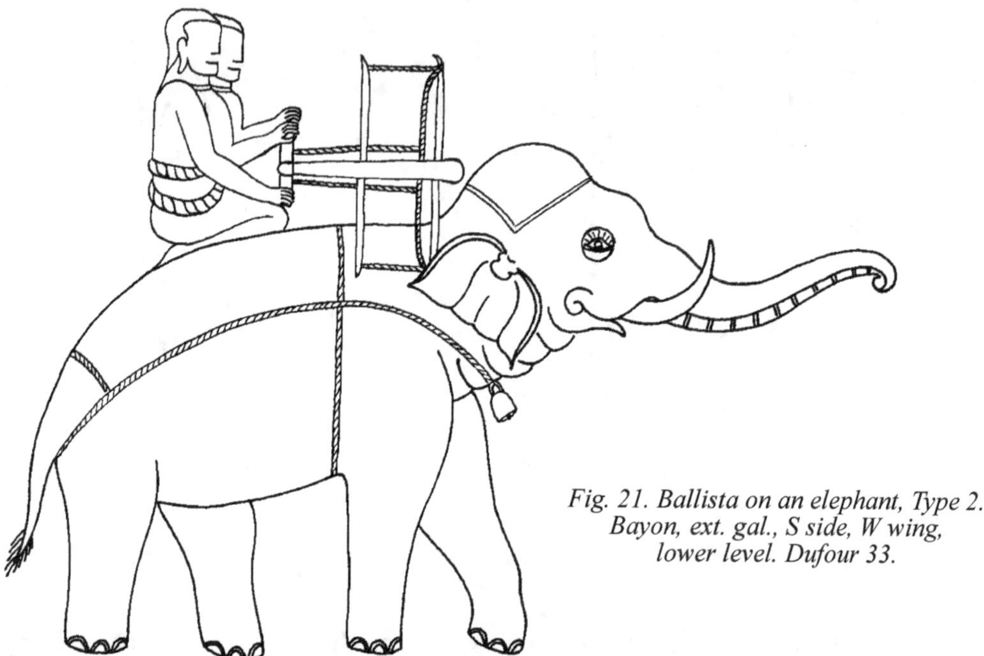

*Fig. 21. Ballista on an elephant, Type 2.
Bayon, ext. gal., S side, W wing,
lower level. Dufour 33.*

A second type of ballista (Figs 20 & 21) is called by Mus a 'ballista with a crank comprising two fixed bows with interconnected release mechanism'. The assembling is the same as for the hand released ballista described by G. Groslier. Added to it is a simple tension and probably a release mechanism. The bow string of the front bow is linked to two stretchers at the back of the machine. The mechanism is not obvious. Possibly the two hands of the person firing hold levers or a crank. Mus thinks that the addition of this presumed mechanism removed the objections he made concerning the type 1 ballista described by Groslier. This type of machine is worked by one or two men, most often two (Fig. 21).

A third type of ballista does not have a crank, but two bows with joint triggers (Fig. 22). The bow at the front is placed as in the other ballistae. The string slides to its ends but, instead of being fixed to the back bow, is hooked over it, and in tension forms a rectangle with variable sides.

In fact, if the person using it pulls back the rear bow with both hands, the transversal elements $\underline{a}$ and $\underline{a}'$ holding the ballista in tension become shorter whilst the longitudinal elements $\underline{b}$ and $\underline{b}'$ are shortened. When the moveable bow is released, the system reverts to its initial state and the double trigger projects the arrow forward, the end of which was touching the string of the rear bow.

This type of ballista is common at Banteay Chmar and is always triggered in this manner, the marksman, always alone, pulling back the rear bow with both hands. A reconstitution of this fairly powerful, simple, and rapid-firing weapon is given in Fig. 22. It should be noted that the elephant's harness is more complicated. The basic ropes

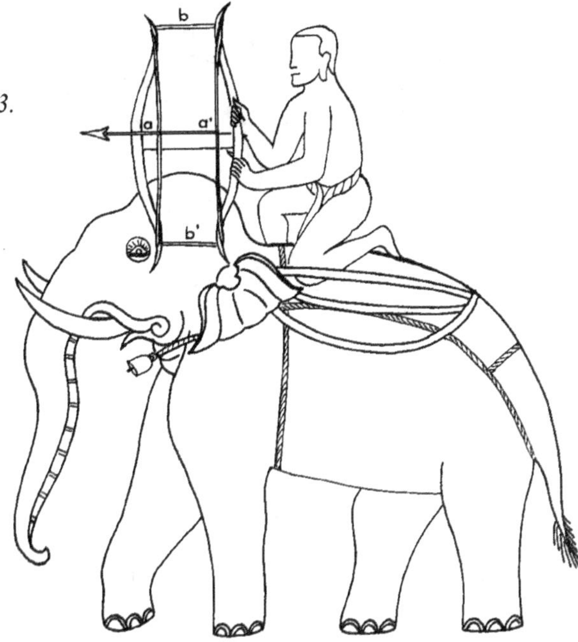

Fig. 22. Ballista on an elephant. Type 3. Banteay Chmar, N gal., E wing, lower level. Beylié 72-3.

remain, but others are added, very badly detailed, which seem to have the purpose of preventing the marksman from falling.

A fourth type of ballista, still on elephant back, has a bar in tension or in traction (Fig. 23). The difference with the other types is that the bow string of the front bow is held in position at its extremities like a normal bow, and instead of a second bow, there is behind it a transverse bar with two hooks which must grasp the bowstring. This bar held in two hands must make the bow taut since the hooks are at each end. Mus[16] writes 'The full cock is obtained by a relatively short rearwards movement. But as the propulsive trajectory is short, the weapon would lack precision even with a powerful release.' This ballista is operated by two men (a third on the elephant's neck directs the animal). One of the two men might use the bar, pulling it with both hands, while the other would stretch the bow string.

These then are the four types of ballistae on the backs of elephants. Their action is far from clear. Boisselier considers that the problem of how they worked can only be resolved if models of them were reconstructed, as has been done for the machines of Leonardo da Vinci. The ballistae are often worked by two men, and the need for the second is not always made clear. Their balance on the back of the beast seems to us precarious (only at Banteay Chmar does a means of protecting the man firing the machine appear), the more so as, apart from a few rare instances, the elephant is not led by a mahout.

---

[16] P. Mus, 'Les balistes…', op. cit., p. 334.

*Fig. 23. Ballista on an elephant. Type 4.
Bayon, ext. gal., S side W wing,
lower level. Dufour 40.*

The bowmen working these machines, except in some special cases we shall describe, are dressed very simply in a loin-cloth; their dress will be considered when we deal with the infantry.

Some types of ballistae we have described are placed on wheels and found in the processions of elephants. The sculptor rendered these very clumsily, vertically, and it is not easy to understand the whole. But it would seem that at the Bayon (Fig. 24.1) the type of ballista on wheels shown is the type 1 already described on an elephant (Fig. 18).

*Fig. 24. Ballistae on wheels.
1. Bayon, ext. gal., S side, W wing, upper level. Dufour 39.
2. Banteay Chmar, N gal, E wing, lower level. Beylié 70-73.*

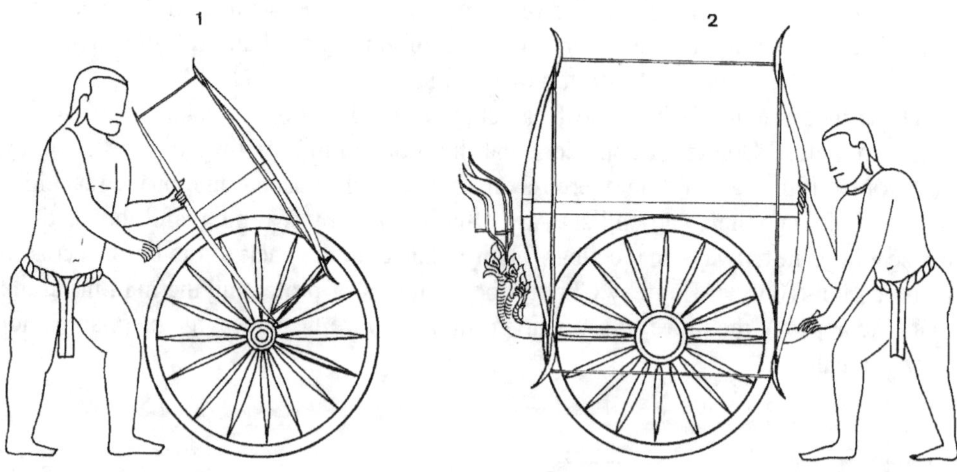

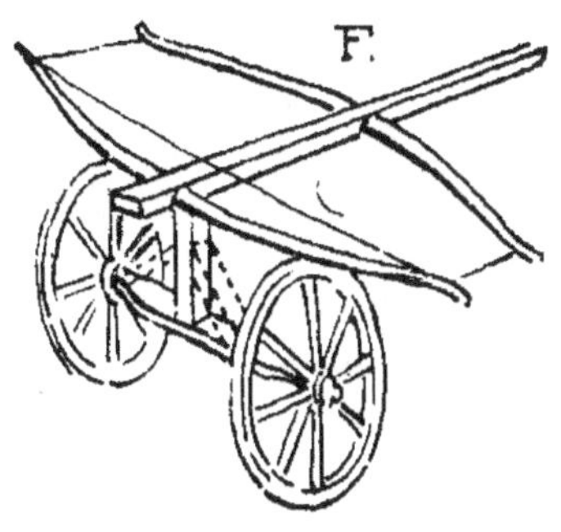
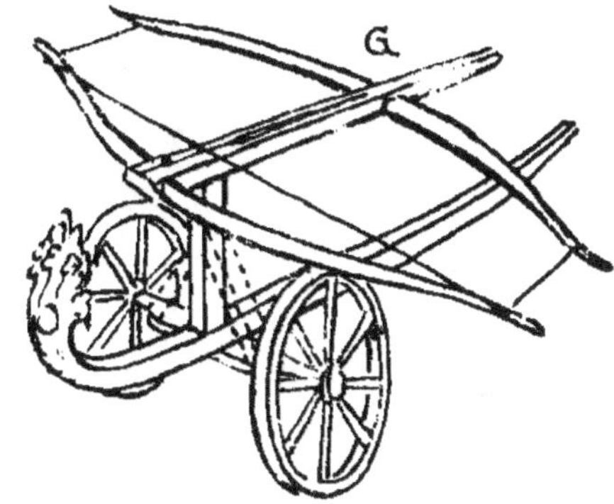

Fig. 25. Reconstitution of ballistae on wheels.
Fig. taken from G. Goslier, Recherches sur les Cambodgiens, *figs 56 F and G, p. 92.*

At Banteay Chmar (Fig. 24.2) the machine on wheels is identical to that described on an elephant at that monument, namely type 3 (Fig. 22).

G. Groslier tried to reconstitute these machines horizontally (Fig. 25), emphasizing that at Banteay Chmar the carriage is decorated at the front with *nāga* heads, but he gave his two drawings the same mechanism which, while acceptable for the ballista found at the Bayon, is not so for that at Banteay Chmar corresponding, as we have said, to type 3 on an elephant's back.

Before finishing with ballistae, we need rapidly to survey the parallels Mus made in his study of them. He compared them to some Chinese weapons, the description and drawing of which appears in the sixth book of the Ming encyclopedia, *San Cai Tu Hei* (三才圖會), cited by Hervey de Saint-Denys in a note in *Méridionaux*.[17]

The *San Cai Tu Hei* calls the machine *shuang gong chuang nu* (雙弓床弩), or 'ballista, literally arbalest, on a chariot'. He gives the following description (Fig. 26): 'Arbalest with two bows on a carriage. They are made taut by turning a winch in parallel. Beneath is a framework (*chuang* 床) supporting the arbalest. When it is armed, ten men and more, uniting their efforts, work together' (*San Cai Tu Hei* VI: *Qiyong* 器用, 19b).

This weapon therefore seems much more powerful than its copy in the Bayon (type 2). The release is caused by the slackening of a strong pin effected by blows from a mallet. Except for this, they are identical.

The same work gives a description of two other machines: the ballista with three bows (*san gong chuang nu* 三弓床弩), the mechanism of which is similar to the previous machine, but there the front bow is doubled, and the 'engineer-powered' bench (*shen bi chuang zi* 神臂床子) (Fig. 27)—a bow placed horizontally on a carriage (a bench: *chuang*)—dispatches a volley of arrows, guided by pipes similar to those found in firearms.

---

[17] Ma Tuan-lin. *Ethnographie des peuples étrangers à la Chine*, translated by H. de Saint-Denys. Geneva, 1873-1883, II.: *Méridionaux*, p. 389 no. 2.

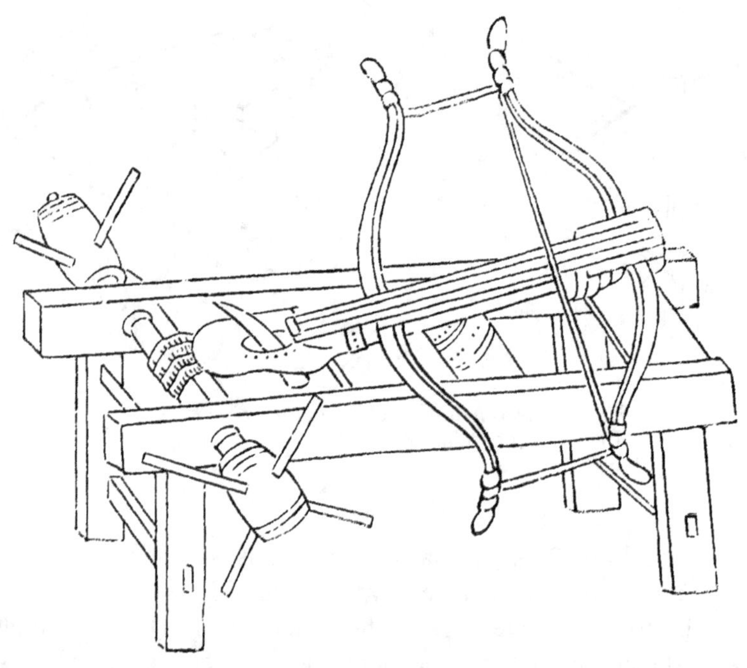

Fig. 26. Arbalest with a double bow.
Fig. taken from article by P. Mus on ballistae, BEFEO, *XXIX, 1929, p. 336.*

Fig. 27 'Engineer-powered bow'.
Fig. taken from the article by P. Mus on ballistae. BEFEO, *XXIX, 1929, p. 336.*

In sum, the arbalest seems to have a long history in Indochina, but the big machines appear to have a Chinese origin towards the end of the twelfth century, perhaps through the Chams, with whom the Khmers were at war. None of these machines is seen at Angkor Wat, the construction of which pre-dates the great battles with the Chams; these people seem to have learnt how to use these weapons from a Chinese instructor who, in 1171, after a journey by boat from Fujian, is said to have landed on the shores of Chen Ching.[18] This hypothesis acquires some weight when one takes into account a bas-relief at the Bayon in which two mercenary Cham warriors, wearing characteristic helmets, are using a weapon of this kind in the Khmer ranks (Fig. 82). The Khmer ballistae seem to derive from these Chinese models, either by imitation, or by a combination of the two types, through the intermediary of the Chams.

It is necessary to point out that these ballistae only appear in processions and they are never seen in action in battles. Perhaps they were only used in sieges, of which these is no illustration in the bas-reliefs.

However, in the thick of the fray, on the outer gallery of the Bayon, E side, N wing, is found a curiously harnessed elephant, ridden by archers, which is similar to the beasts carrying ballistae (Fig. 28).

---

[18] *Méridionaux*, pp. 535-6, in Ma Tuan-lin, op. cit.

Fig. 28. Archers on elephant back.
Bayon, ext. gal., E side, N wing, upper level. Dufour 123.

G. Groslier[19] calls its harnessing *cacolet* ('pack-mule') which, according to the *Petit Larousse* dictionary, is a light seat with a back rest placed on both sides of a special pack-saddle for certain animals used for carrying people. What can be seen on the side of this elephant is rather far removed from this definition. It seems to be a big, elongated semi-spherical and very lightly constructed basket. It is unclear how it was attached to the elephant's harness, which is identical to that of the ballistae-carrying elephants, except that the under-belly rope does not go over the animal's back. This is similar to the harnessing of the ballistae-carrying elephant at Banteay Chmar (Fig. 22).

The purpose of a basket would usually have been to carry objects, but in fact a warrior is found in it. He is not alone; the profile of another man can be seen who must be carried in the same manner on the left side of the elephant. They must have been very uncomfortable. The warrior who is completely visible is kneeling on his right leg and supporting himself against the edge of the contraption with his outstretched left leg, which gives him some stability. He is wearing just a loin-cloth with its two ends falling in front, while another loin-cloth is wrapped around his torso, We shall examine further the clothing worn by the infantry.

Both of them brandish a bow and arrow. No quiver is visible. The mahout only had his goad. In a curious detail, the elephant appears vindictive; during the battle it has seized from the enemy a number of lances and arrows which it holds in its trunk. This is the only example known to us of this disposition on an elephant's back. It is also the only elephant we have encountered to take an active part in battles, though the chronicles often mention this.

We shall complete the study of Khmer weapons by examining a unique war machine, to which we hesitate to give a name (Fig. 29). It is to be seen in the Bayon (ext. gal., E side, N wing, upper level) in a march to battle comprising only war elephants and infantry. It is encircled by warriors armed with lances and bucklers, and like the elephants, is surrounded by a great number of honorific symbols: banners, wicker panels, parasols, etc.

This war machine comprises the body of a cart (the wheel which can be seen includes a side runner, one of the ends of which has upturned *nāga* heads). The visible rail, that is the cart's guard rail, is only shown very incompletely by its upper horizontal side (the rear extremity of the rail is turned up, like the runner, to end in *nāga* heads), and by the rear upright strut which appears to link with the side runner, which makes no sense. But this may represent a raised platform, erected on wheels, which is only viewed, as usual, in profile.

The front of this 'machine' has two unusually tall bucklers (about one and a half times the height of a warrior), which must rest on a stand and be held upright by two soldiers perched on a platform, each on one foot, the other on a kind of stool. Holding the bucklers in their left hands, they brandish their lances in the right.

This 'machine' is moved by a foot soldier who pushes the end of the platform and the side runner. There must have been another person pushing who is not shown. The

---

[19] G. Groslier, *Recherches...*, op. cit., p. 96.

36

Fig. 29. 'War machine' with bucklers.
Bayon, ext. gal.,E side, N wing, upper level. Dufour 124.

bucklers are very richly decorated and topped by banners. It is hard to see wherein lay the efficiency of such a group, undoubtedly difficult to manoeuvre, and cumbersome. It could be that the effort of pulling by the two holding the bucklers improved the aim of their lances. This would be a kind of ancestor of present-day armoured cars or tanks, though at that time, elephants acted as such. This being so, what as the use of this machine? It is certainly unique.

The study of these war machines completes the examination of the armaments of the Khmer army. They are fairly primitive: basic weapons—lances, bows, arrows, bucklers, and, secondarily, cutlasses, sabres, swords, and Khmer axes (*phkā'k*), which only evolve in a few details during the period we are dealing with.

The only major novelty is the appearance at the Bayon and Banteay Chmar of war machines which put the army a step up the ladder of technical prowess. But we are still far from the appearance of firearms.

We are now in a position to study in detail the organization of this army, in its traditional corps, and to see if it corresponds to the schema proposed by the *Arthaśāstra* of Kauṭilya, taken as *a priori* and not critically examined.

PART II

The organization of the army

*Fig. 30. Profile of a chariot harnessed to horses and carrying a warrior.
Angkor Wat, W gal., S wing. Coedès 499.*

1. War chariots

We shall begin by studying the war chariots in detail before considering their real position in the army and in battles. Almost all of them shown on the bas-reliefs are in profile, which makes an understanding of their component parts difficult. A very few examples, where the artists have shown chariots overturned in the conflict, indicate, though rather clumsily, the way the horses were harnessed to the vehicle, which was done by means of a yoke similar to one linking cattle to carts. Two examples are shown from the front, but these are rather vehicles for show than war chariots. All the same, what they tell us about the yoking is precious, because this could not be different from that of a chariot.

Chariots and carts are very similar in their conception. The differences between the two lie in the fact that carts have a roof and, more importantly, have two side runners at the level of the axle, and which protrude beyond it, something the chariots never have. Furthermore chariots are always drawn by horses, whereas carts are pulled by oxen.

These few differences allow the distinction between the vehicles in the bas-reliefs to be obvious.

Seen in profile, as is most often the case, the chariot appears like a kind of cart drawn by two horses, the second animal often merging with the first and being very unclear (Fig. 30).

The body of the vehicle is formed by a platform supporting, in most cases, open-work rails resting on an axle. The ends of the axle pass through the hub of the two high wheels (only one of which is shown) and are held in position by linch pins which are sometimes shown. These wheels have an average of sixteen spokes.

The lateral spars of the platform built over the axle project in front until they meet and are joined in the hoop of the yoke, which keeps the two horses in position; they form the pole or shafts of the vehicle. The end of the yoke is always decorated with more or less exuberant *nāga* motifs.

This joining of the side spars of the platform of the chariot forming the pole is clearly seen in the illustration, which is virtually unique, of two vehicles found on the NW corner pavilion at Angkor Wat (Fig. 31). This concerns, as we have said, vehicles for show, processional carriages, and not war chariots, but the principles should be the same. This seems to be the case with the few examples of overturned chariots which appear in the frays depicted at Angkor Wat (Fig. 32).

In these cases, however, the sculptor only showed one of the presumed lateral spars. From this one could argue that the yoke was linked to a single element, not the double pole like that in Fig. 31. But we shall see that carts on the bas-reliefs are also shown with a single element while their pole or shafts could only be double, like those on contemporary carts, which they are identical to in appearance. This is therefore an error on the part of the sculptor as is found in other representations of chariots in

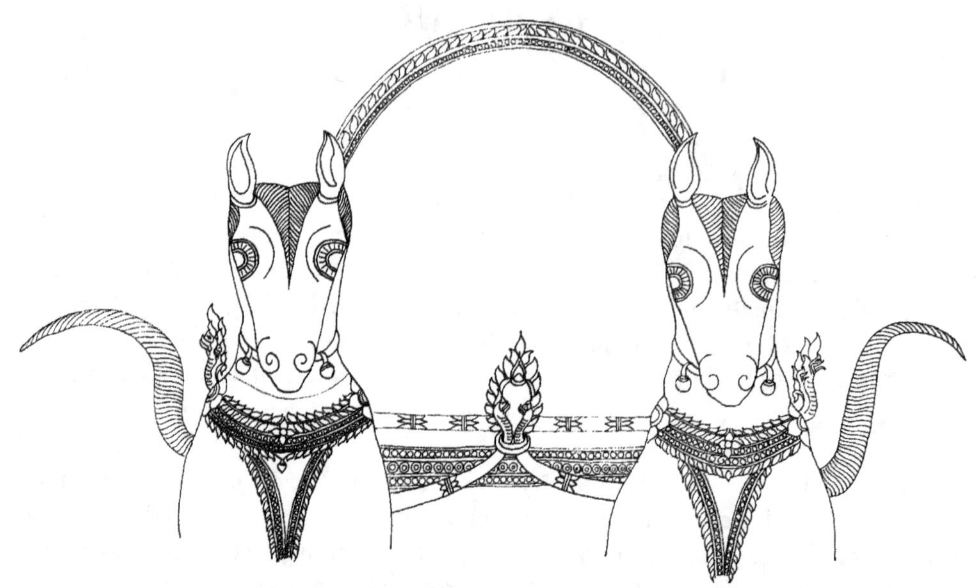

Fig. 31. Cart seen from the front.
Angkor Wat, NW corner pavilion, N wall of E wing. Coedès 326.

Fig. 32. Overturned cart.
Angkor Wat, N gal., W wing. Coedès 450.

profile (Fig. 30). The same inadequacies led the sculptors to depict, at the back of the vehicle, only one of the lateral spars.

These terminate abruptly with a *nāga* motif, also more or less exuberant; and, of course, they are not joined in the front, as that would have hindered access into the chariot (Figs 30 & 32).

The ends of the yoke are slightly bent upwards, and linked to the animal's withers, on which they rested; they were sometimes decorated with a stylized flower motif, and had four hooks. These can be seen in illustrations of overturned chariots we have already spoken about (Fig. 32). Each pair of hooks served to hold the ends of a strap encircling the animal's neck. The outer hook is nearly always shown with a strap on the representations of chariots and horses in profile (Fig. 30).

This way of attaching the animals, taking no advantage of the horse collar, the use of which began to spread in the West at the same period, must have limited the draughting possibilities of the animals, who could only pull light vehicles, as the chariots indeed were.

The two horses of each vehicle were fitted out in the same way as the horses of the cavalry; we shall discuss this later when dealing with this corps. It should be noted that, unlike some horses in the cavalry, the horses pulling the chariots always had a richly decorated collar.

Before describing the different types of chariots, it is appropriate to consider their dimensions, the materials used in their making, and details concerning their construction. Of course, what we can advance concerning these matters is but conjecture.

It is possible to estimate their dimensions by comparing their size with the carts appearing in the bas-reliefs: they are always the same size. Though no war chariot has survived to our times, present-day Khmer carts, as G. Groslier remarked[1] are completely identical to those appearing on the bas-reliefs, and the distance between their wheels coincides with what their models of the twelfth and thirteenth centuries left on the causeway stones at Banteay Chmar and Angkor Wat.

The dimensions Groslier gives are rather picturesque and need explanation. The cart, according to him, measures 'five cubits' in width on the outside, or 2.25 m (one cubit being 45 cm) and '30 to 35 fingers' width between the hubs', or about 55 to 66 cm (the finger's width being estimated as 18-19 mm), which seems narrow to us. But the chariot, without side runners, was not so wide overall, and some 50 cm could be deducted from Groslier's figure, which gives the vehicle a width of about 1.5-2 m which still appears to us excessive.

The basic material used for the chariot's construction could only be wood. Turning again to what Groslier says about the carts on the bas-reliefs, in relation to those found today, it can be presumed, without being far from the mark, that the different parts of the vehicle were held in position by rattan bindings. This is what we have shown on the different drawings in Fig. 33, on the analogy with fig. 61 in Groslier's *Recherches sur les Cambodgiens*, which provides a sketch of a contemporary cart seen from above, below, and in profile (Fig. 140).

---

[1] G. Groslier, *Recherches... op. cit.*, p. 97.

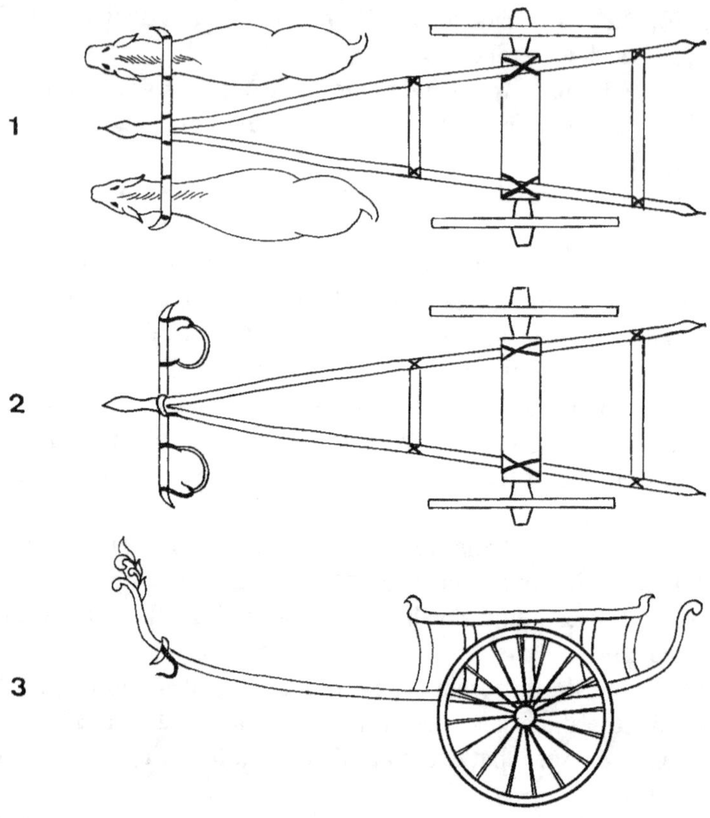

Fig. 33. Schematic view of a war chariot.
1. From above. 2. From below. 3. From the side.

Still on the subject of contemporary carts, G. Groslier[2] specified that the 'rim of the wheel was in four parts, two female and two male' and has sixteen spokes; this number of spokes is also that found most often, not only on the cart wheels in the bas-reliefs, which we shall speak about again, but also on the chariots. The hub, Groslier affirms of these modern carts is long, to prevent it breaking, and no iron at all is used in its construction.

One would like to think that the techniques of construction and the materials used for chariots in the twelfth and thirteenth centuries were the same as those used now for carts. Only the decoration of the chariots was more refined. This would mostly have been wooden carving which would probably have been gilded and have inlaid work of different kinds. The extremities of the rails and the side spars were possibly made of bronze, as some bronzes have been found with similar motifs, all that might remain of such sophisticated vehicles.

In this way the chariots should have been light and readily manoeuvrable, indispensable qualities given the type of traction we have discussed.

---

[2] G. Groslier, *Recherches...*op. cit., p. 98.

We shall now specify a certain number of chariots based on the variations in their decoration and the disposition of their platforms.

The most common type at Angkor Wat (type 1, Fig. 34) has high rails, the frame of which is decorated with various motifs, and extremities ending in *nāga* heads. The openwork frame is formed by carved and indented balusters which can be straight or form harmonious ovals. These usually number four to six. Decorative beading rows of small flowers and leaves, and various decorative rings make these rails carved marvels. The wheels are high and light, their rims unusually thin, their hubs decorated in the same manner as the sides, and the spokes rather thin and sometimes curving outwards in the middle. As we have said, there are usually 16 spokes.

The rear and front ends have a many-headed *nāga* motif carved more or less realistically.

Another type (type 2), still at Angkor Wat, is a more complicated and richer variant of that we have just described (Fig. 35). It is complicated by the fact that the rails, instead of being single as in the preceding example, have at both ends a slight extension, not so high as the central part, but decorated in similar fashion. This form is found on elephant howdahs and also on a number of chariots taking part in the great battles represented at Angkor Wat.

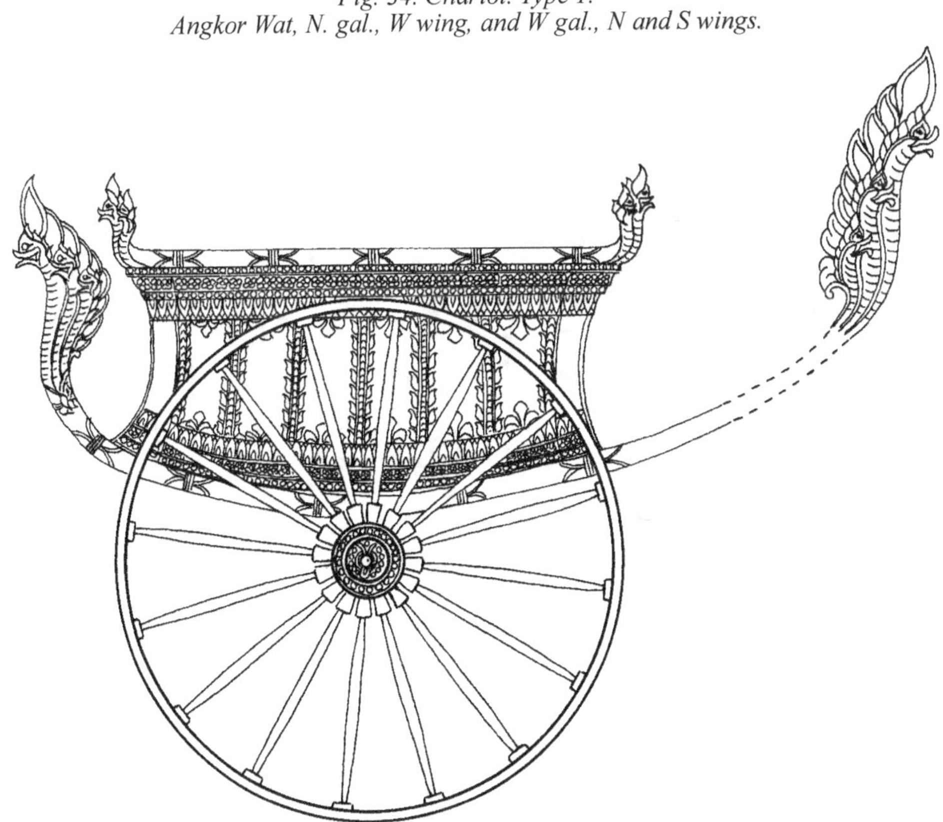

Fig. 34. Chariot. Type 1.
Angkor Wat, N. gal., W wing, and W gal., N and S wings.

It is more embellished, especially in the example we have chosen to illustrate the chariot of Rāvaṇa in the scene of the 'Battle for Laṅkā' at Angkor Wat (W gal., N wing). Models with the same form are decorated like those in type 1, but with RĀvaṇa's chariot the sculptors have gone into great detail in the decoration:

(a) the two rail ends have many-headed *nāga*, the central head having a long tongue hanging out;

(b) the frame of the rails is decorated with a multitude of rows of beading, small flowers, and lotus flowers interrupted at regular intervals by beading rings ornamented with open lotus flowers;

(c) the lattice work has ovals (five for the central part, plus one for each end), decorated top and bottom with lotus motifs;

(d) the axle comes out of a monster's head resembling a *makara*, which can be seen behind the wheel with its particularly well-carved wheel box, and sixteen spokes;

(e)   the rear ends are decorated with the traditional multi-headed *nāga*. The central head of which also disgorges a long tongue. The rear side ends issue from tiny *makara* heads carved at the end of the rails;

(f)   the same arrangement and decoration is found for the front side spars forming a pole, but apart from the *makara* the end parts are difficult to identify, being hidden by the heads of monsters who appear to pull the chariot; again they are multi-headed *nāga*.

Fig. 35. Chariot. Type 2.
Angkor Wat, W gal., N wing. Coedès 483 for the selected model;
and W gal., S wing; N gal., W wing.

Using the same criteria, a third type of chariot can be identified. This type is rare and only found in a few battles on the Angkor Wat reliefs. There is also one example in a parade of warriors at Banteay Chmar.

At Angkor Wat its construction is identical to that of the previously listed types (Fig. 36): a platform with lateral spars bending upwards at the rear and joining at the front to form a pole. The platform rests on an axle, the ends of which enter the hub with wheels of sixteen spokes. The only difference from the preceding types is the absence of rails.

The decoration of the different parts of the vehicle is done with the same motifs as the other types of chariots, with beading, decorative rings, multiple *nāga* heads, sometimes stylized, at the extremities.

The absence of the unusually highly decorated rails makes this type of chariot less attractive. It is sometimes augmented with a mat, only the thickness of which can be seen, decorated with bands of different motifs, These mats may exist on the other types of chariots but the rails prevent one from seeing them.

The chariot at Banteay Chmar (Fig. 37) is poorly outlined and difficult to interpret from the photographs available. It appears to have no decoration in spite of the apparent high rank of its rider. Only the harnessing of the horses shows some refinement.

Only the wheel of the chariot can be clearly seen: one of the rear ends of the platform has been seized by one of the warriors following the chariot. They carry bucklers and lances, and are mixed with numerous bearers of parasols and fans. As it is, the absence of rails assimilates it to the preceding type.

Fig. 36. Chariot. Type 3.
Angkor Wat, W gal., S and N wings; N gal., W wing.

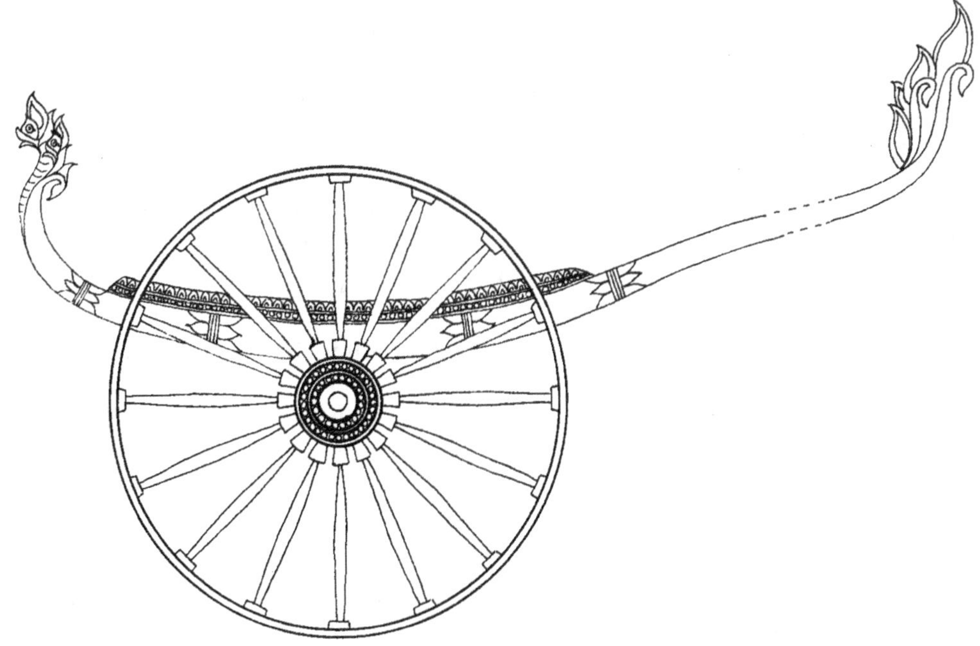

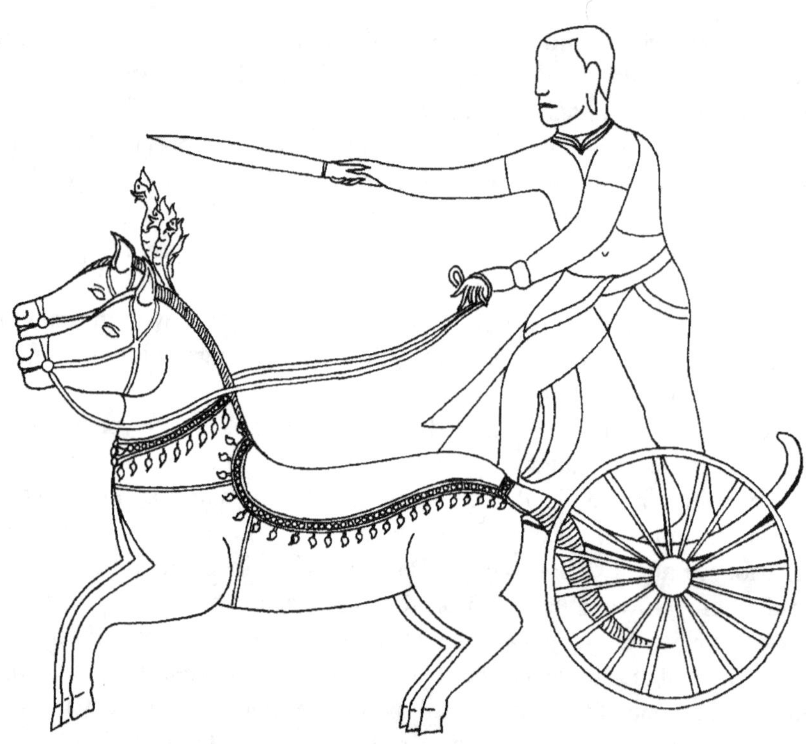

Fig. 37. Chariot. Type 3.
Banteay Chmar, W gal., S wing. Beylié 12.

The rider, standing, holds the reins in one hand, which is not seen elsewhere, and brandishes his weapon. The absence of any driver is perhaps because the chariot is taking part in a religious procession, probably in honour of Viṣṇu, a statue of whom, with four arms, would be borne before.

At the Bayon only a very few chariots are to be found, in the bas-reliefs of the inner gallery (Figs 38 & 39). These chariots, poorly reproduced, have the same characteristics as type 2 of Angkor Wat.

The first chariot we have reproduced (Fig. 38) has double rails, one above the other, the ends of which are upturned in stylized *nāga* heads. The lattice work shown only has undecorated, simple balusters. The extremities of the lateral spars of the platform also end in stylized multi-headed *nāga*. The visible wheel is of very rough workmanship. This chariot is taking part in a mythical combat, drawn by imaginary animals.

The other two chariots shown here (Fig. 39.1 & 2) are closer than the preceding one to type 2 at Angkor Wat but the representation of the rails is clumsy; they have lost the light touch of the earlier models. The shapes are heavy. The decoration is also less rich but uses the same decorative motifs, though simplified or stylized, such as at the extremities.

These two chariots, harnessed, take part in no battle and carry no warriors. They appear in processions, the purpose of which is obscure, but apparently of a religious nature, or linked to the story of a god. The presence of weapons (bow, quiver, club)

48

Fig. 38. Chariot.
Bayon, int. gal., W side, N wing. Dufour 82.

Fig. 39. Chariots.
Bayon. 1. Int. gal., E side, N wing, lower level. Dufour 126.
2. Int. gal., E side, S wing, lower level. Dufour 10.

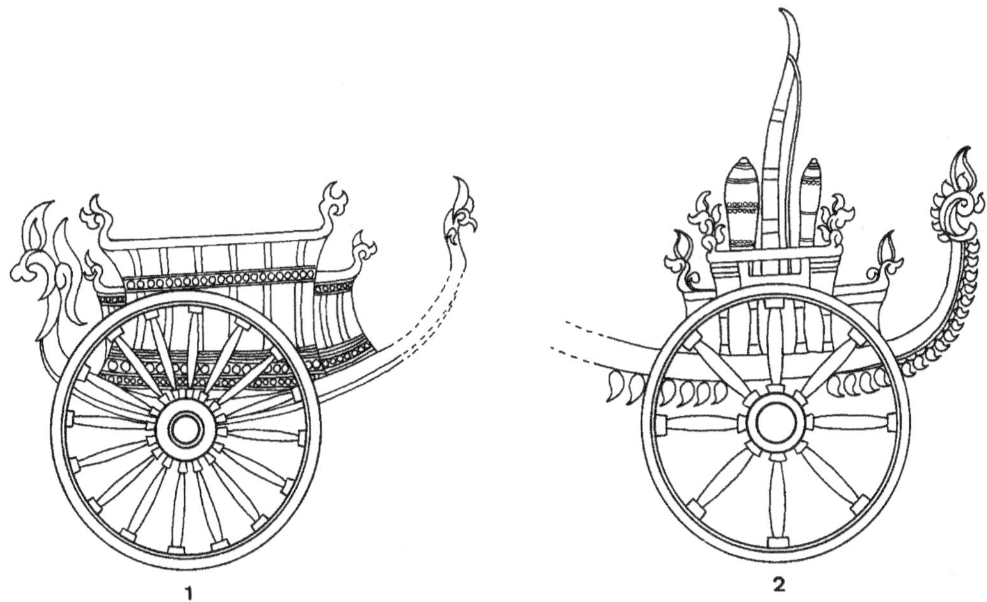

in one of them (Fig. 39.2) indicates that the warrior who would normally occupy it is absent; it may perhaps be the sovereign.

Having described the chariots, we shall now consider the place they occupy in the army and in battles, and the class of the warriors involved with them.

Apart from the warrior on the chariot at Banteay Chmar, who is not identified, all the other chariots are occupied by divinities or mythical heroes from the *Rāmāyana* and the *Mahābhārata.*

They are remarkable for the sumptuousness of their costumes and ornaments, and for the number of honorific insignia (like banners and parasols) surrounding them, even in the height of the fray.

Their weapons are extremely varied: swords, Khmer axes or lances in one hand, round or elongated bucklers in the other. These weapons can be replaced by the bow and quiver; the unoccupied chariot in Fig. 39.2 includes this last weapon, associated with what might be a club. A few rare examples show us warriors carrying clusters of lances which they hurl at the enemy while a bow and quiver are seen at their feet.

Apart from the unoccupied chariots we have indicated in the inner gallery of the Bayon and Banteay Chmar, vehicles manned by a warrior always take part in the most furious combats, mingled with the other corps of the army. The horses are nearly always controlled by a driver (Fig. 30) who takes up acrobatic postures between the two horses, the reins in one hand and a whip in the other. His feet are probably on the lateral spars of the vehicle, forming the pole. The horses neigh and sometimes collapse wounded, which allows us to see more clearly the way the yoke was positioned.

The warrior, for his part (Fig. 30) brandishes his weapons in menacing poses which logically would destabilize him; he often has one foot on one of the lateral spars of the chariot.

All this is rather unrealistic, but this excess seems proportionate to the subjects of the sculptors.

At Angkor Wat, the intense battles that frequently appear are illustrations of the great Indian epics or episodes of Hindu mythology: the 'Battle for Laṅkā' (W gal., N wing) is an episode from the *RĀmĀyana,* the 'Battle of Kurukṣetra' (W gal., N wing) is an episode from the famous *MahĀbhĀrata,* and 'the Combat of the Devas and Asuras' illustrates Hindu mythology. Warriors are also found at the two extremities of the bas-reliefs of the 'Churning of the Sea of Milk'; these show the vehicles which have brought the gods and demons to the place where the action occurs.

The only bas-relief at Angkor Wat (excepting those late reliefs we said we would not study, and that of the 'Heavens and Hells' which subject does not lend itself to chariots) where chariots do not appear is the so-called 'historic' march past in the scene (S gal., W wing) which will form the basis of our study for the other corps in Angkor Wat, and where it would have been appropriate to see chariots coexisting with elephants, the cavalry, and the infantry.

In the Bayon the problem is the same. No chariot appears in the outer gallery in the bas-reliefs which can be considered historic. When one is found in the inner gallery—and they appear rarely—they belong to the gods who rarely mount them.

Apart from the example at Banteay Chmar, then, chariots only appear in scenes relating to mythology or the gods, and never in scenes which could be considered historic.

Can one not deduce from this that the Khmer army did not have a cavalry corps, and if one finds numerous examples of chariots on the bas-reliefs, especially at Angkor Wat, it is only because the sculptors conscientiously illustrated vehicles which the epic or religious texts attributed to this or that personage?

This is the conclusion of H.G. Quaritch Wales[3] from observations identical to ours. He notes, in addition, that Coedès and G. Groslier after him acknowledged that this army had four divisions on the strength of uncertain translations of texts. The first was an eleventh century inscription (AD 1069) known as the 'stele of PĀlhĀl' which Coedès incorrectly translated.

The passage in question is *sa rĀjĀ viṣṇulokakhya caturaṅgavalĀnvitahḥ*[4] which Coedès translated as 'The king Viṣṇuloka with an army of four components' ['quatre membres']. Quaritch Wales questioned the word 'membres', without however proposing an alternative. Coedès was perhaps embarrassed by his translation; he certainly was by a different term in another inscription[5] at Banteay Chmar dating from the reign of Jayavarman VII and also giving an account of an offensive action. He confesses having translated 'in a completely hypothetical manner' the word he stumbled over, and which Aymonier, before him, had translated according to his fashion, by 'division (of an army)' and he adds 'As is known, the armies consisted of four divisions: infantry, cavalry, elephants, and chariots.'

The text he gives of this passage is '(the prince) directed all the royal ceremonies. When he led the four divisions (?) of the Khmer army to do battle in 78 locations…'. In choosing this term, Coedès seems to have been influenced by the fact that no one imagined, at that period, that the Khmer army could not have had four divisions which the Indian texts speak of.

Quaritch Wales goes on to add that in the Siamese army, which he also studies in his book, chariots, as one of the four traditional divisions of the Indian army, had been replaced by artisans and were abandoned in India in the seventh century. This last piece of information was probably provided by R. Dikshitar, who gives proof of this assertion.[6]

S. Sahai all the same considers he 'proposed no convincing argument'.[7] We think his opinion harsh. The study of the war chariots we have just completed seems to us, on the contrary, to confirm Quaritch Wales' viewpoint.

---

[3] H.G. Quaritch Wales, *Ancient South-East Asian Warfare*, London (B. Quaritch), 1952, p. 84 and n. 3.

[4] G. Coedès, 'Etudes cambodgiennes, XI, La stèle de PĀlhĀl', *BEFEO*, XIII, bk 6, p. 29, line XXI and p. 34 line XXI.

[5] G. Coedès, 'Etudes cambodgiennes, XXIX, Nouvelles données chronologiques et généologiques sur la dynastie de Mahīdharapura'. *BEFEO*, XXIX 1929, p. 315 and n. 4.

[6] R. Dikshitar, *War in Ancient India*. London (Macmillan), 1944.

[7] S. Sahai, 'Les institutions politiques et l'organisation administrative du Cambodge ancien (VI-XIIIe siecle)'. Paris, EFEO, 1970, p.134, n.3.

At Angkor Wat there is no carving of a chariot which can be attributed to Sūryavaran's warriors. The bas-reliefs of the 'historic' march past has none, like the external gallery of the Bayon, and we have already considered how examples in the inner gallery should be viewed. The example at Banteay Chmar is of doubtful meaning.

Furthermore, what would the Khmer army have done with a chariot corps in a country where the soil is either clayey or sandy, where ruts quickly form and which periodically becomes a swamp? In contrast to the carts, which are well adapted to the terrain, notably with their side runners, the chariots, drawn by horses more fiery than Khmer cattle, would soon have broken their axles or become stuck in the mud.

We cannot therefore say that there never was a single example of a chariot in Cambodia, but if there were any, they did not take part, in the twelfth or thirteenth centuries, in armed combat.

2. The cavalry

The cavalry is shown fairly frequently in the Khmer bas-reliefs of the twelfth and thirteenth centuries.

At Angkor Wat it appears mixed with the war chariots and elephants in the great mythical battles, but by good fortune, in this monument to see the cavalry, along with the infantry and elephants, on the bas-relief called 'the royal or historic parade', is proof it really existed.

At the Bayon and Banteay Chmar the cavalry is much less visible. It is almost entirely absent from the great battles portrayed on the outer gallery of the Bayon, which emphasize above all the infantry and the elephants of the enemy's armies, and in both monuments few horses appear in the armies' movements.

At first, we shall only look at the externals of this corps, namely the appointments of the horses and the outfits of the horsemen. The relative and real importance of the cavalry which really existed in the Khmer army, unlike the chariots, will only be appreciated in relation to the elephants and the infantry, after we have examined these other two military corps in the same manner.

We shall now examine the appointments of the horses of the military from, initially, a general viewpoint, then in detail, and follow this with the horsemen.

Fig. 40 shows in an ideal fashion the appointments of a cavalry horse. It is rare for all the constituent elements of these appointments to be found on all the horses. This is because the appointments have little evolved from the Angkor Wat period to that of the Bayon, but above all is linked to the work of Khmer sculptors, who were rather forgetful, so to say, of certain details. What is important in our Western logic was not for them, and, for example, the fact of showing a saddle cloth while 'overlooking' showing the harnessing, without which the saddle cloth could not have stayed on the animal's back, did not worry them in the least. To them, it was more important that the saddle be decorated in all its details. The same problems will be encountered when the appointments of the elephants are examined.

For the same period we have had to bring together several examples of horses to be more or less sure of reconstituting their appointments as they probably appeared at that time.

We emphasize in this study that it is the details which most often disappear, in addition to those which vanish from one period to another.

For greater clarity we shall study these appointments in three parts: the bridle, the cloth serving as a saddle, and lastly the decoration around the horse's neck.

The bridle, by which we mean the part of the horse's appointments used for leading the horse, consists of a bit (Fig. 40.1), to which are attached the two cheek straps (2) of the bridle, joined over the head by two rings into which the ears (3) are inserted. A throat lash (4) links the splice of the ear rings. The reins (5), attached to the bit, go over the animal's head.

These elements are never forgotten and appear on all horses in whatever monument.

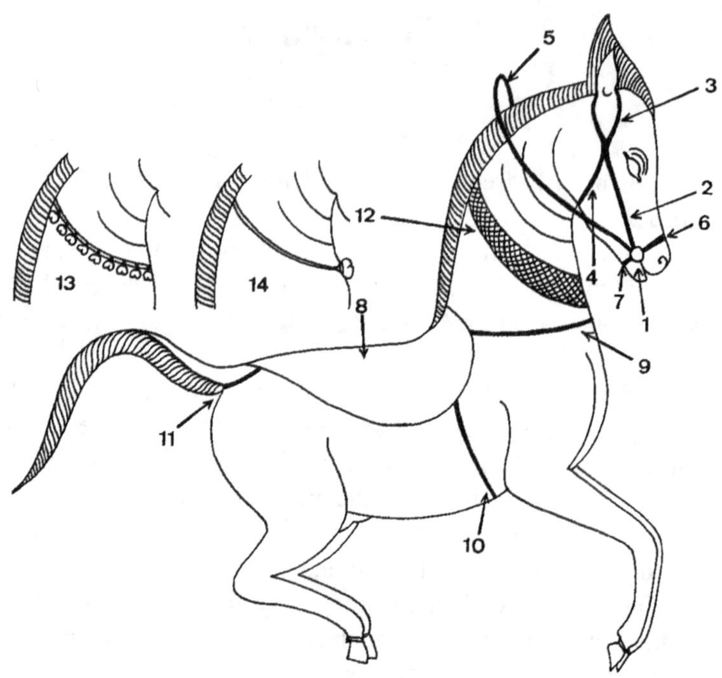

Fig. 40. Schema of appointments of a cavalry horse.

At Angkor Wat there is also a nose-band (6) which is rarely forgotten by the sculptors, but is never found at the Bayon and Banteay Chmar, and a back stay (7), often barely visible, since hidden by the reins, and which is also absent from horses in the other two monuments.

The horse has no saddle, in spite of the assertions of Lefebre de Noëttes,[1] but at Angkor Wat has a circular cloth instead (8), which virtually disappears in the illustrations of the other two monuments. This cloth is, in theory, held in position by three kinds of straps on the horse's back. These are never shown at the Bayon and Banteay Chmar, and they are often completely or partially overlooked at Angkor Wat. They should however normally appear: a breast strap (9), a strap going under the horse's stomach (10), and a crupper (11).

It should, incidentally, be noted that the Khmer horse's tail was not cut, so it was necessary to trim its mane and tail fairly short. One should also point out that there were no stirrups, though these were known in Champa and Siam.

The third part of the appointments of a cavalry horse were the ornaments around the neck and withers. They almost never disappeared completely. They can include a richly decorated horse collar (12), a row of small bells (13), or just a rope with as pendant which looks like a large cow bell (14).

---

[1] Commander Lefebre des Noëttes, *L'attelage, le cheval de selle à travers les âges.* Paris (Picard), 1931, 2 vols, p. 101.

These decorative elements, usually found singly, can exceptionally be combined in twos: for example, a horse collar and a bell rope, or a collar and a row of small bells.

Having completed an overview of the appointments of a cavalry horse, we shall study in details these different elements in the same order.

The bridle (Fig. 41) seems to be made of plaited ropes. The link between several elements (at the level of the rings round the ears and the throat lash) is effected by a splice that is difficult to analyse (Fig. 41.1) or not shown (Fig. 41.3 & 4), or thanks to a buckle, probably of metal, decorated with the motif of an open flower (Fig. 41.2).

The ends of the bit are fairly frequently decorated with a flower motif like that just mentioned (Fig. 41.2 & 3). The nose-band is very frequently decorated with different motifs, including lines of beading or rows of stylized leaves ending in a lotus flower (Fig. 41.1 & 2).

At the Bayon, the mount of someone who appears to be important has unusual appointments not seen elsewhere (Fig. 102): the ears and a tuft of the mane on top of the horse's head are threaded into a ring with a beading motif, and the forehead of the horse is decorated with a floral pendant. But in this monument, as at Banteay Chmar, the horses' bridles only usually have the pieces we have mentioned in Fig. 41.4, and do not have, in contrast to the examples of Angkor Wat, either a nose-band or a back stay.

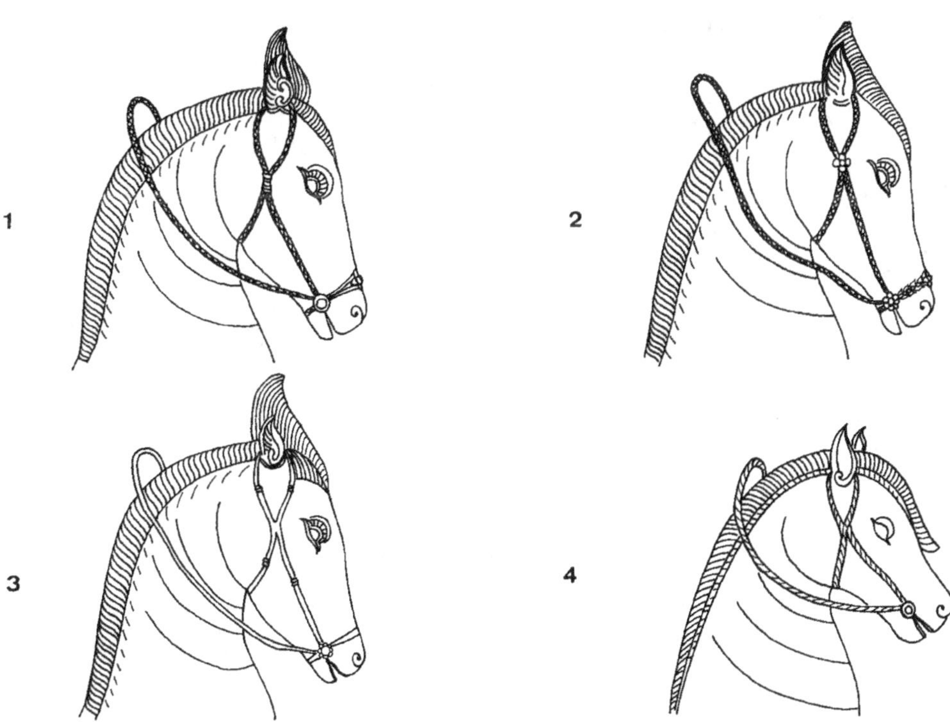

Fig. 41. Bridles for horses.
Angkor Wat, 1, 2, 3. Bayon, Banteay Chmar 4.

We should note that in these four illustrations there is a wide variety in the treatment of the manes, often carefully tended and frequently decorated with a tuft on top of the horse's head between the ears.

The second basic piece of a horse's equipment in the cavalry is the cloth serving as a saddle. Its decoration is extremely varied. It has a fringed edge similar to those found on elephants' saddle cloths, but less rich on the whole: single or double rows of beading, rows of small flowers or stylized leaves dotted with flowers in bloom etc. The material of the saddle cloth is decorated or otherwise with classical Khmer florets. The connections between this cloth and the straps holding it in position are never shown in the bas-reliefs of the twelfth or thirteenth centuries, but, as we have said, these straps were often omitted. The designs in Fig. 42 show the models at Angkor Wat. At the Bayon, with one exception (Fig. 104) and especially at Banteay Chmar, the cloth does not appear, as we have already indicated.

The third and last piece of a horse's equipment are the ornaments at its neck (Fig. 43).

The necklace, where it is found, is decorated to a greater or lesser extent and varies in width. The usual decorative elements are found: beading, rows of stylized leaves, pendants which, at Angkor Wat, end on the breast with a fully opened floral motif (Fig. 43.1 & 2). More unusual at the Bayon and at Banteay Chmar, the collar is less richly elaborated (Fig. 43.3). On some examples the way the collar was held in position is suggested (Fig. 43.2); it was simply knotted.

The little bells only differ in being more or less spherical, as well as more or less numerous—they are rounded and closer to each other at the Bayon and Banteay Chmar than at Angkor Wat (Fig. 43.4-6)—and by the existence, on occasions, on the chest of one bell bigger than the others (Fig. 43.4). The pendant sported by some horses,

Fig. 42. Saddle cloths for horses. Angkor Wat.

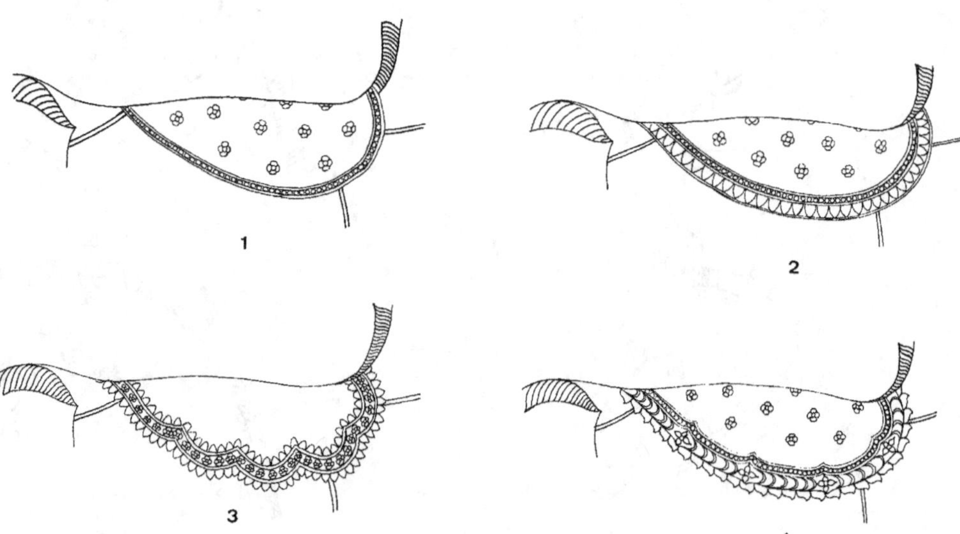

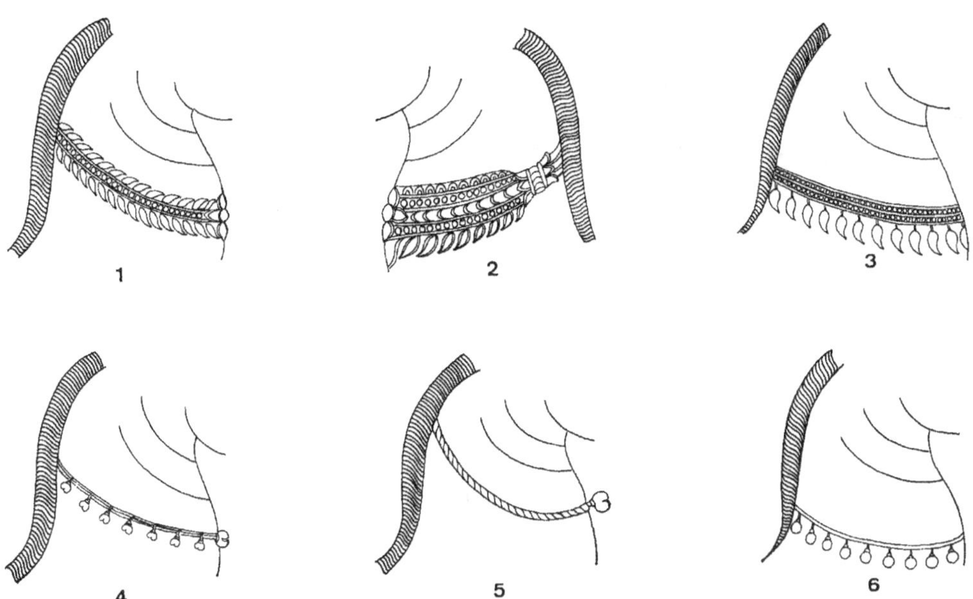

Fig. 43. Horses' neck ornaments.
Angkor Wat, 1, 2, 4, 5. Bayon, Banteay Chmar, 3, 6.

held in place by a rope, is rather difficult to identify, but it must have been a bell (Fig. 43.5). As noted, these neck ornaments could exceptionally be combined in pairs.

The study of the horse's appointments now complete, we shall turn our attention to the riders, dealing with their dress and their weapons.

In the 'historic' march past at Angkor Wat, the horsemen are all dressed in the same fashion (Fig. 44.1). They have a loincloth covering the top of the thighs and held up by a belt, over which flows a broad train on the right side. The chest is covered by a short jacket with the bottom corners rounded off, leaving the stomach exposed; one side of the jacket folds over the other. The neckline forms a 'V' and the sleeves are short. Around the neck, the horsemen wear a pendant necklace, or sometimes carry a small cutlass in its sheath which we have already mentioned. The material of these clothes is as usual very varied, but with cloth decorated with florets dominating. The piping is always emphasized with bead-like decoration.

At the Bayon and Banteay Chmar the dress of some horsemen is similar to the infantry. There is, therefore, some diversity which is not the case at Angkor Wat. The rider wears a loincloth, the two front ends of which are squashed between the side of the horse and the soldier's leg, and he has a short jacket with front tails having rounded corners, whose two sides meet but do not fold over each other; the neckline is 'V'-shaped and the sleeves are short. A pendant necklace around the neck is never omitted. The materials are similar to those at Angkor Wat and the piping on the jacket almost always emphasized by beading.

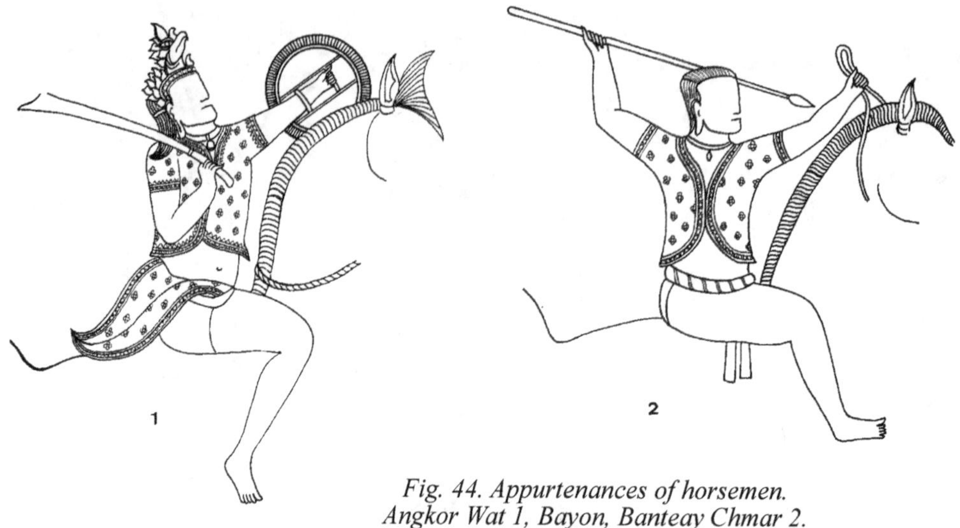

Fig. 44. Appurtenances of horsemen.
Angkor Wat 1, Bayon, Banteay Chmar 2.

The jacket can be longer, and occasionally the loincloth is replaced by a kind of pleated breeches with the edges piped with beading, and a belt, which cannot be seen, ending with a twisted flap of cloth (Fig. 101).

This jacket can even sport double sleeves (Fig. 102), the loincloth becoming a sarong with a side train, draped like the horsemen at Angkor Wat. This last example is unique.

At the Bayon and Banteay Chmar, we can find some diversity of dress, unlike the uniformity prevailing at Angkor Wat. But for headdresses, the opposite is true.

At Angkor Wat the headdress of the horsemen is extremely curious and very varied. Two general categories emerge: the hairstyle proper and the headdress with an animal tiara (Fig. 45).

Some horsemen have their hair combed and knotted at the top of the nape of the neck like a little bun. This is the hair style of the warriors on elephant back or the mahouts (Figs 56 & 59). There are some variations here. The hairstyle in Fig. 45.1 has the hair fairly long, reaching the shoulders, and simply thrown back, the forehead being girt with a narrow beaded band. The second hair style (2) has the hair just as long and also combed back, but a few locks are gathered together at the top of the head, and tied at their base to form a little quiff. The band holding the quiff has beading, with lotus petals all round forming a corolla. But these hair styles are often unique and the horsemen more commonly wear animal tiaras on their heads.

One of these tiara headdresses, the simplest and that seen most often, is found in (3): the hair is long and thrown back, reaching down the shoulders and slightly upturned at the end. The forehead sports a tiara in two parts: a band decorated with small leaves going behind the ear, and marking it with a larger leaf; and the head a bird with a predatory beak, markedly indented at the crest, and with stylized plumage at the neck.

Headdress (4) is a variant on this; the diadem is more richly decorated and the hair cannot be seen, but the same predatory beak is found, with a few modifications, and here with outstretched wings.

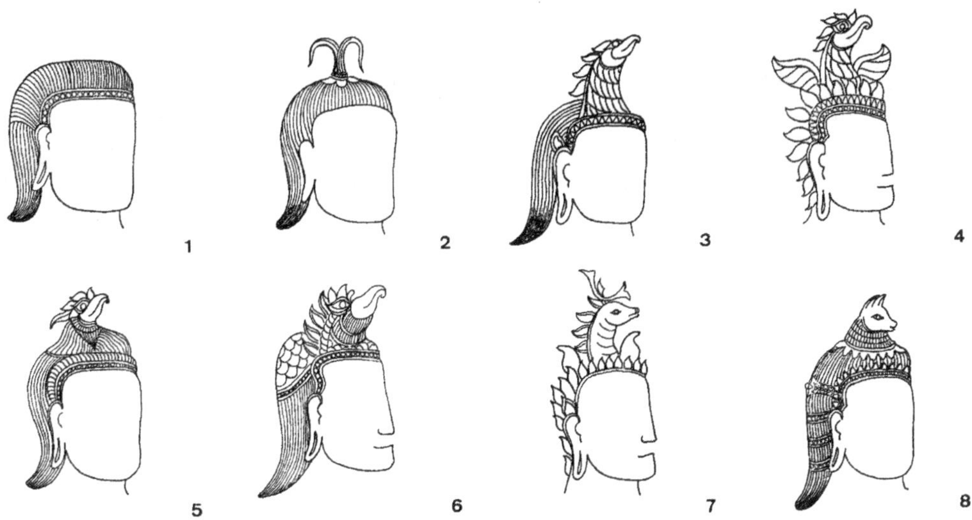

Fig. 45. Headdresses with an animal tiara.
Angkor Wat, S gal., W wing.

On headdress (5), the tiara is more modest (a beaded row, and a row of leaves); the hair can be seen again, covering the nape and reaching the shoulders. The tiara is topped by the same bird's head, and its wings seem to be folded back.

A final version on the predatory beak is model (6) which, in addition to the bird's head, tops the head with a skullcap with a beaded edge and a scaly surface.

This type of headdress, with a predatory bird's head, is notably predominant among the cavalry. There are numerous variants, a few of which we have indicated. But each warrior had an original headdress, the theme of which is above all as outlined here.

Yet other animals on top of the headdress are found. That of (7) has an antlered deer, and is fairly frequently seen. The antlers are treated more or less realistically. The hair is sometimes seen on the nape of the warrior's neck, sometimes not.

We shall not venture to identify the animal's head on the headdress (8), which is sometimes seen. But one should notice that, for this headdress, the bands with beading decoration and lotus flowers tie the thrown-back hair without bunching it up.

All these animal headdresses are found among the foot soldiers at Angkor Wat. We shall consider later the materials which could have been used to make them and their possible meaning.

At the Bayon and Banteay Chmar, the horsemen have most commonly short hair which is carefully combed. The important person on horseback (Fig. 102), about whom we shall speak again later, has a little bun at the nape of his neck, a rare detail which appears to be a sign of his caste. At the inner gallery of the Bayon, a few horsemen have a coiffure of lotus flowers, a motif which will be considered when dealing with the foot soldiers.

We will close this section on the cavalry with a few words about the arms carried by the horsemen.

At Angkor Wat, these arms are above all offensive; the lance is common, as are also the sabre and the Khmer axe (Fig. 44.1). The only weapon they never carry is the bow. In addition, they can be sometimes seen with a round buckler (Fig. 44.1). At the scenes of the great battles in the other galleries, there is more variety, but we have already expressed reservations about these scenes.

At the Bayon and Banteay Chmar, the horsemen only carry a lance and never a buckler (Fig. 44.2).

3. War elephants

Throughout all the military scenes in the bas-reliefs at Angkor Wat, the Bayon and Banteay Chmar, elephants are the animals most often illustrated. They fill various roles—we saw some of them when considering weapons; others will be seen when examining the commissariat.

But their chief role, to be examined here, was to serve as the mounts of high-ranking warriors, if one judges by the multitude of honorific emblems surrounding them. They thus constituted a military corps which could be called the 'elephantery'.

As with the cavalry, we shall only examine the externals, that is the equipment of the animals and that of the warriors, generally at first, then in greater detail.

As the appointments of the elephants varied somewhat in the details from one monument to the other, we encountered in reconstituting them the same difficulties as for the cavalry. So to simplify matters, we have at first schematized these appointments which ought in all cases to have existed—in Angkor Wat, the Bayon and Banteay Chmar—if the sculptors had not been 'forgetful' of certain details in all their carvings.

At Angkor Wat (Fig. 46) the essential parts of the elephant's harnesses are:

(a) a howdah, or pack, placed on the animal's back, coming in various forms, but which always has a platform with a side balustrade carved in different fashions; this platform also had at its four corners hooks when seen from the front, but which G. Groslier[1] thinks were perpendicular to the horizontal axis of the whole. They were linked by curved cross-braces probably meant to stabilize the howdah on the elephant's back;

(b) the howdah is placed on a mat covering the elephant's back, the mat being always round. Groslier[2] thinks there was also some padding, which is not shown in the bas-reliefs, to protect the animal's delicate back;

(c) the howdah is held in position by ropes linked to the hooks. At Angkor Wat they are independent of each other; in spite of the sculptor's blunders, over-sights or incomprehension, one can distinguish the rope of the breast strap, the underbelly rope (linked to the front hooks of the howdah), and the crupper.

Apart from these essentials, the elephant's appointments included a number of secondary accessories, among them a mat inside the howdah, the end of which goes over the crupper, a headpiece like a bonnet, occasionally the *mukuṭa*, the diadem on the forehead (though how it was held in position is a mystery), a very rich collar, bells hanging from the howdah by thin ropes, the bell at the neck tied to the breast strap or to the collar, and restraining straps inside the howdah which are sometimes held by

---

[1] G. Groslier, *Recherches…* op. cit., p. 105.
[2] G. Groslier, *Recherches…* op. cit., p. 105.

Fig. 46. Schema of an elephant's appointments at Angkor Wat.

warriors standing on the animal's back. It would seem that paint was placed around the eyes of some elephants.

The elephant's appointments at the Bayon and Banteay Chmar (Fig. 47) also have as the most important the howdah, much the same as that seen at Angkor Wat. Like those, it is placed on a round mat, but is held in position on the animal's back, not by a separate system of ropes independent of each other, as at Angkor Wat, but by a holding rope going round the animal, linking up with the hooks, and becoming finally the equivalent of a breast strap, an underbelly rope and a crupper.

As secondary accessories one should mention a headpiece and very exceptionally a *mukuṭa*, a rope round the neck from which is hung a bell, small bells fixed to the howdah's hooks, and some paint occasionally around the eyes of some beasts. One should note the absence of decoration on the tusks though they are found in carving in the round and in royal treasuries.

Let us now examine in details the elephant's appointments: the howdah, the mats of the howdahs, and the accessories.

The howdahs always have the same elements but their form and decoration change. Several types can be distinguished. The most common in all the bas-reliefs is that with the curving balustrade (type 1).

62

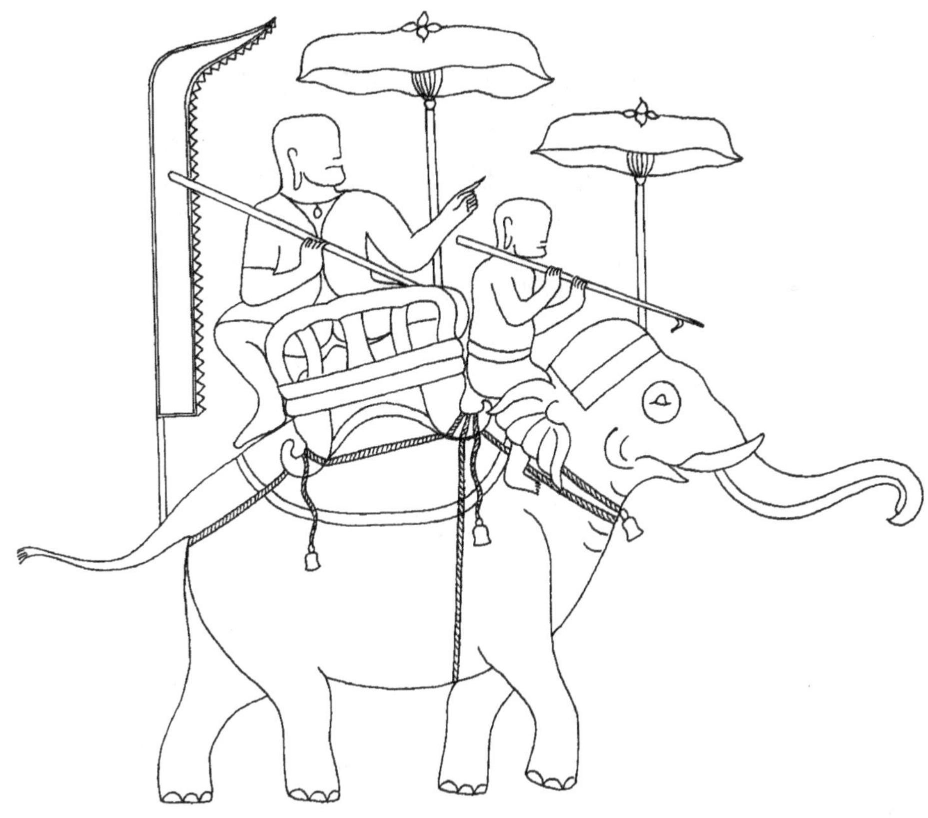

Fig. 47. Schema of an elephant's appointments at the Bayon and Banteay Chmar.

At Angkor Wat, where one sees it first (Fig. 48A) the shape is elegant and graceful. The side view is redented with various carved motifs arranged in horizontal lines. The platform extends below to four decorated hooks, with the ends upturned.

G. Groslier, as we mentioned, thinks the hooks were perpendicular to the long sides of the platform but not in their extension. These hooks are linked two by two by double curved cross-pieces which give stability to the howdah on the elephant's back. The howdah has on the sides a balustrade, formed here by two open-work parts, one above the other. The lower part is narrow and separated by a decorative band from the upper part with a curved profile, with three elaborate balusters.

This type sometimes has an additional motif: the hooks, instead of being merely bent back, are decorated with raised *nāga* heads coming from tiny *makara* (Fig. 48B).

This basic type at Angkor Wat is broadly found at the Bayon and Banteay Chmar, though its silhouette becomes rather heavier (Fig. 49A). The side view of the platform is more solid, the hooks are identical, but more massive. There is only one thick cross-piece with decorative rings, the top curve of which touches the platform. The balustrade, viewed from the side, has a bent outline and is less elegant and simpler, and is no longer lightened by a lower open-work band. It also has three balusters.

63

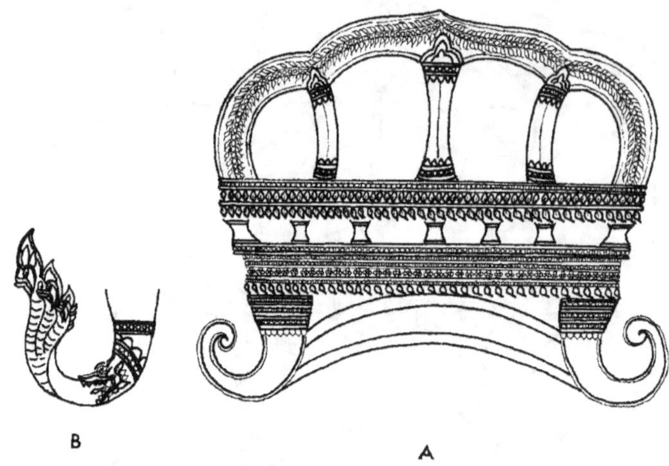

Fig. 48. Elephant howdah. Type 1.
Angkor Wat.

All the illustrations of numerous elephant howdahs in these two monuments, but, as at Angkor Wat, show several variants on the basic type in the details, notably seen at the Bayon on the N panel of the E side of the outer gallery: they are mostly evident in the cross-pieces. Thus (Fig. 49B 1-3) the cross-piece, instead of connecting directly to the platform is linked to it by a rather elegant leaf motif. Some of these howdahs have hooks decorated with *nāga* heads (Fig. 49C).

There are other variants on this type, still at the Bayon but in the inner gallery (Fig. 50A, B). The general shape of the howdah is made to appear lighter. The balustrade

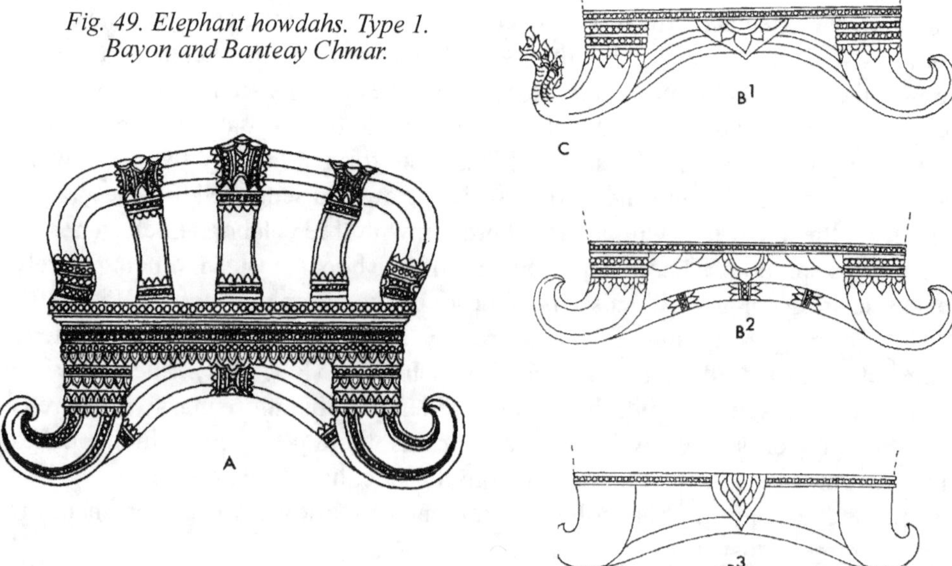

Fig. 49. Elephant howdahs. Type 1.
Bayon and Banteay Chmar.

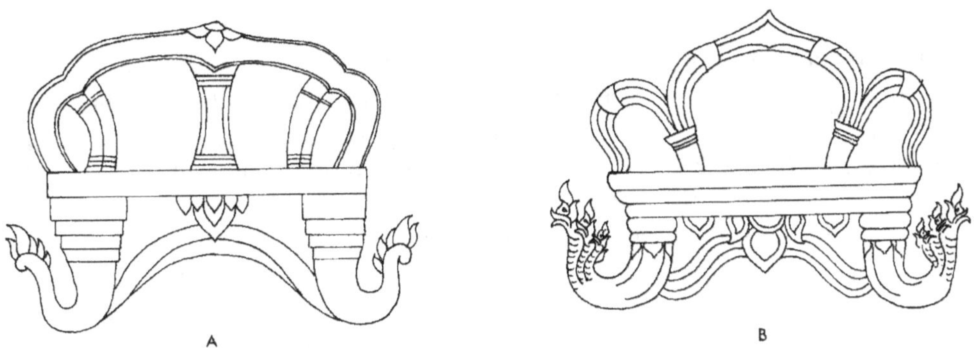

Fig. 50. Elephant howdahs. Type 1.
Bayon, inner gallery.

can be markedly curved (Fig. 50B). It has two or more, most often three, balusters. The cross-pieces are like those of the earlier models. The hooks are decorated with simple and complex *nāga* heads. The decorative detail is, however, much less rich then the earlier examples in the outer gallery, but this could be said of all the bas-reliefs in the inner gallery of the Bayon.

A different type of howdah, with a straight balustrade (type 2) is found much less frequently than type 1.

At Angkor Wat it is, however, found more or less everywhere, but especially in the 'historic' march past relief in the S gallery, W wing. There are several variants. The most frequent, and simplest, has a straight balustrade with six elaborate balusters, with both ends having raised *nāga* heads, and the hooks also raised in the same way, a double cross-piece with three curves, and very rich decoration (Fig. 51A).

A first variant (Fig. 51B) has the general characteristics of the previous model, but the balustrade is raised at the level of the platform by a narrow lattice strip similar to the model in Fig. 48A with curved balusters.

A second variant on Fig. 51A (Fig. 51C) has the same general form, but the balustrade consists of three parts: the central element, slightly higher than the side

Fig. 51. Elephant howdahs. Type 2.
Angkor Wat.

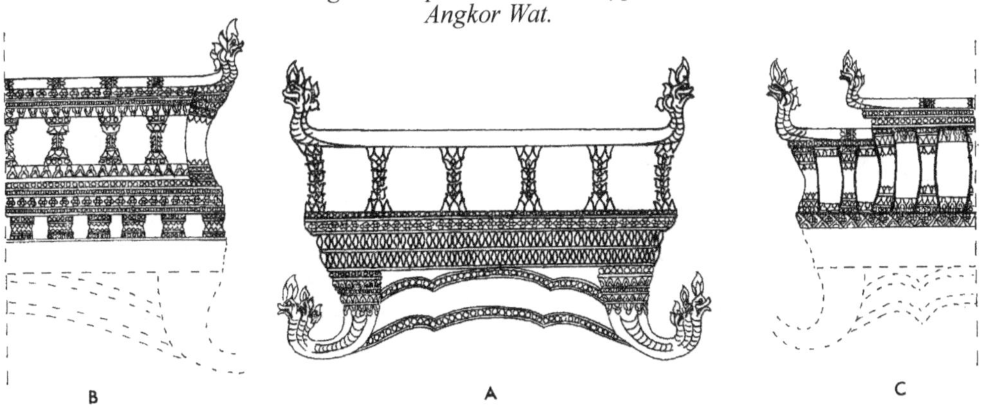

elements, comes in front of these. The ends also have *nāga* heads. This is the type of howdah on the mount of King Paramaviṣṇuloka in the 'historic' march past.

A richer variant of this type is found on the mount of Indra in the bas-relief of the 'Battle between the Deva and the Asura' (N gallery, W wing) (Fig. 52A). The central part of this howdah, corresponding to the raised part of the balustrade, seems clearly detached from the side elements; the ends of the balustrades are supported by a frieze of telamones taking the form of small monsters. The balustrade of the central part bears, folded over, a kind of small rectangular mat found on no other howdah.

Yet another type (Fig. 52B) is similar to the type 2 howdah and to type 1 with the curved balustrade. Some examples can be seen in the bas-relief of the 'Battle between the Deva and the Asura'.

The ends of the upper part of this howdah are formed from the same balustrade ends as the rectilinear model found in Figs 51C and 52A. But the raised central part, instead of having another element of the rectilinear balustrade, curves in the same way as the types with curved balustrades. The hooks are of both types. This is a kind of composite model.

At the Bayon the howdahs with rectangular balustrades are only seen in the reliefs on the inner gallery. The workmanship is often indifferent, like much else in this gallery.

Most often the model derives, in simplified form, from the single balustrade at Angkor Wat (Fig. 53A). Other forms have the balustrade diminishing in breadth (Fig. 53B), a heightening of the howdah with an additional element (Fig. 53C), and other variations of greater of lesser felicity (Fig. 53D).

Another of the appointments of the war elephants is the harnessing. These were described in the general introductory section, and we have seen differences between what was found at Angkor Wat and the Bayon and Banteay Chmar.

It should be recalled, in relation to the harnessing, that in all the monuments they are extremely difficult to study because of the 'oversights' of the sculptors.

The third element in the appointments of the war elephants is the mat on the howdah, which was essential to protect the elephants' backs. Perhaps they also had some

Fig. 52. Elephant howdahs.
Angkor Wat, N gal, W wing Coedès 447. Bayon, N gal, W wing.

Fig. 53. Elephant howdahs.
Bayon, inner gal.

padding, as G. Groslier suggests, but that is never evident, except perhaps in the patterns of the checks on some of them (Fig. 54D).

They are always roughly circular in shape and are more or less rich. Very elaborate at Angkor Wat (Fig. 54A, B), they are simpler at the Bayon (Fig. 54C, D). The decorative motifs beloved by Khmer sculptors are all found there—florets, various forms of beading, lotus flowers, rows of leaves, and pendants.

The accessories for these appointments for war elephants are numerous, as we have seen (Fig. 55).

The mats extending beyond the howdah to the rear on the elephant's rump are always to be seen at Angkor Wat, but their decoration hardly evolves (Figs 88-92); at the Bayon they are absent, with certain exceptions (Fig. 53C). The elephants always have a headdress. In most cases it is in the form of a cap or bonnet, both at Angkor Wat and the Bayon and Banteay Chmar. This can be round with a wavy edge (Fig. 55A), like a skullcap, and can also have a more rectangular border forming a right angle on each side of the head (at the Bayon especially). Whatever its form, it has an embroidered border decorated with florets. When the elephant belongs to the king or a god, its headdress becomes more elaborate. It then has a *mukuṭa* including a diadem and a raised conical part, the whole being highly decorated (Fig. 55C). The upper part of this type of coiffure sometimes has three decorated cones (Fig. 55D). But it can

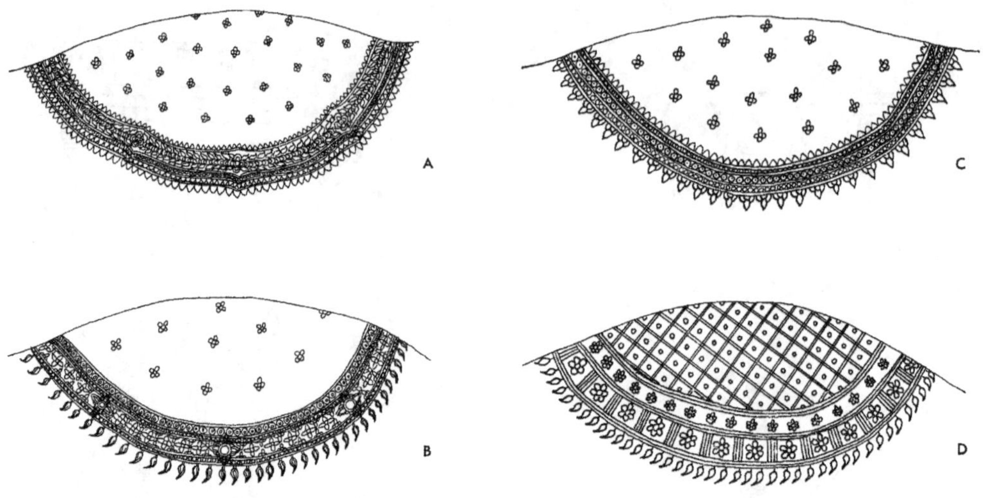

Fig. 54. Mats for elephants' howdahs.
Angkor Wat, A, B. Bayon, Banteay Chmar, C, D.

also take the form of a tiara, either simple or complex in its elaboration (Fig. 55E, F), or be a pointed head decoration made of scales cut like lotus leaves (Fig. 55G).

Collars are worn by the elephants at Angkor Wat only. They are very richly decorated (Fig. 55A, B, C). Only they have the prerogative of tiaras. They take the form of narrow bands, tapering towards the ends, and sometimes decorated with rosettes. They gird the animal's forehead and it is not clear how they were held in position (Fig. 55A, B, C).

It seems that around the eyes and the cheeks some elephants were painted (Fig. 55A) but one can say little about this.

Small bells appear at two specific places: at the elephant's neck there is usually one, tied to the breast-strap rope holding the howdah in position—this is the case at Angkor Wat (Fig. 55A, B, C), or tied with a special rope, as at the Bayon and Banteay Chmar (Fig. 47). Other bells are found against the elephant's flanks, hung by small ropes from the hooks of the howdah. These are found in every carving of an elephant.

This completes the study of the war elephants' appointments. We shall now turn to the warriors who mounted the animals and the mahouts who directed them. Each elephant had one warrior, never more, who took up his position on the howdah, and a mahout was seated cross-legged on the beast's head. We are unaware of any example which does not include the mahout.

The study of the warriors, in their dress and weapons, will be exclusively based, as at Angkor, on the bas-reliefs of the 'historical' march past; precisely because of

Right. Fig. 55. Elephant accessories. Angkor Wat, A, B, C, D. Bayon. E, F, G.
C. N gal, W wing, Angkor Wat (Coedès 447 for this sketch); D. W gal., N wing, Angkor Wat (Coedès 482 for this sketch); E. int. gal. E side, S wing (Dufour 9 for this sketch); F. int. gal., E side, S wing, Bayon (Dufour 12 for this sketch); G. int. gal, N side, E wing, Bayon (Dufour 115 for this sketch).

68

A

B

C

D

E

F

G

the nature of the work, it is more likely to present a more or less realistic image of the appearance of persons depicted.

The dress of the warriors, in general, was fairly uniform (Fig. 56A, B, C, D).

The material of the sarong, after being wrapped around the top of the thighs, extends to the right in a huge side train, reaching down to the warrior's ankles. It is held in position by a belt which holds, at the back, two flaps of cloth which appear between the legs and float freely. The warrior in Fig. 56C has brought one of these pointed flaps over his left thigh. Apart from the sarong of this person, the material of the other three costumes is strangely lacking in decoration. This is probably a sculptor's oversight.

The top of the body was protected by a breastplate; these were discussed when considering weapons. Fig. 56A, B, C reconstitute the complete dress. The first two, which show the warriors from the front and in profile, are sufficient to make the point; we have added Fig. 56C on account of the most unusual dress depicted. It shows King Sūryavarman II, who ordered the construction of Angkor Wat, designated by his posthumous name of Paramaviṣṇuloka in the inscription of the bas-relief. It is the richest dress we have seen. The cloth appears sumptuous, the breastplate is extremely detailed in its decoration, and, in addition to the headdress, which we shall discuss later, the king wears many jewels: rich bracelets at the biceps, bracelets on his wrists and ankles, a wrought belt holding up the sarong, and earrings in the shape of lotus buds.

In the whole march past, which has a score of mounted elephants, he is the only person to have these costume accessories like the heroes or gods in the great battles depicted in the other galleries. One is reminded of the description Zhou Daguan has left us of the king's dress in the thirteenth century.[3]

A very small number of warriors do not wear a breastplate, so one can see their jacket (Fig. 56D). It is simple, short, with cut-away front tails and a round neckline revealing a typical necklace with a pendant. One front panel of the jackets covers the other. The material is thin, except where the jacket sleeves are covered by a breastplate.

All the warriors are bare-headed except for the king and the head of the Siamese troops who takes part in the march past.

Contrary to the horsemen and the foot soldiers, whose exuberant head pieces we shall soon observe, their hair is not smoothed down but thrown back and knotted at the top of the nape of the neck into a small tight round bun. They do not wear earrings (Fig. 56A, B, D).

The king though (Fig. 56C) wears a wrought tiara which curves at the ears and appears to enclose the back of the skull; the diadem is topped by an engraved conical *mukuṭa*.

The weapons carried by these warriors are extremely diverse. Apart from the breastplate, as a defensive weapon they often carry in the left hand a round or long buckler (Fig. 56A, B, D). These bucklers are in most cases coupled with a lance

---

[3] Zhou, *Mémoires… op. cit.*, pp. 145-7.

70

Fig. 56. Weapons used by warriors on elephants.
Angkor Wat, S gal, W wing. Coedès 541 for sketch C.

(Fig. 56A, B, D), or sometimes with a Khmer axe (Fig. 90) which can be the only weapon carried (Fig. 56C).

In addition to these two weapons, the lance being most common, the warriors can also carry a sabre (Fig. 91), though very rarely, or more commonly a bow and arrow (Fig. 94); in this case a quiver placed on the howdah is visible.

Apart from the knives of the breastplate, which we have already discussed, one sometimes sees on some warriors a cutlass at the belt, the sheath of which is slipped inside the sarong on the right side, and which is held in position by the belt (Fig. 56B, C).

Very unusually a warrior has two offensive weapons. Thus in Fig. 90 the warrior has a Khmer axe and a buckler, in addition to his cutlass, and at the front of the howdah can be seen a quiver and a bow which he could also use.

Having completed the study of the warriors at Angkor Wat, we shall look at those in the other two monuments.

At Angkor Wat, the warriors perched on these elephants are also important persons; the abundance of honorific insignia around them shows this. Their dress is also according to their rank.

In the overwhelming majority of cases they wear a long jacket with short sleeves, made of various materials, checked, or dotted with florets, or just plain. The hems of the sleeves and the jacket are trimmed with a single or sometimes double rows of beading (Figs 57D, 58A) which can be replaced by a simple selvage (Fig. 57D).

This jacket has several variants. It can be shorter (Fig. 58A) and its hemline can be wavy (Fig. 57F). It can be very short, clinging to the body, leaving the belly exposed (Fig. 57A). On the other hand, it can have double front tails (Fig. 58B) or even triple ones (Fig. 58C, D). The jacket can be covered by a breastplate (Fig. 57B); these we have considered along with the weapons, indicating these examples were few and difficult to comprehend.

To summarize the discussion about jackets, we can say that in the majority of cases jackets take the form of a long coat with short sleeves and rounded front tails, the front edges do not overlap and the neckline leaves the neck exposed. The modifications we have mentioned only concern a minority of warriors.

The second part of the dress is more difficult to interpret because it is frequently hidden by the howdah or the jacket itself. This is the cloth which girds the loins. Sometimes it seems to be knee breeches without side flaps, covering the top of the thighs (Figs 57 E, F and 58B). Or it can be a draped sarong with side flaps, the disposition of which is incomprehensible, because of the attitudes struck by the warriors or because of simplifications introduced by the sculptors. A small flap is most common, going beyond the bottom of the jacket (Fig. 57A, B, C), and through the balustrade of the howdah one can glimpse in the background the sarong.

When the jacket is short, the sarong is more readily visible (Fig. 58A) or totally exposed (Figs 57A and 58E, F). It is difficult to understand the way it is worn: a cloth

Right. Fig. 57. Equipment of warriors on elephants, Bayon.

A
B
C
D
E
F

belt at the hip holds some material which, after going between the legs, covers the tops of the thighs and falls in multiple lappets to the sides; the belt itself must be part of these flap.

The warriors are nearly always bare-headed. In the outer gallery at the Bayon there is one example in a poor condition of a headdress (Fig. 58E). In the inner gallery, the analysis is made more difficult because mythological scenes are introduced into what one could consider representations of warriors of the period.

The hair is not cut but combed back and arranged on the head. Quite often, it forms a small round bun at the nape of the neck, held in position by what appears to be a long comb (Figs 57E and 58C).

The headdress of the warrior we wrote about in the outer gallery of the Bayon is effaced, but we thought it could be compared to the pointed headdress sported by a high-ranking warrior in the inner gallery (Fig. 58F). The head and nape of the neck seem to be covered by a kind of helmet with three protuberances: the central one is highest, and all three are embossed with regular concentric circles. In the same gallery can be found, more or less distinguishable, other renderings of this headdress.

All the warriors, like the rest of the Khmer army, go barefoot, though sandals form part of the regalia. The essential accessory to their dress is the pendant necklace at the neckline of the jacket. This is the only piece of jewellery they wear, with the exception of the warrior with the breastplate in the outer gallery of the Bayon who, apart from the necklace he seems to wear but which his breastplate hides, has a bracelet on each wrist and earrings in the shape of lotus buds (Fig. 58E). There are other exceptions among the warriors wearing head-pieces in the inner gallery at the Bayon, of which we have given an example (Fig. 58F). The earrings are similar to those already mentioned but the necklace is much more opulent and comes down to a point on his bare chest; the biceps are encased in worked bracelets decorated with an open lotus flower.

These warriors on elephants mostly carry a bow. The bows are all the same shape. Only the warrior in Fig. 58F has one with decorated ends. During marches, they hold their bow in the middle with one hand, and in the other have several arrows; beside them are one or two quivers (Fig. 58C, D). In battles, they pull the bowstring back with an arrow, ready to aim at the enemy; next to them can be seen the open quiver and the tops of arrows in it, though sometimes it is closed (Fig. 57A, B). They sometimes replace the bow and arrows with a lance or can have a number of arrows held in a large sized quiver (Fig. 57C). In the inner gallery of the Bayon, and very rarely in the outer gallery and at Banteay Chmar, they sometimes carry the Khmer axe on their shoulders (Fig. 57D). They only carry a buckler very rarely at the Bayon or at Banteay Chmar. With very few exceptions they only have offensive weapons.

These are the most common weapons carried by the warriors mounted on elephants. But there are other weapons.

In the inner gallery at the Bayon some warriors can be seen on elephants with a club or a sword, but we have expressed our reservations about this gallery.

Right. Fig. 58. Equipment of warriors on elephants. Bayon, ext. gal., W side, N wing. Dufour 62 for sketch E, and int. gal. E side, S wing. Dufour 9 for sketch F.

A

B

C

D

E

F

What one should rather note is that the howdahs of several warriors often carry another weapon than the one they are using, In Fig. 58C the quiver is next to a sword; in Fig. 57A it is next to a big cutlass. Sometimes the bow and quiver are placed in reserve and the warrior brandishes a lance.

To conclude this section, it should be noted that some warriors at the Bayon, in both inner and outer galleries, brandish in one hand a kind of triple-banded flag which floats in the wind and merges with the honorific insignia surrounding the elephants (Fig. 57F).

The other person on the elephant's back is the mahout. At Angkor Wat we shall, as for the warriors, study those appearing in the 'historic' march past (Fig. 58A, B, C).

His position is always the same: the mahout is seated cross-legged on the nape of the elephant's neck, wedged between the beast's head and the warrior's howdah behind him. He therefore always appears in profile or at an angle, his legs behind the elephant's ears; the feet, though, and part of his leg, reappear beneath the lower part of the ear. At the Bayon, however, this particular detail is mostly overlooked.

His dress is more regular at Angkor Wat than at the Bayon and Banteay Chmar. All the mahouts have the same type of sarong; one can see the material which girds the thighs, the side train is thrown back to the right as well as sometimes a part of the belt holding everything up. There may be a flap at the back or in front, because of too much cloth forming the belt, which cannot be seen in the carvings. The train on the right side, often partially hidden by the howdah, must have been joined to the cloth girding the thighs (Fig. 59A, B, C).

This type of sarong, also worn by the foot soldiers, is not easy to comprehend in the way it is worn, in spite of its apparent simplicity.

Fig. 59. Mahouts.
Angkor Wat, S gal., W wing.

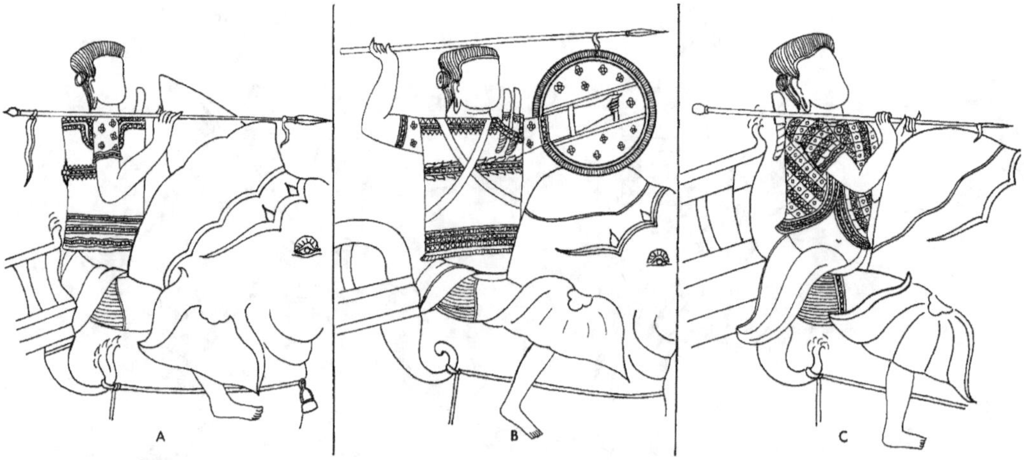

All the mahouts wear a short jacket with short sleeves and rounded front tails, leaving the belly exposed (Fig. 59C). But at the Bayon and Banteay Chmar one of the sides folds over the other and there is no neckline, but the sides of the jackets are straight, forming an opening at the base of the neck which has a pendant necklace on a thin cord, with a kind of small knife. This detail can also be seen among the foot soldiers.

Special to some of them is a knife, bigger than those seen on the pendants, carried on the back, probably held in position by string (Fig. 59C).

A fairly large number of mahouts cover their jackets with armour identical to that of the warriors on elephant back (Fig. 59A, B).

They have no headdress and their hair is thrown back and gathered into a small bun at the nape.

The arms carried in addition sometimes include a buckler (Fig. 59B). These are defensive weapons linked to their function which was not to fight but to control and direct their elephant according to the warrior on the howdah, during marches or in battle, in the course of which the weapons and the buckler would be useful. As for the knives at their neck, on their back or their left side, these were not really weapons, but tools in the broad sense of the word.

However, their essential attribute, which all have, is the elephant crook, the *aṅkuḌa*, used to control the animal. It looks like a lance with a hook at one side (Fig. 59A, B, C). This crook, which is bent to difference degrees, would also have been useful in battle.

The bas-reliefs at the Bayon and Banteay Chmar, especially at the former, are better than those at Angkor Wat in the sense that, even if they are poorly carved, they show scenes which are very realistic. In the inner gallery at the Bayon (Fig. 60) can be seen an elephant on whose back the mahout has finished fastening the howdah, and one of his assistants is getting ready to pass him his crook.

Once the warrior is in position, the mahout takes up his position which does not change, whether on a march or in a battle; this is the same at Angkor Wat. He is thus stuck between the elephant's head and the howdah; though his possibilities of movement are very limited, that does not stop him turning sometimes to the warrior to receive his orders or draw his attention to something (Fig. 61C).

Unlike the mahouts at Angkor Wat, those of the other two monuments have very varied dress and headpieces.

One of the most common is linked to the simple sarong of the foot soldiers with its visible front ends, and a short jacket leaving the belly exposed but which is sometimes longer than normal (Fig. 61A). This jacket is made in the same way as those worn by all the people in the bas-reliefs, decorated with florets and various checks; the piping of the jacket, the sleeves as well, are beaded at the edges.

Fig. 61B allows us to see not only the position of the mahout with his back to us, almost the only one in the bas-reliefs, but also the arrangement of his dress, entirely similar to that worn by the foot soldiers, as will be seen. It also shows the hair combed in the standard manner.

The mahout in Fig. 61C has a longer jacket and a headdress which seems to cover the entire head and nape of the neck. It appears to be made of cloth pulled onto the

head like a skullcap, taking on the shape of the head. In fact two skullcaps seem to be discernable, one on top of the other, the second being topped with a lotus flower motif, the petals of which spread out around the skull, while in the central part, the middle of the flower emerges from the middle of the smaller petals in a sort of horn than bends backwards.

The model in Fig. 61D has a similar headpiece, a jacket and a loincloth, but also a kind of short breeches which seems to be pleated and have beaded piping. These breeches must in fact be a length of cloth worn like breeches.

The model in Fig. 61E has a loincloth which when rolled up shows it to have been printed with squares on a plain background; the jacket is short. The mahout's headpiece is most unusual. The hair is combed back but the forehead has a tiara with beading, the ends of which disappear into the hair behind the ears; the front is decorated with a short bent-back horn, the end of which curls up.

Right. Fig. 61. Mahouts. Bayon, ext. gal., (especially E side, S wing) except for sketch J (int. gal.).

A
B
C
D
E
F
G
H
I
J
K
L

With model Fig. 61F we start to see a series of special headdresses, resembling the Cham head gear, which will be examined later. These have given rise to the suggestion that the Chams were enrolled in the Khmer army, which is not impossible, since the Cambodian army must have had mercenaries and it is known that Cham princes fought for Jayavarman VII as vassals.

On the head of this mahout, who is wearing a jacket that covers his belly and what seems like short breeches, are the elements of the Cham headdress. The sides and rear of the head are covered with a double row of narrow, curved scales, a chin piece, and the whole is topped by a lotus flower. But is he really a Cham? Probably not.

A variation of this Cham headdress, or something Cham-inspired, is provided by the model seen in Fig. 61G. The lotus flower is in full bloom: the petals are well arranged and the centre of the motif rises and bends back exuberantly. This model is interesting and individual from another point of view. The mahout has breeches similar to Fig. 61D and a fairly long jacket comparable to that in Fig. 61C; its originality comes from the jacket being largely covered by a kind of form-clinging tunic covering the upper arms as well. It appears to be made of oblong strips, perhaps metal, rounded at the end; the rows of strips are placed on top of each other, like scales.

The model in Fig. 61H is dressed just like the model in Fig. 61D but the headdress again seems to be Cham-derived. It has three rows of scale-like unlinked strips, but sharpened and bent back at the ends, with a lotus flower on top of the head but no chin piece.

The model in Fig. 61I also has a Cham type of headdress with three rows of superposed strips joined to each other. There is no chin piece, but a lotus flower on top of the head, the top of which bends backwards like the models in Fig. 61C and D. This model is more original in its costume, which includes a closely pleated pair of breeches and a loincloth belt with a design like that in Fig. 61E. In addition the mahout has wound round his chest and neck what in the foot soldiers seems to us to be a spare loincloth.

The model in Fig. 61J is found in the inner gallery at the Bayon, whereas the earlier ones appear in the outer gallery. He has, in addition to a fairly long jacket which conceals his breeches or his loincloth, a headdress which seems to be of Cham inspiration and is found on the foot soldiers in that gallery. Large bent petals frame the face, and a lotus flower tops the whole. But on this model, which seems to us unique, the centre of the lotus seems to take on the form of a beaked bird's head, like a Garuḍa. Perhaps this is a distant throwback to the zoomorphic head pieces of Angkor Wat which we have seen, up to now, worn by the cavalry but which the infantry in the Bayon also frequently wear.

Lastly the models Fig. 61K and L, especially K, take on the characteristics of the classic foot soldiers of the Bayon in the outer gallery. They are often found. Model K is one of the most frequent, with those of Fig. 61A and B in the outer gallery of the Bayon. In the inner gallery the dress of the mahouts is more like those in Fig. 61 J. For Banteay Chmar we have supplied no model because the dress of the mahouts there is similar to those found in the outer gallery of the Bayon.

Some mahouts at Angkor Wat wear armour. None is found at the Bayon or Banteay Chmar (except perhaps the model in Fig. 61G). But as at Angkor Wat they sometimes sport a round buckler which they brandish in their left hand (Fig. 61A, E) and which in truth would not have been useless. However, they are rare, and in most cases only have in their hands the *aṇkuḐa*, the goad, the pointed tip of which had a hook and sometimes, in addition, a kind of twisted sharpened point (Fig. 61H).

4. The infantry

The infantry constitutes the bulk of the army shown on the bas-reliefs at Angkor Wat, the Bayon and Banteay Chmar, where it almost eclipses the others corps in the army.

It is rather difficult to indicate the common characteristics of their accoutrements or their arms, because they vary enormously, not only from one monument to another, but also from one bas-relief to another in the same building.

At Angkor Wat we shall restrict our study to the bas-reliefs on the 'historic' march past for the reasons already often stated.

In this long procession, of which we have already studied the cavalry and the elephant corps, the foot soldiers are very well represented. We shall consider later what seems to be their position in relation to the other army corps. As for their arms, they are both varied and uniform, depending on the type of weapon being considered.

Their dress varies little, and the few variations primarily concern the sarong. The variations of the upper part concern the breastplate or a short jacket with founded front tails and a round neckline.

On the other hand, their headdresses are extremely varied and complex, unlike the warriors mounted on elephants who, as we have seen, with the exception of the king, only have their hair gathered into a bun, but which brings them close to the cavalry, having the same hair style.

If one considers their weapons, there are two types of foot soldiers: those who carry a lance and a buckler, by far the most numerous and almost all wearing armour which the archers never have; they rely on their bows and the few arrows they have in their hand, but no quiver is to be seen.

These two types of foot soldiers do not mingle, but in the close order of this gallery, they follow on the heels of each other. One should also mention the very few carrying the Khmer axe at the end of the march past.

Let us now look more closely at the foot soldiers' accoutrements.

We have just said that there was little variation in their costume, but six variants can be observed.

In the dress of Fig. 62A, the sarong covers the tops of the thighs; it seems to be pleated, or at least printed with parallel stripes and edged with beaded piping. The excess cloth falls to the right in the single lappet, the hems of which have decorative beading. The rolled cloth belt holding it up is striped, and after probably passing between the legs, flows down at the back as a lappet which can be seen between the thighs. The chest is encased in a breastplate, the nature of which we have already considered. The breastplate here shows nothing of the jacket except the sleeves.

The dress of Fig. 62B has a sarong fairly similar to the preceding model, except that the right lappet extends, taking on the appearance of a side train, like most of the foot soldiers' sarongs, and the rear flap comes round to the front, apparently connected to the belt, and passing beneath it. The cloth clinging to the top of the thighs is not much in evidence and as will be seen is not shown on most of the models. The upper

Fig. 62. Foot soldiers. Angkor Wat, S gal., W wing.

part of the body, as in the previous model, has armour which only allows one to see the short sleeves of the jacket. One detail often observed at Angkor Wat with many foot soldiers and some mahouts is the small knife in its sheath hung round the neck, in addition to the knives going with the breastplate.

The sarong of Fig. 62C is the simplest of all: a length of cloth around the top of the thighs and the buttocks, a belt with a single front flap going over it. The breastplate completes the attire, but this sarong is coupled with the typical short jacket, like that worn by the foot soldiers in Fig. 62E. Another variant of this model, still with no breastplate but with the jacket, has a train on the right side linked to the sarong.

These two variants to the model in Fig. 62C, although without the breastplate, are worn by foot soldiers armed with lances and bucklers, which is rare.

The dress in Fig. 62D shows one of the most frequently depicted sarongs: the cloth girding the thighs can no longer be seen but certainly exists; a train falls to the right, the belt passes between the thighs and ends in a single fall of cloth, visible between the legs. The soldier also wears a breastplate which apparently conceals no jacket, for there are no short sleeves to be seen.

Up to this point, the clothing considered has been that of the foot soldiers armed with a lance and a buckler, and wearing a breastplate, apart from some very rare exceptions. The next two models considered are the archers' dress.

The dress of model Fig. 62E has a sarong with a train on the right side and a twisted belt going between the thighs. On the model shown there is no lappet coming from the belt, but some do have one in front or to the rear. This sarong is accompanied by a short sleeved jacket with rounded front tails, but one of the sides covers the other; the neckline is at the base of the neck which here has a string with a small knife as a pendant, similar to that of Fig. 62B. The edges of the jacket are emphasized with beading. The material is usually decorated with florets.

This is the dress of most of the archers. Some, though, at the head of the march past, wear a long jacket (Fig. 62F) with short sleeves, the fronts of which are rounded over the thighs. The right front covers the left and the neckline is the same as the previous model. The cloth is dotted with small flowers and its edges emphasized with beading. The jacket is tied by a cloth belt with one end falling in front. Nothing can be seen of the sarong.

We must now discuss the headdresses of these foot soldiers which we have already said are very varied. Apart from some extremely rare hairstyles of some of them (Fig. 62A), the rest can be grouped into three types: those with the hair thrown back with a topknot on the top of the head, those with their hair also thrown back but with a headband topped by a tiara, and those with hair combed back and a headband topped by an animal figure.

We shall study these three types of coiffures by dividing them into three parts: the front part with a headband on the forehead, the upper part with a top knot, a tiara, or an animal head, and the rear part comprising the hair thrown back, sometimes tied up or concealed by additional decoration.

The first type of headdress of the foot soldiers at Angkor Wat has a headband on the forehead. Fig. 63A, B, C show fairly clearly this headdress: the long hair is combed back, reaching the shoulders; the hair is gathered into a topknot on the top of the head, generally held in position by a decorative beaded band. The topknot varies in size. The rest of the hair is gathered by other bands, usually similarly decorated. The forehead has a headband going behind the ears; it is decorated to a greater or lesser extent, but the decorative elements are always the same—rows of beading, of lotus leaves, and loops.

Variants of this type of headdress can be seen in Fig. 63D, E. The hair is thrown back in the same fashion and tied; a headband goes across the forehead, single in Fig. 63E or more elaborate (Fig. 63D), but in addition a tuft of hair appears at the top of the head, tied by a ribbon in Fig. 63D; it becomes bigger in E where its base has a decorative ring, the edges of which form loops all around the top of the head.

The second type of headdress of the foot soldier, well shown in Fig. 63F, still has the hair thrown back, tied together, and the headband. The difference from the previous type lies in the appearance of a kind of tiara rising from the headband and probably hiding the topknot of hair in the first type of headdress. This tiara is decorated with the usual rows of leaves or beading.

The headdresses in Fig. 63G and H are similar to the last, except that the tiara has a decoration of narrow strips decreasing in height from the top of the head to the ears. It could almost be said that these last three headdresses have been given high tiaras.

Models in Fig. 63I and J are more complex. It is rather difficult to interpret headdress I, the headband of which is simply beaded; it has a topknot of hair decorated with beading and enclosed by a beaded band with lotus leaves above and below. The hair falling down to the neck is emphasized by successive rows of beading forming loops. This headdress could be considered a type 1 model but for the special treatment of the topknot.

Headdress J, though, emphasizes the headband, which goes very low behind the ears down to the shoulders. It is topped by a pyramid of loops and leaves which, decorating the lower part, hide the hair, which cannot be seen.

The third type of headdress, the most common, adds to the thrown-back hair and the headband an animal figure rising on top of the head of the foot soldier; the exuberance of this decoration conceals the hair, as in examples Fig. 63S and T.

In most cases, the figure shown is the head of an imaginary bird with a hooked beak and ornamental comb (Fig. 63K), sometimes with wings (Fig. 63L). There are very many variants. Some have already been seen in the headdress of the cavalry.

Another theme that reappears fairly often is the deer's head with more or less well-developed antlers (Fig. 63M).

Sometimes one sees above the headband the head of a scowling monster (Fig. 63N) or a horse's head (Fig. 63O), a wood owl with horns (Fig. 63P), a cow (Fig. 63Q), or animal heads which cannot be readily identified (Fig. 63R, S, T) and which might be does or hares.

What can one say about this imaginative explosion in the headdresses of the foot soldiers, like that of the cavalry? We hesitate to give an opinion. Perhaps these animal

figures corresponded to the desire of the warriors to place themselves under the protection of this or that revered animal, perhaps even to assimilate themselves to this animal.

The fact that the imaginary bird, similar in some respects to a Garuḍa, is a recurring theme is significant. The Garuḍa in Cambodia is the mythical bird which is the sworn enemy of snakes, and is associated with Viṣṇu, the god defending good causes, supporting Good over Evil. But perhaps these warriors with exuberant headgear had other intentions than seeking to protect themselves. The taste of the Khmers for showiness and colour is well known, and, if an idea of the probable appearance of these headpieces is wanted, one must, like G. Groslier,[1] bear in mind the extremely complicated and glittering headpieces of Khmer actresses in our time. The materials used are probably the same: cut-out leather, cardboard, papier mâché, and carved wood, the whole covered with gold lead and studded with frippery.

At the Bayon and Banteay Chmar, it is rather difficult to define the common characteristics of the foot soldiers. The most obvious, without any doubt, is their weapons, as in nearly all cases they carry a lance and a buckler in their left hand, which can be round or long. The lancer is brandished or, more often, carried on the shoulder, with the tip facing down.

It is more difficult to discover commonalities in the dress. They all go barefoot, and probably all wear the tight necklace with a central pendant, but their clothes and headdresses are extremely varied.

At the outer gallery of the Bayon, they nearly all have short combed hair, but in the inner gallery mixed headdresses appear, involving both the hair and headpieces, alongside short combed hair. At Banteay Chmar most heads have short hair, and though there are also some examples of headpieces and longer hair styles, in spite of everything in these two monuments of the same period there is a general tendency towards short combed hair. At for the dress, there is no uniformity, only the greatest variety. It would seem, though, that the variations in the dress of the foot soldiers is due to the inclinations of this or that team of sculptors to show one particular type of dress and not another. Thus in the outer gallery at the Bayon, the clothing varies less from one panel to another or from one wing to another. This said, the range of clothing seen in this gallery is extremely varied. It goes from the loincloth tied around the loins, or course, passing between the legs, and having two loose-hanging ends in front, to the long jackets with short sleeves. Between these two extremes there is a whole range of jackets with short sleeves, of variable length and fullness. Depending on the scene depicted, this or that item of clothing dominates, but they are all more or less equally represented.

In the inner gallery at the Bayon the earlier types of clothing are seen, but the long jacket, together with loincloth worn in different fashions, seems to dominate.

---

[1] G. Groslier, *Recherches…* op. cit., p. 70.

Left. Fig. 63. Headdresses of foot soldiers. Angkor Wat S gal., W wing.

At Banteay Chmar, the foot soldiers mostly wear a kind of loincloth-cum-jacket, more elaborate than those found at the Bayon, but that does not exclude the appearance of types of dress found there, nor other new types.

It is therefore not possible to define the foot soldiers' dress and the variations in the clothing do not appear to be linked to rank in the army; whatever their accoutrements, they occupy identical positions in the order of march and have the same weapons, the buckler and the lance.

To complete the subject, we need to multiply the examples, indicating whether any one is generally found or unusual. We shall consider the clothes in each group: the outer gallery of the Bayon, its inner gallery, and at Banteay Chmar, moving from the simplest seen to the most complicated.

At the external gallery of the Bayon, the clothing of type 1 (Fig. 64A) is the simplest imaginable. It comprises a cloth around the loins, which must have been a long piece of cotton. G. Groslier[2] compares it to what the Moi wore at the time he was writing and which they may still wear; he describes the loincloth as being a length of thick cloth 3.5-5 m long and 0.28-0.32 m wide, 'decorated at both ends with one or two red transversal bands, and woven geometric designs in black and light blue. A fringe made of warp threads completes the belt, forming a small ornament of dried seeds threaded like pearls.'

On the bas-reliefs, the band of cloth, after going round the loins, passes between the legs, rolled up all the way. The two free ends are turned down in front in two parallel

---

[2] G. Groslier, *Recherches… op. cit.*, p. 44.

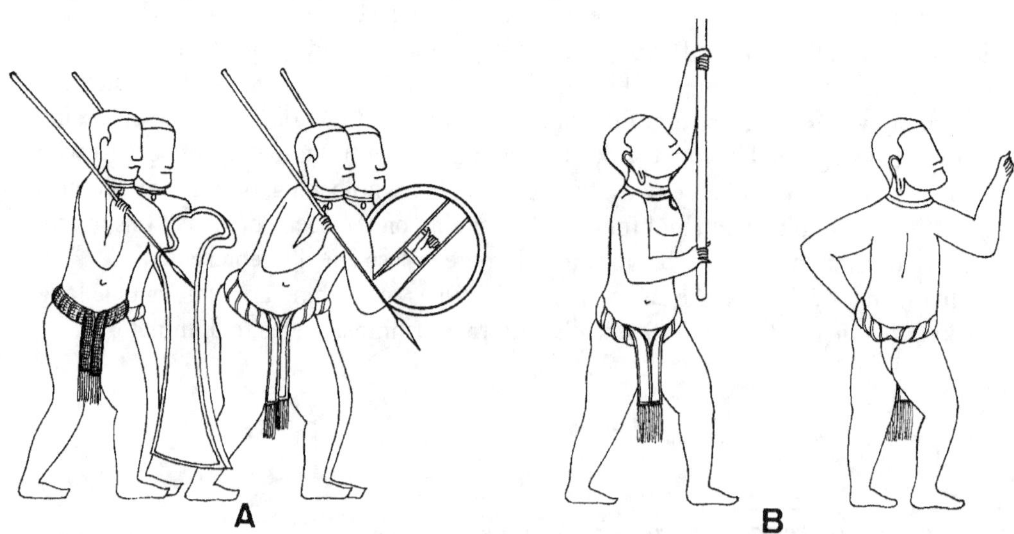

Fig. 64. Foot soldiers. Type 1.
Bayon, ext. gal.

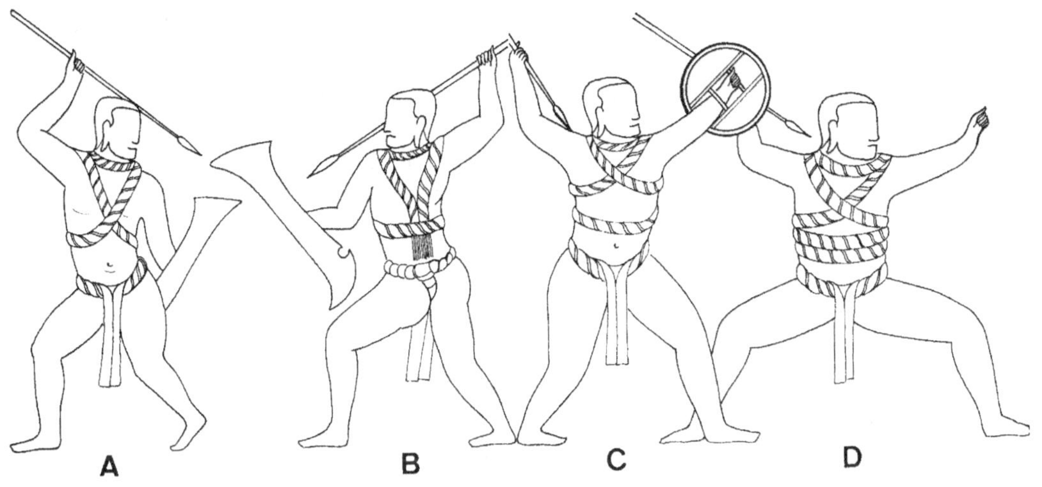

Fig. 65. Foot soldiers. Type 2.
Bayon, ext. gal.

flaps, with the end fringed and sometimes decorated with various geometric motifs.

As we shall note in the third part of this work, this is the dress worn by a series of persons marginal to the army. They carry parasols and insignia, are musicians, or work in the commissariat (Fig. 64B). They are always seen from the front.

The second type of dress (Fig. 65) has an identical loincloth to the preceding type, but also had around the warrior's torso a roll of cloth similar to that of the loincloth, twisted in the same fashion. Commaille must have noted the way this was worn from fairly far off, since he wrote in his guide[3] about this band of cloth, which he likened to a rope. 'The usefulness of these ropes can be understood when one thinks of all the prisoners of war taken into slavery.' Subsequently the men so dressed he called slaves. The fact that they bear arms and take part in battles does not seem to have worried him.

In the simplest arrangement (Fig. 65A, B) the roll of cloth goes round the back, then its ends cross on the chest, and go over the shoulders to come down the back again, where they are held in position by the band of cloth itself. Before this, one of the rolled ends was passed round the neck. This neck roll is found in almost every case; only a few warriors dressed in this way replace the roll with the classic pendant necklace, or still more rarely have both.

Things become slightly more complicated when the cloth roll goes round the chest once (Fig. 65C) or even twice (Fig. 65D) before crossing itself as in the preceding arrangement.

What is the meaning of this cloth roll? It hardly seems to protect the torso. It was probably a spare loincloth which the foot soldiers carried in this way, without getting tired.

---

[3] J. Commaille, *Guide aux ruines d'Angkor*. Paris, Hachette, 1912, p. 122.

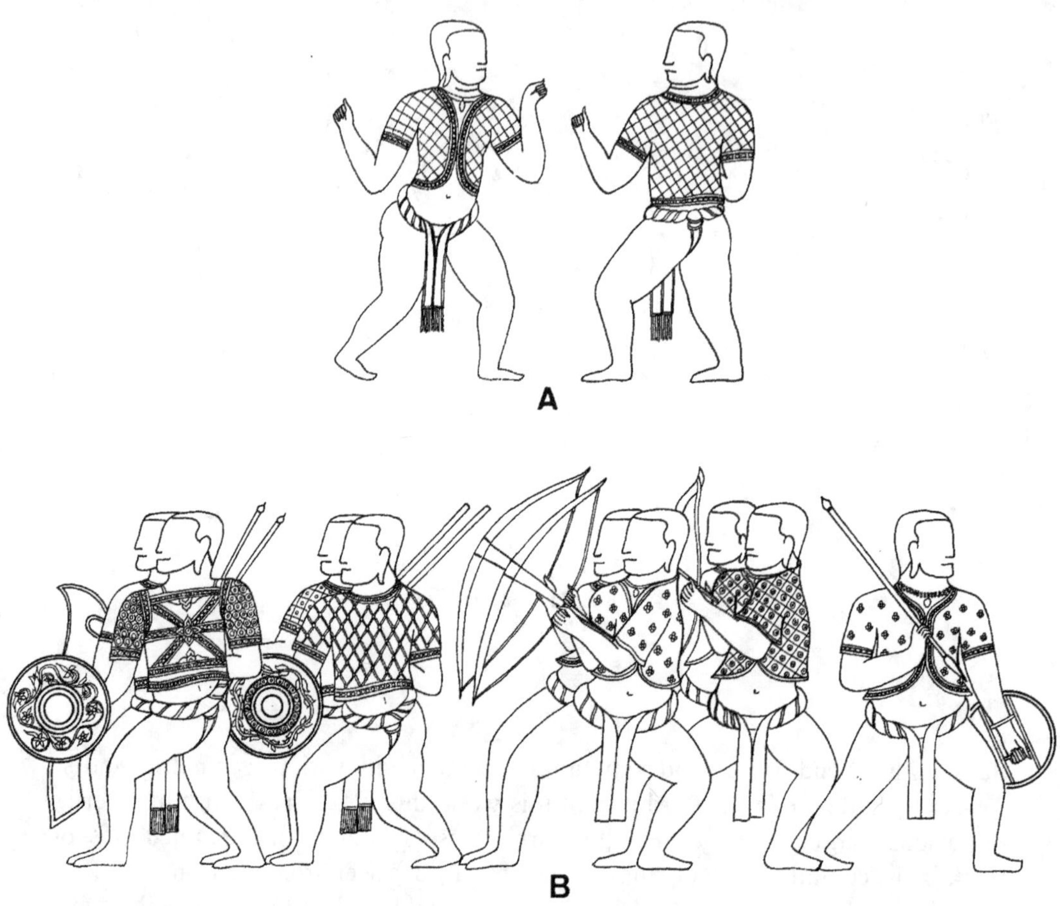

Fig. 66. Foot soldiers. Type 3.
Bayon, ext. gal.

This dress is seen quite often and is worn in numerous battles, notably those depicted in the east gallery, north wing, but it is also the dress of the porters or parasol bearers, but less often than with type 1.

Type 3 dress (Fig. 66A) has the same loincloth in common with the two previous types. It is embellished with a short jacket showing the whole loincloth, the bottom of the back, and the belly. This jacket has no collar and the neckline reveals a short necklace with the pendant worn by all the warriors. The two sides of the jacket are joined by no visible means and then become rounded at the bottom. The sleeves are short. The jacket is made of very different materials—checks, and flower or leaf decoration. The selvages, including the sleeves, are decorated with a beading in most cases. The jacket can be close-fitting and cling to the body, or be more free, showing the belly less, but just as much of the back (Fig. 66B). The front tails, always rounded, are then slightly higher. Covering this jacket, a very few foot soldiers wear

90

a breastplate similar to those described already for this monument. This type of dress is mostly seen from the back.

The dress of type 4 (Fig. 67) is similar to type 3B in its conception but the jacket is longer. It covers a large part of the loincloth at the back (Fig. 67B), and in front (Fig. 67A) the front tails broaden out and are longer on both sides.

Similar to the preceding type, the jacket of type 4A is still longer; the front tails move away from the body though continue to show the belly and the loincloth (Fig. 68A). The rear views, fairly rare for this type, show the edge of the jacket continuing to move up, while hiding the loincloth (Fig. 68B).

The main characteristic of type 5 is the lengthening of the jacket, which reaches its maximum. The rounded front tails reach down to the knees. The jacket is identical in concept to preceding types. The loincloth can hardly be seen (Fig. 69A, B). At most, when the jacket is very long, the loincloth, where it exists, can only be seen in the two ends hanging down in front (Fig. 69C). The lower back line of the jacket can then sometimes be seen between the legs (Fig. 69C).

This type of dress is particularly well represented in a related concept on the bas-reliefs of the internal gallery.

Type 6 (Fig. 70) seems to be conceived as two jackets, one on top of the other, of different lengths, the topmost being the shorter. Both are fairly long. The difference in height between the two ends is variable (Fig. 70A, B, C, D, E). The jacket therefore has double front tails which open out broadly in front. The opening reveals the typical two ends of the loincloth (Fig. 70A, B), or the crotch without the flaps (Fig. 70D), or just one flap, larger than the others, which must be part of a more elaborate loincloth

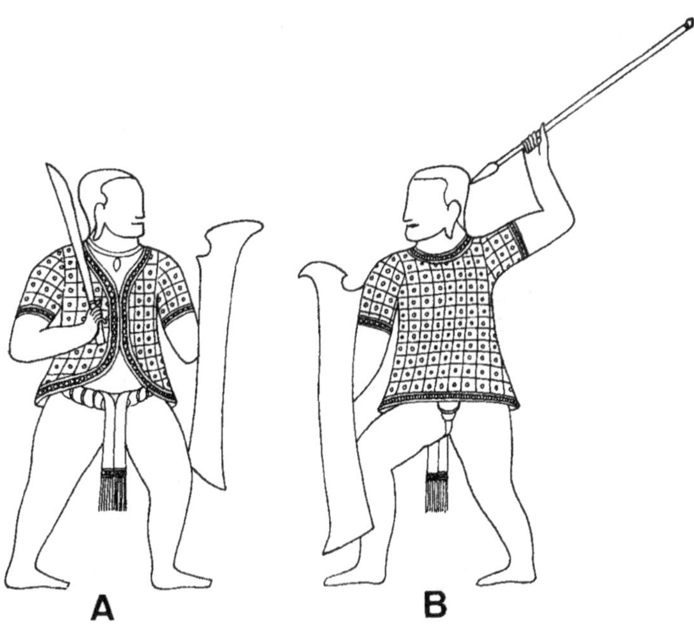

Fig. 67. Foot soldiers. Type 4.
Bayon, ext. gal.

A　　　　　　　**B**

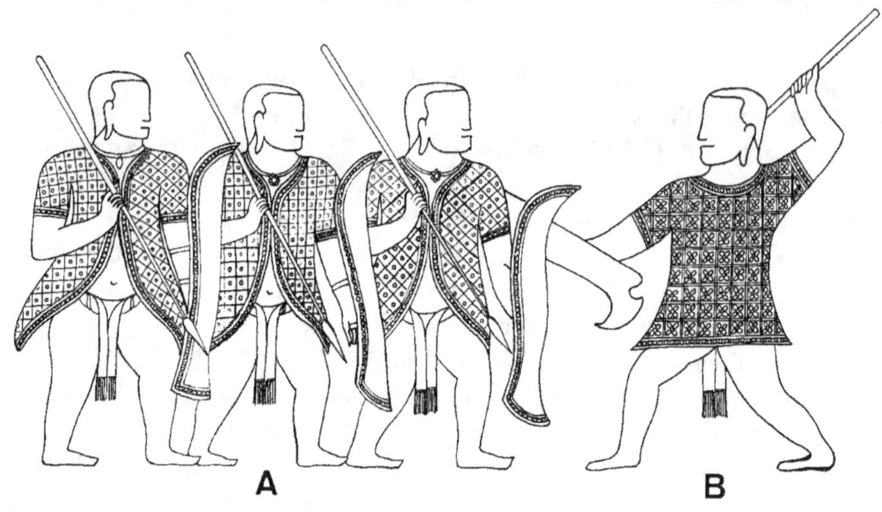

Fig. 68. Foot soldiers. Type 4. Bayon, ext. gal.

(Fig. 70E). But sometimes nothing can be seen of the loincloth, and through the crotch one can see the inside of the back part of the jackets (Fig. 70C). The materials used in making these jackets are very varied, and can be two different kinds for the same article, the lower part being cut from material with different patterns from those on the upper part (Fig. 70B, C).

Type 7 dress (Fig. 71) is quite separate. They are only worn by a few warriors, and are very few indeed when compared to the hundreds of foot soldiers appearing in the bas-reliefs of this gallery. Most are found on the north wing of the west gallery.

Fig. 71A shows a warrior wearing striped or pleated breeches, held in position by a twisted belt passing between the legs. This belt is similar to the loincloth of type 1 (Fig. 64) but has no lappets. The torso is bare.

Fig. 69. Foot soldiers. Type 5. Bayon, ext. gal.

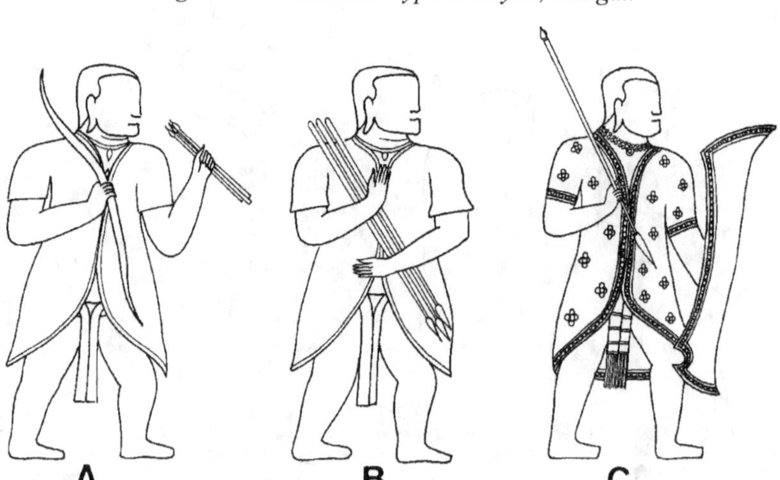

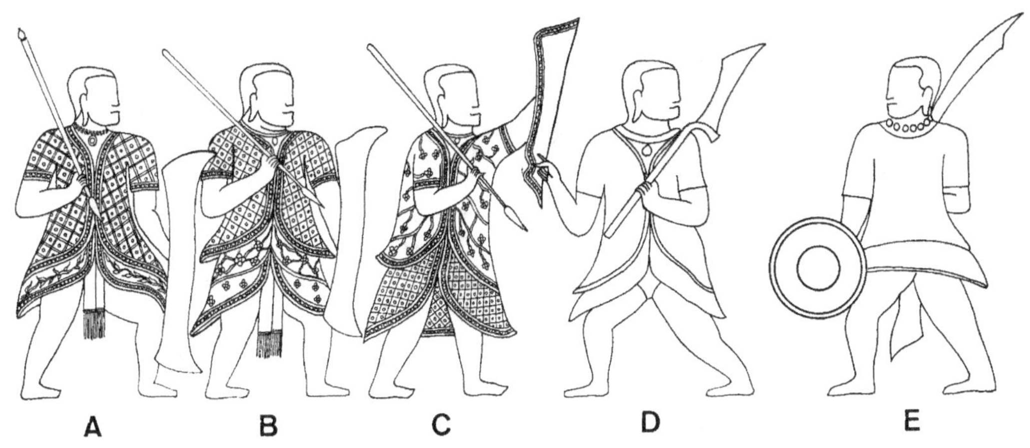

Fig. 70. Foot soldiers. Type 6. Bayon, ext. gal.

In Fig. 71B the same kind of 'breeches' held up by the same kind of belt is seen, but the warrior also wears a short jacket similar to that of type 3 (Fig. 66B).

In Fig. 71C the same kind of jacket can be found but associated with a loincloth with multiple lappets, which are impossible to comprehend.

Fig. 71D has a unique arrangement of a type 1 (Fig. 64) loincloth worn with a short jacket girded with a twisted band of cloth of the same type as 2A (Fig. 65A).

Lastly comes the final variant of type 7 (Fig. 147) comprising a loincloth with

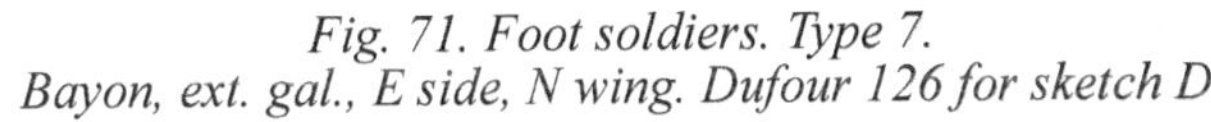

Fig. 71. Foot soldiers. Type 7.
Bayon, ext. gal., E side, N wing. Dufour 126 for sketch D.

multiple end lappets, less complicated than type 7C, but also with a bare torso. It is worn by warriors practicing for a fight, about which we shall speak in part 3.

In all, the clothes most often depicted in this gallery are types 2A (Fig. 65A), 3B (Fig. 66B), and 4 (Fig. 67), though others are to be found, not including type 7 (Fig. 71) shown here.

The clothes worn in the inner gallery of the Bayon are markedly different from those shown in the outer gallery (Fig. 72). Certain types of the same kind of dress are found, such as just the loincloth in type 1 (Fig. 64), with two parallel flaps in front, sometimes replaced, though, by a single twisted flap. The short tight-fitting jacket of type 3A (Fig. 66A) with a loincloth and parallel flaps or a single twisted flap, and the semi-long front tails of type 6 (Fig. 70) are also found. But in general the dress of the foot soldiers seems different. Firstly there are very many long jackets, with or without the lappets of twisted cloth (Fig. 72A, B), sometimes covering a bell-bottomed skirt (Fig. 72C). There are also a number is short jackets and loincloths with complex knotting and multiple side flaps (Fig. 72D, E, F, G). Lastly just these loincloths can be worn in the same complex arrangements which are very difficult to interpret (Fig. 72H, I).

At Banteay Chmar, all the types of clothing found at the Bayon are to be seen. But a large majority of foot soldiers wear just the loincloth of type 1 (Fig. 64) found in the outer gallery of the Bayon, like the archer of Fig. 73A, which we have copied because most unusually he had a quiver on his back. He is part of the scene showing archers fighting on both sides of tall bucklers driven in the ground, which we have touched upon and shown in part one (Fig. 9.1).

The foot soldier in Fig. 73B adds to his typical loincloth with two front flaps a rolled loincloth over his abdomen like the foot soldiers in the outer gallery of the Bayon, but worn in a different manner (Fig. 65).

The foot soldier in Fig. 73C wears the kind of loincloth-cum-breeches, with complicated falling lappets, glimpsed at in the Bayon (Fig. 71C) and also found in the inner gallery (Fig. 72F) of the same monument in great numbers. Understanding how these different types were arranged would be guesswork and we give up trying to comprehend it. This type is found quite frequently at Banteay Chmar; it is sometimes found with a short jacket (Fig. 73D).

One also finds there long clothes, some similar to those at the Bayon, others more original, like the model in Fig. 73E which, as shown, is like a long skirt with a long slit at the front. Perhaps it is only a long coat like those on type 5 models (Fig. 69) of the outer gallery of the Bayon, or those in Fig. 72A-B found in the inner gallery.

There are also long clothes, a kind of skirt slit to the thighs, worn with a semi-long jacket (Fig. 73F).

Perhaps this is a model similar to Fig. 72C of the inner gallery of the Bayon, which also comes in two clearly separate parts; but in this example it is seen from the front and it is not clear if the skirt is slit; moreover the jacket is longer than the model in Banteay Chmar.

94

Fig. 72. Foot soldiers.
Bayon, inner gallery.

To complete this section on the foot soldiers' dress in these two monuments, we must say something about their headdresses.

Most at the inner gallery have nothing, simply short hair combed back in different styles, but always neat (Fig. 74A, B, C). Sometimes they have a trimmed beard, which can hardly be seen, but no moustache.

Quite exceptionally one sees hairstyles completely similar to these but with a tuft tied by a ribbon or a ring (Fig. 74D), or a decoration deriving from a lotus flower fixed about the forehead (Fig. 74E).

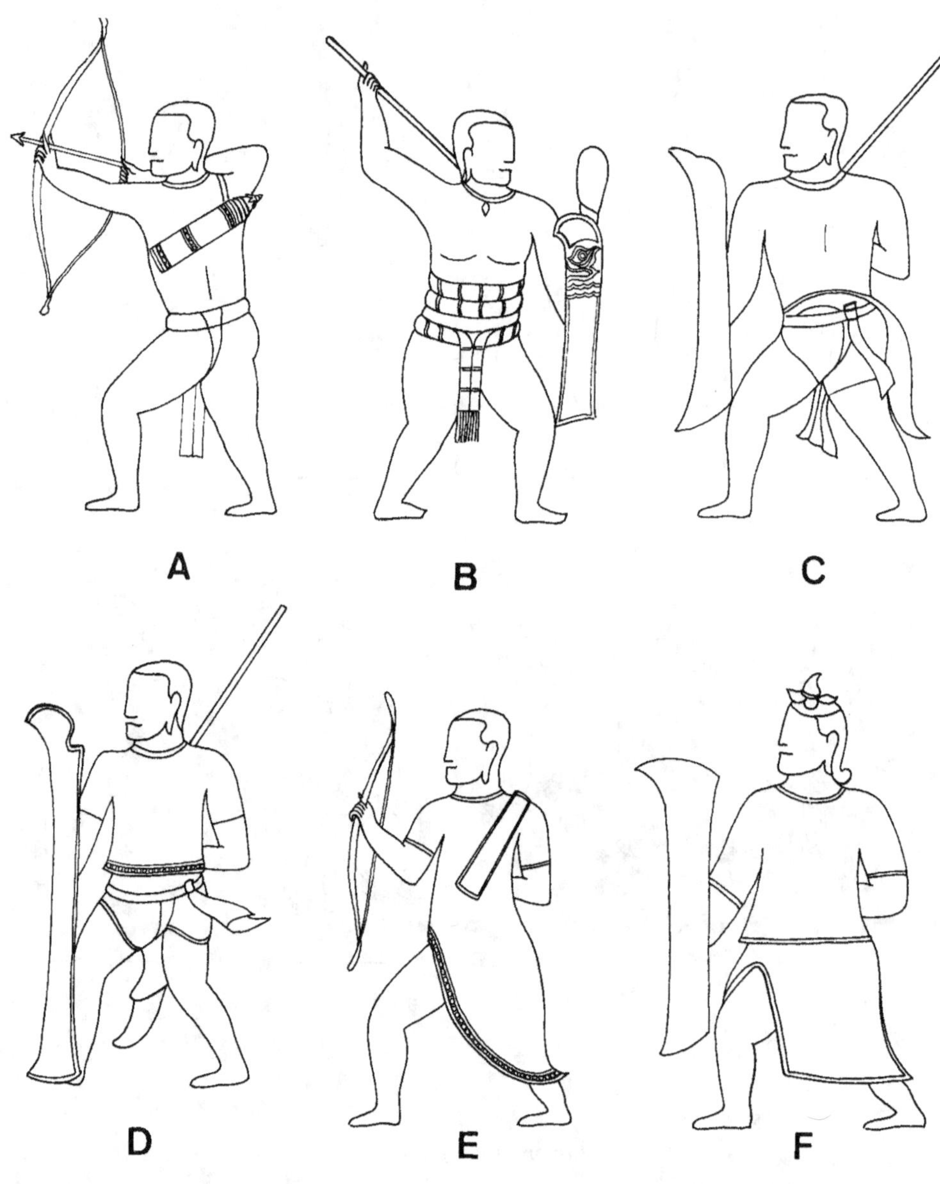

Fig. 73. Foot soldiers.
Banteay Chmar.

In the inner gallery, the coiffures of the foot soldiers are more varied. Most of them, though, consist of either short combed hair, as in the outer gallery, or have a headpiece which hides the hair (Fig. 74F, G). The top of this headdress is in the form of a lotus flower with wide open petals covering the whole of the top of the head. The sides and rear are formed by linked lotus petals which go down to the nape of the neck and the bottom of the extended ears. This headdress recalls that of the Cham, as will be seen; it is different in the arrangement at the sides and the back.

Apart from these two types of headdress, there are in this gallery some with hair gathered into a bun, of greater or lesser importance (Fig. 74H, I), placed on top of the head; one lock, probably plaited, is wound once or several times on itself and passed through the loop thus created.

Another headdress (Fig. 74J) seems to link the lotus flower stuck on top of the forehead to a kind of 'crew-cut' hair-do; a narrow band surrounds the top of the forehead.

The last type among the foot soldiers (Fig. 74K) combines elements of the preceding type (with band and lotus) but replaces the 'crew-cut' with broad pointed leaves of diminishing size towards the neck.

It should be emphasized that these last types of coiffure only exist in a few examples among the hundreds of foot-soldiers appearing in the reliefs.

At Banteay Chmar, in most cases by far, one finds the short combed hair of the outer gallery of the Bayon. Exceptionally, among the foot soldiers assigned to look after the horses, which they restrain by the bridle, as at the Bayon, outer gallery (Fig. 105), the same hairstyles with tufts are found (Fig. 71D, E). Some warriors, to conclude, combine the lotus flower on the top of the forehead with a kind of bonnet, leaving the back of the head free; the hair is visible and falls, to rise like a duck's tail at the nape (Fig. 74L).

Fig. 74. Headdresses of foot soldiers.
Bayon and Banteay Chmar.

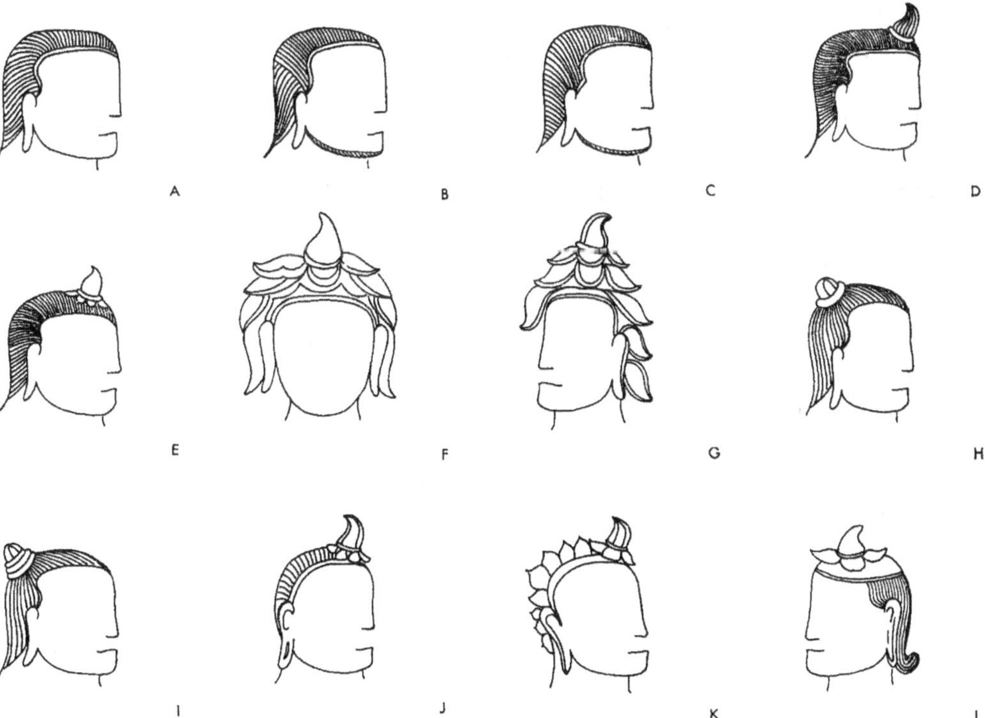

5. Allies, mercenaries, and enemies

Having now completed the study of the different corps in the Khmer army, and before considering the importance of the role of the different corps in relation to each other, we shall briefly consider the foreigners fighting alongside the Khmer, and the enemy troops opposed to them.

At Angkor Wat, at the head of the 'historic' march past, appears a foreign contingent identified by an epigraphic inscription as the chief of the Siamese and his troops. Is this mercenary chief in the service of Sūryavarman II, part of the king's own Siamese guard, similar to the Japanese and even Portuguese guards which some post-Angkorean rulers possessed, or a military contingent from a Siamese principality then a vassal of Cambodia, as S. Sahai suggests?[1] We cannot decide.

The organization of this small band is, in any case, completely identical to that of the Khmer. It comprises a warrior mounted on an elephant led by a mahout, four horsemen, and a score of foot soldiers.

The elephant (Fig. 75) is harnessed in the same manner as the mounts of the Khmer warriors. They have the howdah with its mat inside going beyond the animal's rump, the mat covering the back on which the howdah is placed, held in position by incompletely illustrated ropes, the elephant's richly decorated necklace, the bonnet and the sort of headband decorating some of the Khmer mounts. There is nothing new here. The only accessory which is a little different is the howdah (Fig. 76): its shape is similar to the howdahs with rectilinear balustrades, but its decorations are distinctive.

The Siamese chief (Fig. 75) is striking in his accoutrements. He is standing, with his left leg in the howdah, the right resting on the elephant's back. He is wearing an ankle-length skirt, held in position by a wrought belt from which hang two strings of beads, one above the other, of different lengths, ending in a leaf motif. At his back, level with the belt, is a cloth lappet.

The upper part of the body is covered with a close-fitting singlet with short sleeves, which goes to the middle of the chest; this is decorated with a beaded band hanging down, similar to those of the skirt. The edge of the short sleeves also has several rows of beads hanging down. The neckline is enhanced by a beaded collar as its central motif, to which are also attached tear-drops.

The headdress has a bead-covered helmet, the tear-drops of which frame the face and cover the nape of the neck. The upper part has a series of vanes inserted one into the other, from which feathers float.

To all this must be added double rows of beads of different lengths at the back, and several rows of beads at the wrists and ankles.

This chief is holding a fairly short bow in his hand, into which he had placed an arrow; there is no quiver to be seen. He is also carrying a cutlass in its sheath at his belt.

---

[1] S. Sahai, *Les institutions politiques … op. cit.*, p. 135.

Fig. 75. The Siamese chief.
Angkor Wat, S gal., W wing. Coedès 558-9.

Fig. 76. Siamese elephant howdah.
Angkor Wat, S. gal., W wing. Coedès, 558-9.

The mahout (Fig. 75) occupies the same position as his Khmer confrères. His dress is identical to that of the chief, except that the skirt seems to have two layers of cloth and to open in front. The upper part of his headdress, in the same style as the warrior, is still more exuberant. He carries a cutlass at his belt and in his hand is a goad that is more like a lance, because it has no hook, only a blade. The shaft is decorated with the same feathers as the headpieces and the weapon ends in feathers like the headdresses.

The four horsemen who go two by two and their mounts are harnessed in the same way as the horsemen who follow them or the two who come before them. Only their dress is unusual (Fig. 77).

The skirt seems to have been abandoned in favour of 'breeches' with a turned down train on the right side. Another single cloth lappet is tied to the belt behind. It is the same kind of lappet we have seen worn by the warrior on the elephant, and his mahout, and which the foot soldiers wear.

The worked belt, decorated with strings of beads, is identical to the others. The torso is tightly enclosed in a jacket which has the two front sides meeting and short sleeves. It covers the belly and its lower beaded end is decorated with a string of beads which can also be seen around the circular neckline. A loose cloth flap is attached at the back at the level of the lower edge of the shirt.

The headdress is different from those already observed or yet to come: the hair is thrown back to reach the shoulders, like the Khmer foot soldiers and horsemen, but is topped by a platformed headdress similar to those already seen, but the forehead has a headband. The ears are decorated with earrings of hanging beads.

Fig. 77. Siamese horsemen.
Angkor Wat, S gal., W wing. Coedès 559.

Two horsemen carry a sabre on their shoulders and hold the reins in the other hand. The other two, in the same position, have a lance decorated with a few feathers on the haft.

Some twenty foot soldiers can be seen, as we have said. They surround the elephant, proceeded by four horsemen; here too what singles them out from the Khmers is their dress (Fig. 78). At their hips is a long skirt kept in position by a worked belt. The shirt, as can be seen in Fig. 78D, E, has a floating train tied at the rear to the belt, similar to that of the warriors and the mahout. The models in Fig. 78A, B are pleated, the folds sometimes covered with florets, and the end of the skirt has a beaded band not found on the others. Like the mahout's skirt, the models in Fig. 78C, D, E show a double layer of cloth, the top layer opening in front. Surrounding the belt, and attached to it, are found strings of beads which for the models in Fig. 78D, E form two rows of different lengths. The torso is tightly enclosed in short-sleeved jackets. For the models in Fig. 78A, B, C the shirt is tucked into the belt. The edges of these shirt fronts do not overlap and are brought into relief by a beaded selvedge. The material can be decorated with florets (Fig. 78B). On the models in Fig. 78D, E the shirt is identical to the others, except that it reveals the belly, and the bottom selvedge is decorated with beads hanging from it.

These foot soldiers have beaded helmets covering the head and the nape of the neck, topped by a skullcap of different levels ending in feathers of greater or lesser number. In addition to the worked belt, they have at the ears large rings to which

Fig. 78. Siamese foot soldiers.
Angkor Wat, S gal., W wing. Coedès 558-9.

strings of beads are attached. One of them (Fig. 78D) has a necklace, but this is rare.

For weapons, they carry a lance by the shaft decorated with feathers at the end; in the other hand they hold a long buckler like the Khmer examples, the edge of which is bordered by beading.

One thing is special about these warriors; they often wear trimmed beards like some of the Khmer warriors, as well as, sometimes, a moustache or even as goatee. Their features in particular are quite different from the Khmer; they have a marked mandibular protrusion which must be a local characteristic rather than an ethnic marker.

At the Bayon foreigners in the army's ranks appear several times. They appear twice in the long military march pasts and combats in the east outer gallery, north and south wings. Their first appearance, in the south wing, comprises, grouped around an elephant, some thirty foot soldiers and two horsemen. They are closely integrated with the Khmer warriors and are only different from them in their headdresses and their markedly Chinese features.

Also the harnessing of the elephant and the two horses does not differ from Khmer models. The weapons they carry are not new: bows and arrows for the warrior on the elephant, goad and buckler for the mahout, lance for the horsemen, lance and long buckler in different Khmer forms, for the foot soldiers. The dress of the different elements of this corps also corresponds to their Khmer counterparts: a jacket with double front tails and double sleeves linked to a loincloth, with a lappet for the warrior on the elephant; short jacket and small 'breeches' for the mahout; long jacket and 'breeches' with lappets for the horsemen; long jacket and loincloth, of which we can only see the two front ends, for the foot soldiers.

Nothing unusual therefore among these foreigners, probably mercenaries or vassal allies of the Khmer, except their features and their headdress. They have very slit eyes and a beard and a pointed goatee; their ears are small and do not have distended lobes; they could be Vietnamese.

The headdresses are most extraordinary. The hair is drawn back and gathered on the top of the head (which emphasizes still further the Mongolian features) into a bun or a plait to which is added a hair piece to keep everything in place (Fig. 71). In Fig. 79A, B, C, D, E the chief part of the hair piece is a beaded ring decorated with lotus leaves, the lower row taking on the form of the head. In the simplest case (D.79E) the plait comes out of the ring to form a handle; in Fig. 79D the hair forms a bun encircled by a beaded handle; the headdress in Fig. 79A, B, C presents original if barely realistic topknots. The headdress of Fig. 79F is that of the elephant's warrior; the basic elements of the headdress are the same as the others, but various decorative ornaments are added.

The second representation of foreigners in the north wing is in the middle of the fight against the Cham, and grouped around an elephant is a small military band of three musicians and some ten foot soldiers.

Like the previous group, the elephant's harness is identical to Khmer types. The weapons are not original either: the warrior on the elephant has a bow, a quiver in the howdah, and all bear lances and long or round bucklers.

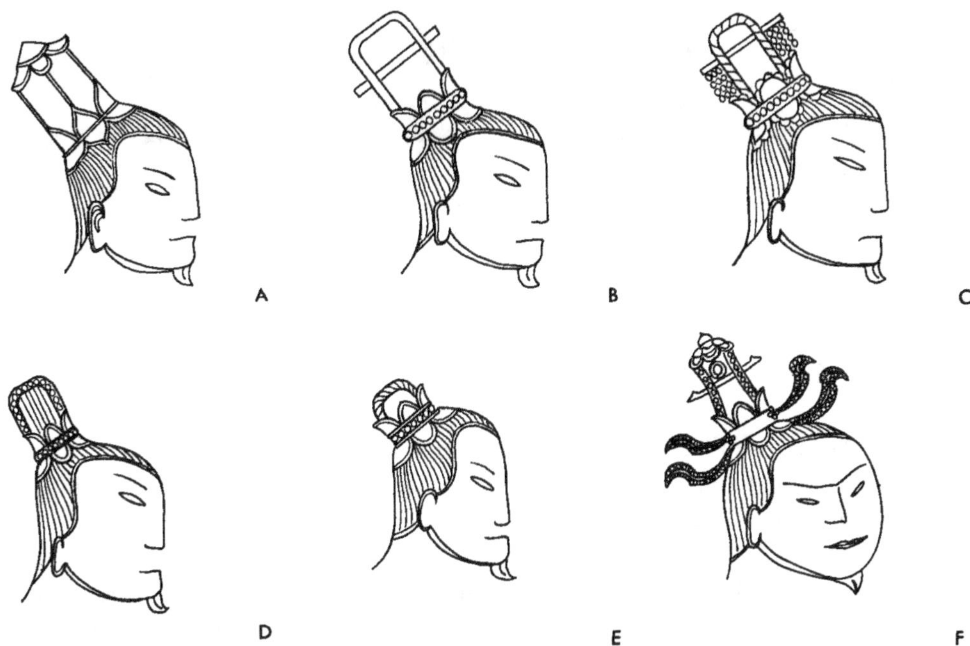

Fig. 79. Headdresses of mercenaries.
Bayon, ext. gal., E side, S wing, lower level. Dufour 2.

Their dress is not fundamentally different either. There are some variants in details on a few of them; the double shirt front tails of the elephant's warrior's jacket are not rounded but cut straight like those of the Cham, as we shall see. This is also true of some of the foot soldiers who replace the loincloth by 'breeches' with trains, in the Cham fashion. But some other warriors have exactly the same dress as their Khmer counterparts.

Their great originality, once again, is found in their physical appearance, the same as that in the first group, and in their still more exotic headdresses (Fig. 80). The hair is still drawn to the top of the head, which carries fragile and airy constructions, from which come what appear to be vegetal stalks ending in flower motifs. One of them (Fig. 80A) has an image of what is probably a Buddha or a Bodhisattva.

The musicians accompanying these warriors include a trumpet player who can hardly be seen in the crush (his trumpet is identical to those we shall study when dealing with Khmer military musicians), a portable gong player, and another playing an unidentified instrument (Fig. 81).

These two groups of foreigners are probably only the symbolic representation of allied or mercenary troops who join the Khmer during conflicts; they must have been much more numerous.

Much has been said about the Cham troops among the Khmer ranks. We believe that these comments are essentially based on an incorrect examination of the bas-reliefs of the inner gallery of the Bayon, where we have seen many Khmer foot soldiers

A   B   C   D

Fig. 80. Coiffures of mercenaries.
Bayon, ext. gal., E side, N wing, lower level. Dufour 125.

wear headdresses similar to those of the Cham; the headdress they wear is the chief criterion for recognizing them. But we think we have only positively identified them at the Bayon at one place, the outer gallery, S side, E wing (Fig. 82).

There, on an elephant carrying a ballista, are two warriors whose clothes (even though they are not wearing the Cham 'breeches'), headdress, and physical appearance make them look like Cham. Their role as ballista attendants in a march past with several other machines confirms this hypothesis. When studying weapons in part one, we had, in fact, following the research of Mus, accepted the hypothesis that the ballistae, of Chinese origin, unknown at the Angkor Wat period, might well have been introduced to the Khmer army through the intermediary of Cham instructors in the service of the Cambodian king; given this hypothesis, it is not surprising to see these two warriors among the Khmer troops. Perhaps in reality there were others. Hostile

Fig. 81. Mercenary musicians.
Bayon, ext. gal., E side, N wing, lower level.
Dufour 125.

104

Fig. 82. Cham fighting on the Khmer side.
Bayon, ext. gal., S side, W wing, lower level. Dufour 37.

monarchs readily welcomed deserters from the enemy camp; but we only know of these two examples in the bas-reliefs at the Bayon.

As for Banteay Chmar, we have observed no foreign troops in the Khmer ranks.

Now we shall turn to the enemy troops to be seen in the bas-reliefs who oppose the Khmer in the great battles depicted at the Bayon and Banteay Chmar.

How were they organized? If one considers the details, it soon becomes evident that their organization is on every count the same as their adversaries. One finds in their ranks a high proportion of foot soldiers closely surrounding as many elephants as among the Khmer (Fig. 85). Likewise, they had few horses, apart from some isolated examples we shall not concern ourselves with. But when the details are examined, many things are different, though not all.

Unlike the Khmer foot soldiers, whose dress varied greatly, the Cham foot soldiers are always dressed in the same fashion, apart from a few details, and their dress hardly differed from that of higher ranking warriors (Fig. 83). They wear small pleated 'breeches' held in position by a belt that goes between the legs and sometimes ends at the front or the back as a single lappet, but in some cases as two flaps by the lower

Fig. 83. Cham foot soldiers.
Bayon, Banteay Chmar.

part of the jacket. This jacket is fairly long, with short sleeves, and differs from the Khmer model in that the neckline is hardly marked and the lower front tails are not rounded off, but join, except for some drummers at the Bayon (Fig. 83D) and some warriors at Banteay Chmar (Fig. 83E).

These jackets, generally with headed edges, are cut from very varied cloth, often checked, as with the Khmer, which indicated padding.

Fig. 84. Cham coiffures.
Bayon, Banteay Chmar.

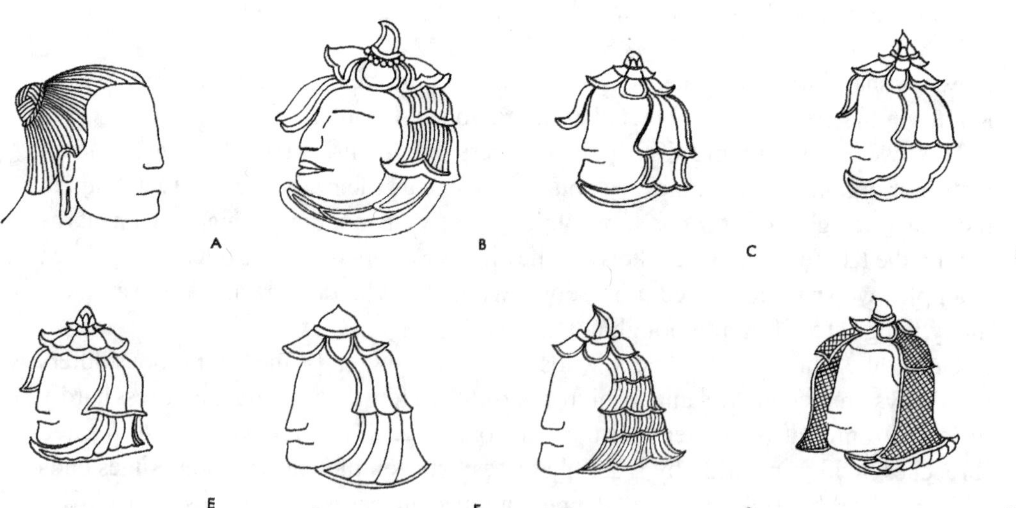

These foot soldiers never go bare-headed, like the other warriors, even of the highest rank. Only a few oarsmen in battleships have tightly dressed hair in a bun at the top of the nape of the neck (Fig. 84A). All the other individuals in the army sport very similar headdresses. Several elements of these headdresses can be distinguished: on top of the head is an open lotus flower motif, of greater or smaller size, while the rest of the head is hooded down to the shoulders by from one to four lengths of probably stiffened material, cut in narrow bands which undulate (Fig. 84B, C, D, E). The chin and neck are very often marked by a chin piece looking like a half-crescent with the other end disappearing under the headdress. This piece must be doubled but only one part can be seen. The chin piece is sometimes absent or only indicated by the top of the lowest part of the headpiece (Fig. 84F, G) or is part of the headpiece proper (Fig. 84E). The headdress of Fig. 84H is unusual in that it replaces the cut strips by two sections of material which cover the head and to which the chin piece is attached.

The foot soldiers only carry a lance together with a long buckler, the bottom part of which is scalloped.

The elephants (Fig. 85) are harnessed as with the Khmer, and with the same omissions on the part of the sculptors (mostly the strap passing under the animal's belly). But, this apart, the howdah is positioned on the elephant's back in the same fashion, the straps are attached to big hooks, joined by a brace with rosettes, just the

Fig. 85. Cham elephants and foot soldiers.
Bayon, ext. gal., E side, N wing, lower level. Dufour 122.

same as with Khmer howdahs. Only the form changes; it is like a box with rectangular sides, with the front part projecting (Fig. 86). The sides of this howdah are decorated with broad foliated scrolls; the rectangular central part is often decorated with the mouth of the grimacing monster. This howdah, like the Khmer howdahs, is placed on a richly decorated mat and the hooks have small bells at the end of ropes. But the elephant only rarely has a headpiece, and when it does it is like Khmer models; neither does it have a decorative collar; only the breast strap which helps hold the howdah in position often has a small bell.

On this elephant, harnessed in this manner, poised on the neck, is the mahout who controls it with the help of a goad (Fig. 85); he sometimes has on occasions, as does his Khmer counterpart, a long buckler.

The warrior on the howdah is upright (Fig. 85). His dress does not differ from that of the foot soldiers; though perhaps he is a little more refined in his ornamentation. He holds in his left hand a long buckler, of the same type as the foot soldiers; and brandishes in his right hand javelins which are unusual in that they have symmetrical 'spurs' all the way down the haft. He draws these javelins from a big quiver outside the howdah, but the lower end seems to be inserted in an opening in the side wall of the howdah. The way this quiver is held in position is never clearly shown (Fig. 86).

For a Khmer elephant, the enumeration of the persons it carried would stop there, but the Cham have a third person, the parasol bearer (Fig. 85), kneeling on the crupper of the elephant, at the back of the howdah, on a kind of mat with raised sides that are richly decorated. Dressed exactly like a foot soldier, he holds over his master a parasol like those we shall examine among the Khmer. This position seems most uncomfortable but, in spite of that, these bearers maintain it during marches as well as in the fiercest battles, in which they are for good measure often killed.

It should be added that, apart from the parasol carried by this bearer, other honorific totems surround the elephant, indicating the high rank of its chief occupant. They take the form of parasols, banners etc, also similar to Khmer models (Fig. 85).

The Cham army thus moves to confront the Khmer, its massive elephants surrounded on all sides by foot soldiers, marching to the rhythm of a drum (Fig. 83D).

*Fig. 86. Howdah of Cham elephant.
Bayon.*

6. The importance and function of the field forces in relation to each other

Apart from the chariots, which we have shown could not have formed a corps in the Khmer army, we have described, from an external viewpoint, the three other army corps: the cavalry, the elephant corps, and the infantry, as they can be seen in the bas-reliefs of Angkor Wat, the Bayon, and Banteay Chmar.

Now we shall attempt, basing our study on the bas-reliefs, to give an idea of the importance and the role which each of the three army corps had in relation to each other.

At Angkor Wat, the descriptive study we conducted is essentially based on the bas-relief of the west wing of the south gallery, called the 'historic' march past. This bas-relief has the inestimable advantage for this study of providing, with verisimilitude and without excessive exaggeration, a faithful image of the different army corps in the reign of Sūryavarman II.

But this is an ideal march past, arranged by the sculptors. And even if they reproduced the reality they witnessed, an image of an army on the march is not presented, but a parade of a religious inclination (indicated by the presence of the sacred fire and priests) in which appear only the essential elements of the army, the king, and his chiefs on their mounts, surrounded by an élite guard of foot soldiers, the numerical size of which is probably altered.

We can, therefore, reach no definitive conclusion, in examining this bas-relief, about the importance and the role of the three corps in relation to each other, but we can make some observations.

The march past is continual but in fact constituted by a score of groups which, in the reality of the army, could constitute the nucleus, the élite troops, of what we would today call a combat unit.

Each group comprises a single elephant, cavalrymen, and foot soldiers (Fig. 87).

The warriors mounted on elephants adopt very varied poses in spite of the fact that they are only taking part in a parade, and so one can have an idea of their behaviour not only when in a march past but also during marches and battles.

The attitudes which seem to us the most appropriate in the circumstances of the parade are those in Figs 88, 89, and 90: the warrior is standing, his right leg is on the rump of the elephant, the left leg is bent and finds support inside the howdah. To keep their balance, the warrior in Fig. 88, who is the king, and the person in Fig. 89, hold onto a strap fixed in front of the howdah, which they hold in the left hand (the right hand in the case of the king), holding a Khmer axe, the *phkā'k*, which rests on the shoulder, and a cutlass for the warrior in Fig. 89. Another possible attitude for a parade is shown by the warrior in Fig. 90: his legs are in the same position; he had in his right hand a Khmer axe which rests on his shoulder, and instead of holding a strap in his left hand, like the other two, he brandishes a round buckler but his attitude has nothing menacing about it.

110

Fig. 87. A combat unit.
Angkor Wat, S gal., W wing. Coedès 530.

Fig. 88. Parade position on an elephant.
Angkor Wat, S gal., W wing. Coedès 541.

Fig. 89. Parade position on an elephant.
Angkor Wat, S gal., W wing. Coedès 543.

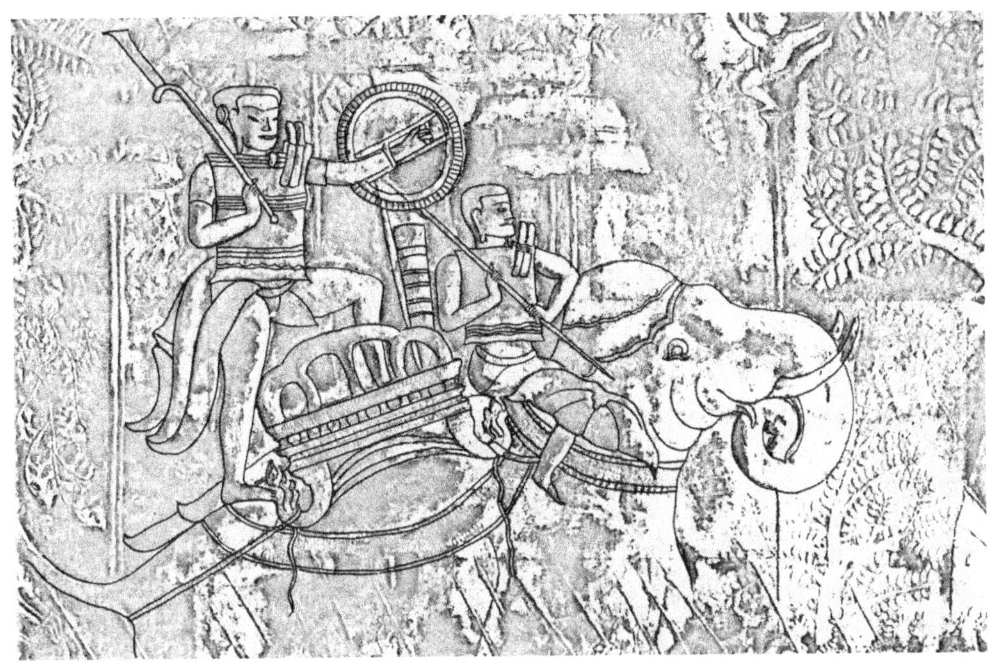

Fig. 90. Parade position on an elephant.
Angkor Wat, S gal., W wing, Coedès 531.

Fig. 91. Resting position on an elephant.
Angkor Wat, S gal., W wing. Coedès 517.

When marching to the site of a battle, the warrior would assume on the elephant's back a comfortable position, as appears in Fig. 91. He is seated on the howdah, his left leg is pulled back under him, the right leg is outside the howdah, seeking support with his foot on the elephant's rump. He holds his weapon in one hand, in this case a sabre balanced on his shoulder. With the other hand he holds on to the balustrade of the howdah.

During combat, however, their attitudes must have been as animated as suggested in Figs 92, 93, and 94. These are also the attitudes of the warriors in the great mythological battles, though perhaps rather calmer. The warrior still has one foot in the howdah and another on the elephant's rump. But this time his legs are bent and he appears to be about to leap at the enemy. His weapons are brandished: lance and buckler for the warriors in Figs 92 and 93; bows and arrows for the person in Fig. 94.

The mahout keeps his cross-legged position on the elephant's neck, already described, his goad in his hand. Sometimes though (Fig. 94) he complements the menacing attitudes of his master, brandishing his goad or the buckler he sometimes sports.

The elephant, in each group is preceded by cavalrymen. There can be from two to six or even seven of them, but these three figures represent the extreme case we prefer to put to one side; in half of the groups remaining there are three horses in front, except for one of the horses slightly apart, either ahead or in the rear of the others (Fig. 95). The other half has either four horses in front in pairs (Fig. 96) or five horses variously positioned (Fig. 87).

The cavalrymen are usually seated on their mounts, surrounded by parasols, which indicate their important rank. They either hold the reins of their horses in the left hand and brandish in the right a sabre, a lance or any other weapon, or simply hold it in their hands or rest it on their shoulders. When they have a buckler, the reins are left free on the horse's neck.

Fig. 92. Fighting position on an elephant.
Angkor Wat, S side, W wing, Coedès 538.

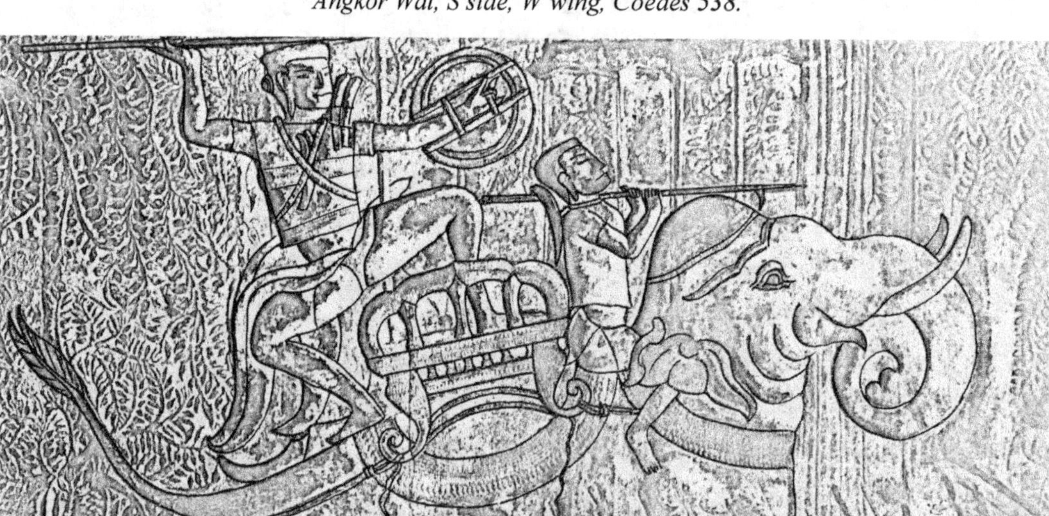

Fig. 93. Fighting position on an elephant.
Angkor Wat, S gal., W wing. Coedès 555.

Fig. 94. Fighting position on an elephant.
Angkor Wat, S gal., W wing. Coedès 530.

Fig. 95. Group of three horsemen.
Angkor Wat, S gal., W wing. Coedès 554.

Fig. 97. Cavalryman in battle.
Angkor Wat, N gal., W wing. Coedès 443.

Like the warriors mounted on elephants in the same march past, the attitudes vary between calm and menacing, when anticipating a future battle, but the horsemen have, of course, infinitely less possibility of movement than the warriors on elephants.

However, if one studies the great battles in the other galleries, one can see horsemen who seem to abandon prudence in the heat of the combat (Fig. 97); standing on the backs of horses, the reins floating in the wind, they brandish their arms against a nearby combatant. This could be one of these exaggerations special to the epics which the bas-reliefs refer to, which is why we have mostly put them to one side in our study.

Each group includes foot soldiers who seem to head the march, flanked by cavalrymen who rise beside them (Fig. 87). Perhaps there were also some on the other side which sculpting conventions in bas-reliefs, given the limitations of Khmer artists, prevent us from seeing. These foot soldiers rarely march alone, but mostly in twos, even in threes or fours, in one row, with their weapons in their hand.

When level with the elephant, they continue to march two by two, and probably encircle it. It should be mentioned that if the cavalrymen and their mounts are shown in entirety, one only sees the upper parts of the bodies of the elephants, their feet being always hidden by rows of foot soldiers. They complete the march past in the centre of the group.

Left. Fig. 96. Group of four horsemen. Angkor Wat, S gal., W wing. Coedès 547.

This is the organization each unit shows in the long march past. It may be wondered if this corresponds to a theoretical view of an ideal army the Khmer might have been aware of and wished to imitate. One is forced to consider, once again, the *Arthaśāstra* of Kauṭilya and the numerous passages in this work concerning the good organization of an army, a manifestation of the king's security.

In Book 10, we learn[1] that the army must be formed of combat units centred on an elephant or a chariot, surrounded by five horsemen and thirty foot soldiers, fifteen in front of the elephant and fifteen behind.

One is struck by the similarity between this ideal viewpoint and the scenes we have just analysed at Angkor Wat. True, there is no chariot, the numbers of horsemen varies and the number of foot soldiers is difficult to estimate, but these similarities cause us to think that this march past, in spite of the idealized nature we have at first attributed to it, nevertheless provides a not excessively inexact image of the organization of the army at the time of Sūryavarman II. We can therefore say, without taking serious risks, that it was composed of combat units centred on an elephant ridden by a chief, and that this elephant was preceded, surrounded, and followed by foot soldiers, who protected it, and that three to four cavalrymen, on average, surrounded the foot soldiers at the head of the group.

In this organization there is a striking contrast between the mass of the elephant, seemingly invulnerable, and the diminutive size of the foot soldiers who, in spite of everything, seem to protect it efficiently by surrounding it and forming a block with it. Besides them, the horsemen seem to play a small role, in spite of their number. They provide a contrast by opposing their mobility, well indicated by the postures of the horses, to the heaviness and supposed slowness of the group constituted by the elephant and foot soldiers. Perhaps their function was only secondary. The *Arthaśāstra* tells us,[2] it is true, that they broke the enemy's lines, but, more importantly, they supervised discipline in the ranks, played the part of scouts in advance of the army, ensured quick connections between the diverse elements of this army—all tasks emanating from their principal advantage of mobility. The result of a battle would not depend on them but on the combined action of the elephant corps and the infantry, which does not detract from the real services they could provide.

It would seem that this organization was made systematic in the following period, to judge from the scenes at the Bayon and Banteay Chmar.

As we have already indicated in the first part, we have in these two monuments a large number of bas-reliefs which can be considered historic and illustrate military marches and fierce battles.

The marches, putting aside the bearers of honorific emblems and the army bandsmen, who we shall discuss in part three, are almost all an uninterrupted march past of very many elephants surrounded by foot soldiers.

---

[1] *The Kauṭilya...* op. cit., vol. II, Bk 10, ch. 3, §9-13.

[2] *The Kauṭilya...* op. cit., vol. II, Bk 10, ch. 5, §53-56.

118

*Fig. 98. Departure of one of the 'elephant-cum-infantry' groups.
Bayon, ext. gal., S side, W wing, lower level. Dufour 38.*

The often anecdotal nature of the bas-reliefs at the Bayon allow us to witness a scene illustrating the departure of one of these elephant-infantry groups (Fig. 98); the warrior is mounting the back of this elephant by the rump and reaches the howdah, where his weapons are waiting for him; the mahout is waiting for his orders. The foot soldiers, weapons in their hands, surround the elephant; one of them, arriving a little late, is drinking from his gourd, his buckler casually hanging from his shoulder. The moment of departure is near.

During the marches, the warriors on the elephants take up comfortable positions (Fig. 99). They sit in the howdah on the heel of their bent right or left leg, while the other leg rests firmly on the elephant's back. This position probably ensured good stability without tiring them.

They hold their weapons in their hands and often point out, with their free hand, the direction the mahout should take. The foot soldiers, wisely, march two by two or three by three beside the elephant, in front and behind him. It is hard to calculate how many they are are; between twenty and thirty, on average, it would seem.

What is clearly striking, in comparison to Angkor Wat, is the almost complete disappearance of the cavalry, only represented here in these long marches by a few isolated horsemen (Fig. 100). They go alongside the rows of foot soldiers, their weapons on their shoulders, or else brandished aloft; as they never have a buckler, they always hold the horse's reins in their left hand (Figs 101 & 102). More than at Angkor Wat, their function indeed seems to be to control the order and discipline in the ranks, to act as scouts ahead of the army, and to ensure the transmission of orders to the various parts of the heavy and ponderous column which formed the Khmer army.

*Fig. 99. Example of 'elephant-cum-infantry' groups on the march.
Bayon, ext. gal., E side, N wing, upper level. Dufour 118.*

We cannot give valid reasons for this depletion of horses, except perhaps that they were not native to the country, and had to be brought in over dangerous routes. Ma Tuan-lin, thanks to whom we already know that the Cham learnt about the use of ballistae from a Chinese instructor shipwrecked off their coast (cf. part 1, section 2, n.17), also mentions in the same passage that this Chinese incited the Cham to go and obtain horses in China, and he taught them to fight on elephant back with a bow or an arbalest (Ma Tuan-lin, *Méridionaux*, pp. 555-6).

This is the proof that the Cham, though not unfamiliar with horses, did not make much use of them. On the Khmer side the situation was not so extreme but it should be admitted that they could have experienced difficulties, which we do not know about, in replenishing their stables, which would account for this depletion of horses in the bas-reliefs at the Bayon and Banteay Chmar.

Though reduced in number, the horse remains a noble mount. The grand person surrounded by a cohort of horsemen bearing honorific insignia uses horses to move around quickly (Fig. 103).

120

Fig. 100. Fighting unit with a horseman.
Bayon, ext. gal., E side, S wing. Dufour 4.

Before considering the army in its battles, a few words about the harnessed horses without riders, restrained by their reins, which appear several times at the Bayon, in the outer gallery, mixed in with the foot soldiers and the elephants. The warriors bearing a lance hold them by the bridle and appear to be only foot soldiers, possibly attached to look after the mount belonging to a high ranking warrior, like grooms in short (Figs 104 & 105).

When the Khmer army meets the enemy's army, which it does on several occasions in the bas-reliefs of the two monuments, its organization is unaffected; each fights in his own fashion. The warriors mounted on elephants assume agitated positions (Figs

121

*Fig. 101. Horseman.
Bayon.*

*Fig. 102. Horsman of high rank.
Bayon, ext. gal., E side, S wing, upper level. Dufour 3.*

122

Fig. 103. Important person on horseback and his followers.
Bayon, ext. gal., E side, S wing, upper level. Dufour 3.

Fig. 104. Horse without rider restrained by its reins.
Bayon.

Fig. 105. Horse without rider restrained by its reins.
Bayon.

57A, B, C, 58A, B, 92, 93, 94). They raise themselves on their bent leg, sometimes going as far as almost standing (Fig. 57A), while still keeping one foot on the back of the elephant. In relation to this, it is curious to note that to avoid their foot slipping, it is sometimes restrained by a kind of cord loop attached to the rear hooks of the howdah (Fig. 57A). At the same time, they pull back their bows or brandish their other weapons, such as their lances.

At their feet are the foot soldiers of both sides, not losing sight of the elephant they surround, and who boldly kill each other, and bodies strewn around the ground—enemy corpses, of course, for these are battles th depict the greater glory of the Khmer army (Fig. 106).

The cavalrymen, though few, are also involved and we have seen at the Bayon, in one of the battles on the east outer gallery a confrontation between a Khmer and a Cham horseman which ends with the unseating of the Cham (Fig. 107).

Fig. 108 summarizes in some degree all the fighting aspects of the two armies. We should point out that it is exceptional because of two details: the confrontation with enemy elephants, which is rare (the warriors mounted in the rear in general limit themselves to firing arrows from a distance) and that of two horsemen, which is unique (Fig. 107).

In sum, the combat is settled by furious hand-to-hand fighting with the enemy foot soldiers and a more 'distant' confrontation of the elephants. There can be no doubt that if the foot soldiers were in difficulty, the elephants became, in spite of their size, very vulnerable. This doubtless incites the enemy leaders to beat a retreat, on several occasions; they are intact, though somewhat roughed up, but the Khmer foot soldiers carry the day (Fig. 109), and this appears to justify the enemy's panic and flight.

124

Fig. 106. Foot soldiers in combat.
Bayon, ext. gal., E side, N wing, lower level. Dufour 124.

Fig. 107. Confrontation of two horsemen.
Bayon, ext. gal., E side, N wing, lower level. Dufour 122.

We believe that we can propose, after studying the bas-reliefs, that the Khmer army comprised essentially elephants and foot soldiers. This is somewhat corroborated by epigraphic texts.

S. Sahai[3] emphasizes that these introduce several officials belonging to the elephant corps: 'the Brahmin BrahmarĀśika, head of the royal elephant hunters (*NrpahastigahĀdhipa*), the *VĀp śrī* Niketa of the elephant corps (*anak vra½ tamraya*) and the *mrtĀñ śrī SalyĀyuddha, khloñ mukka* of the elephants' and he adds in a footnote that 'several inscriptions speak of capturing elephants'.

As for the foot soldiers, if no source or text indicates their number in the Khmer army, their importance, which was vital in the conclusion of a campaign, seems attested by the remark of Zhou Daguan, who notes that 'in the war with the Siamese they (?) forced everyone to fight'.[4] An epigraphic inscription also noted by Sahai[5] points in the same direction. It says:

'The supreme king of the land should not employ in his own service any of the slaves of Śrī Indreśvara, nor of other gods. Should an army invade the kingdom, but only in this case, they can be called upon for the destruction of this army.'

Two facts can at least be deduced; one was that the army never had enough foot soldiers for the king's liking, to the extent that some religious institutions had to oppose his requisitioning of slaves by issuing consecrated edicts, and the other being that foot soldiers were very useful in desperate situations.

An army in which the foot soldiers play the leading part, in spite of appearances, is not, after all, very original; this was the case with armies in medieval Europe in which weighty horsemen enveloped in their armour, the equivalent of Khmer elephants, were often only there to rain mighty blows on each other, which had no influence on the outcomes of battles that were lost or won by the foot soldiers whom they hindered more often than helped. Perhaps this was also the case of elephants in the Khmer army, so impressive, so numerous, so cumbersome, and possible so useless.

The small Khmer foot soldiers did not only fight on dry land. We shall now find them, just as intrepid, on water. The study of the fleet which follows will complete the second part given over to the examination of the different army corps.

---

[3] S. Sahai, *Les institutions politiques…* op. cit., p. 134.
[4] Zhou, *Mémoires…* op.cit., p.176.
[5] S. Sahai, *Les institutions politiques…* op. cit., p. 135.

Fig. 108. *Khmero-Cham combat.*
Bayon, ext. gal., E side, N wing, lower level. Dufour 122-3.

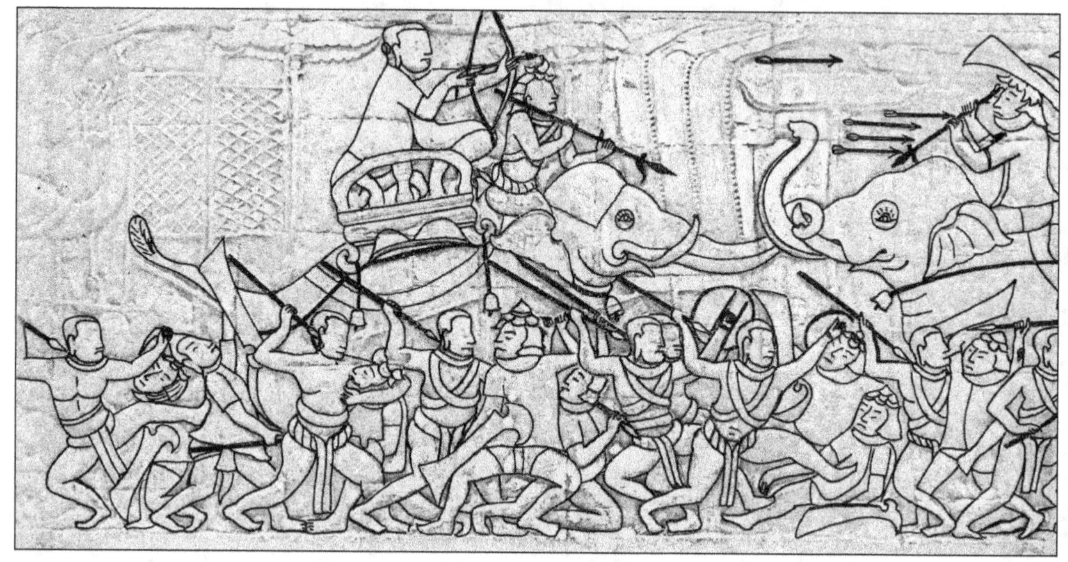

Fig. 108 Detail. Khmero-Cham combat.
Above – detail of left half of relief
Below – detail of right half of relief

Fig. 109. Khmero-Cham combat.
Bayon, ext. gal., E side, N wing, lower level. Dufour 124-5.

Fig. 109 Detail. Khmero-Cham combat.
Above – detail of left half of relief
Below – detail of right half of relief

7. Boats used in warfare

The representation of naval craft used in war, on their own or taking part in a naval battle, is found twice in the Khmer bas-reliefs we are studying: once at the Bayon on the end wall of the outer gallery, S side, E wing (Fig. 111), a scene whose portrayals of naval vessels can be linked to those in the same wing but farther west (Fig. 110), and those on some panels on the south-east corner of the same gallery. The other is found at Banteay Chmar where another naval battle fills a panel on the outer east gallery, south wing (Fig. 112).

These two great naval encounters will provide the basis of our study of Khmer naval craft; we shall not concern ourselves with other vessels which might appear on the bas-reliefs but which indicate civilian use.

On the two ensembles of bas-reliefs, the Khmer fleet is pitted against the Cham fleet. The Cham are clearly at a disadvantage in the furious engagements. At the Bayon, their vessels are invaded by Khmer warriors; one of the vessels is beginning to sink, and the Cham are tipped into the water on all sides; the losses they inflict on the Khmer are minimal.

Fig. 110. Cham naval attack.
Bayon, ext. gal, S side, E wing. Dufour 27.

At Banteay Chmar, the scenario is the same. The Cham are in complete confusion; the commanders prepare to flee and the oarsmen who normally row facing the back of the boat have all changed position as if they wished to leave their boats and flee as quickly as possible; their losses are considerable.

These two battles described by numerous authors have been compared to each other, and G. Coedès in 1929, in an article in *BEFEO*,[1] and again in 1932, in another article,[2] proposed that these bas-reliefs represented the naval victory of Jayavarman VII over the Cham invaders shortly after 1177, a victory which ended their occupation of Cambodia and was a prelude to the restoration of the country under the shrewd government of the new king.

This battle could only have taken place around the vital centre of the country, that is Angkor; it was therefore inland and possibly occurred on the Tonle Sap. The boats shown are, in consequence, light gellerys which we shall examine and we do not intend to advance further the meaning of the scenes depicted on the bas-reliefs.

In the two battles, on the Khmer side, 29 boats are shown, more or less completely. Often only the prow or the stern is shown, sometimes neither, but only the central part of the vessel. But of the 29 boats, 26 have at least their prow or stern represented, and 15 are complete.

These vessels have the same common characteristics:

(a) they are all low in the water;

(b) they are elongated, 'broad in the centre and tapering at the two ends' as Zhou Daguan has it;[3]

(c) 'they have no sails and can carry several persons; they are propelled by oars' as he says.[4] We should add that the oarsmen are replaced by paddlers. Rowers or paddlers are divided into two symmetrical rows.

(d) they are steered by a helmsman positioned at the rear end possessing one big oar which acts as a rudder;

(e) lastly, they are all laden with warriors ready for the fight.

The differences between the vessels are seen above all in the carvings on the prow and stern and incidentally in the ways they are propelled and protected.

Six types of Khmer boats can be distinguished on these criteria (especially the first). In describing these types we shall not repeat the general characteristics already covered, but will emphasize the originality of each (an example of each type is located in the photographic copies of the naval battles, Figs 110-112).

Type 1 (Fig. 113) is the simplest; it has no decoration on the prow or stern; they are plain. It is rarely seen; there is only one vessel and one isolated prow.

---

[1] G. Coedès, 'Nouvelles données chronologiques...' op. cit., p. 326.

[2] G. Coedès, Etudes cambodgiennes XXVII 'Quelques suggestions sur la méthode à suivre pour interpréter les bas-reliefs de Banteay Chmar et de la galerie extérieure du Bayon', *BEFEO*, XXXII, 1932, pp. 71-81.

[3] Zhou, *Mémoires...* op. cit., p.172.

[4] idem.

Fig. 111. Bayon, ext. gal. S side, E wing. Dufour 22-24.

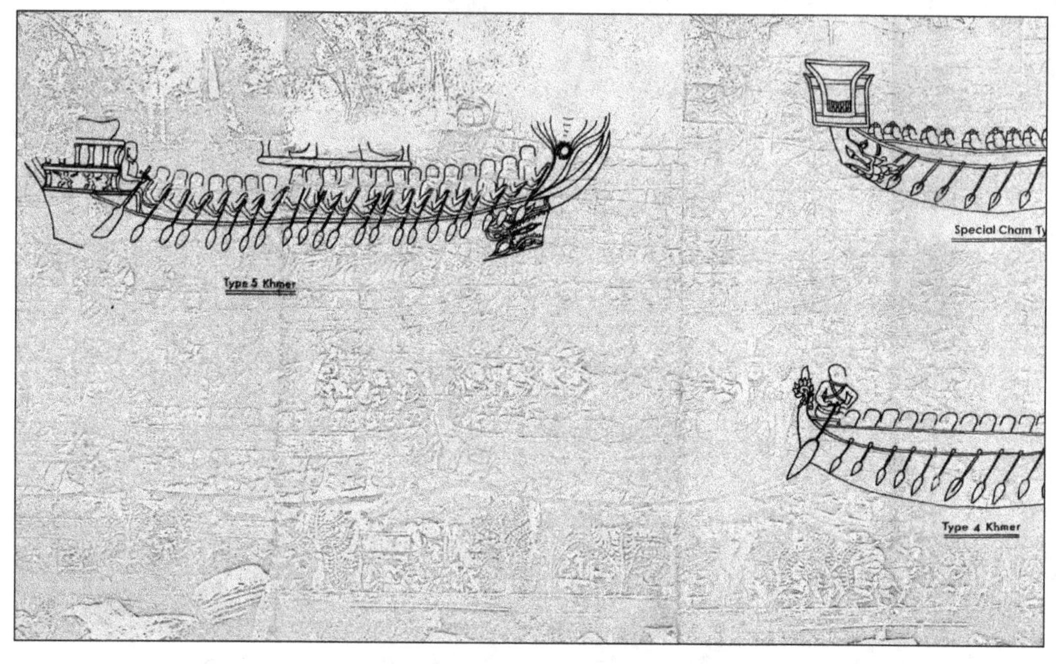

Fig. 111. Detail. Above – detail of left half of relief
Below – detail of right half of relief

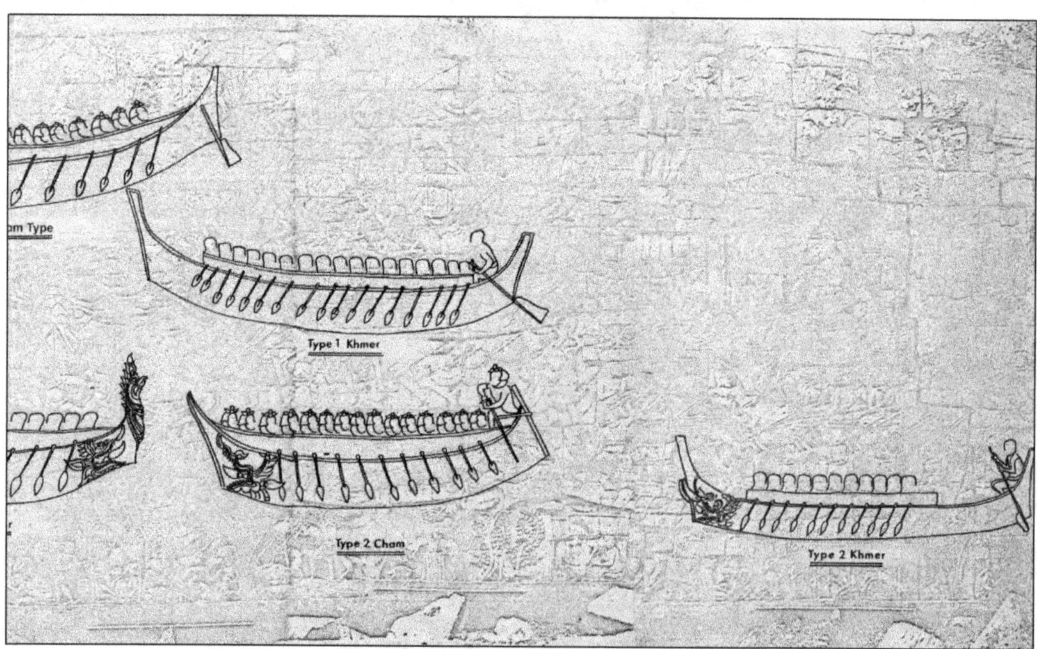

Fig. 112. Naval battle. Banteay Chmar, E gal.. Beylié 61-64.

Fig. 112. Detail. Above – detail of left half of relief
Below – detail of right half of relief

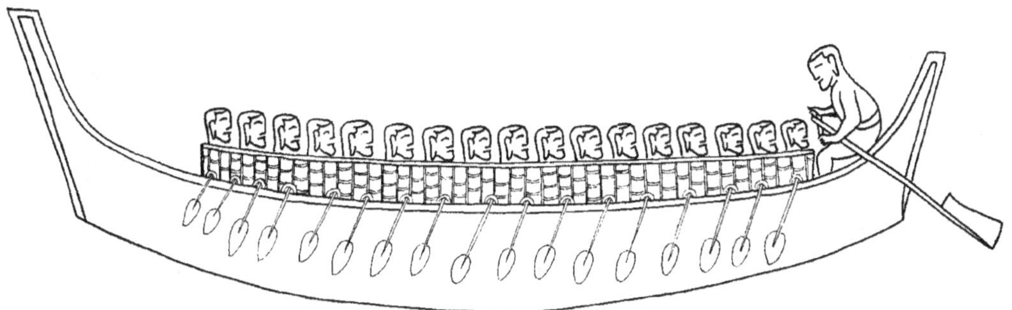

Fig. 113. Khmer war vessel. Type 1.
Bayon, ext. gal, S side, E wing, lower level. Dufour 22-23.

The second type (Fig. 114) has decoration on the prow in the form of a *makara* head, jaw open, with prominent tusks which perhaps serve as battering rams; but the upper part of the prow is as unadorned as the stern. This type is also rare, consisting of one vessel and two isolated prows.

Type 3 (Fig. 115) does not appear in any battles but is found on the panels of the south-east corner of the outer gallery of the Bayon. The prow has lost its *makara* but has a proud head of Garuḍa topped by oriflammes which we shall discuss later. The stern is raised and carved in what we can call a tail of a *nāga*, or perhaps of the Garuḍa. This type is found in two complete vessels and in six identical prows.

Type 4 is one of the richest and is most often found (Fig. 116). At the prow, the carved *makara* found on type 2 reappears, but sports in addition a Garuḍa or possibly a *haṃsa* head. At the stern is a motif similar to that in type 3 (Fig. 115). Six complete vessels of this type can be found, to which should be added two prows of the same type.

In addition to these four types, there are two exceptional craft, one at the Bayon the other at Banteay Chmar, which appear to belong to the commander of the Khmer

Fig. 114. Khmer war vessel. Type 2.
Bayon, ext. gal., S side, E wing, lower level. Dufour 22.

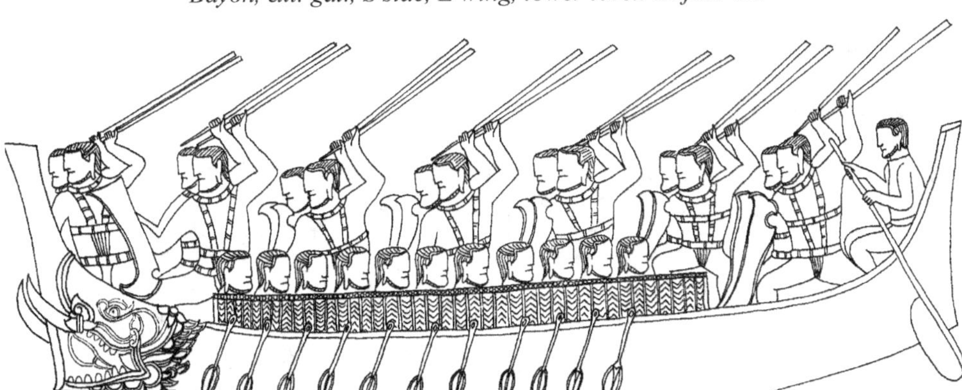

Fig. 115. Khmer war vessel. Type 3.
Bayon, ext. gal, S side, E wing. Dufour 18.

naval forces, Jayavarman VII himself, perhaps. Unfortunately they are both extremely difficult to comprehend because of the poor quality of the photographic reproductions and, at the Bayon, because the upper part of the bas-relief is missing.

The last of these (type 5, Fig. 117) has a *makara* at the prow with very long tusks which indeed look like rams. It disgorges what must be a many-headed *nāga* instead of a Garuḍa. At the stern is a quite richly decorated covered cabin. The steersman is in front of this. In the centre is what seems to be a platform where the commander should take his position, as will be seen at Banteay Chmar with the second exceptional craft (type 6, Fig. 118).

Fig. 116. Khmer war vessel. Type 4.
Bayon, ext. gal, S side, E wing, lower level. Dufour 23.

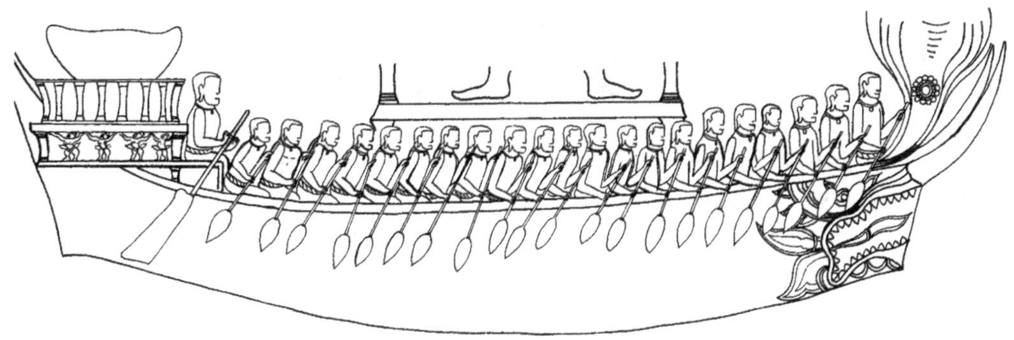

Fig. 117. Khmer admiral's vessel. Type 5.
Bayon, ext. gal., S side, E wing, upper level. Dufour 23-24.

At the prow is the same type of *makara* as before, with tusks like rams, also disgorging the same *nāga*, but the multiple heads give way to a small mitred feminine figure. G. Groslier[5] produced an approximate sketch. The stern curves back in the form of a *nāga*'s tail. In the centre is a balustrade, with *nāga*-headed ends, carrying the chief, armed with his bow and breastplate. This, and the previous vessel, is definitely a flagship.

Apart from these differences in the carvings on the vessels, giving rise to these types, as defined, they also differ in the various ways they are propelled, and in certain dispositions.

---

[5] G. Groslier, *Recherches....* op. cit., p. 110, fig. 72G.

Fig. 118. Khmer admiral's vessel. Type 6.
Banteay Chmar, E gal, upper level. Beylié 62.

On 29 vessels, 19 are moved by rowers with paddles, of which one can only see one row (Figs 113, 114 & 116). There is only one oarsman per paddle. Very occasionally, one can see the profile of the oarsman on the other side. The oarsmen face the stern. Their paddles protrude from rowlocks serving as thole pins, arranged between the upper level of the planking and a plaited wattle screen forming a washboard; this only allows one to see the heads of the oarsmen.

The paddles often have a fairly pointed tip; but sometimes they are rounded. The join with the haft can be seen in some of the types we have presented (Figs 113, 114 & 116).

In the stern is the steersman who may be provided with a low seat on which he is seated or squatting (Fig. 116). He holds a long oar which is used as a rudder. Its end is generally rectangular, broadening at the base (Fig. 113). The top end most often has a transversal bar which helps in handling the oar. It is placed either on the port or starboard side, as necessary. The occasionally curious positions taken up by the steersman, with his hands behind his back (Fig. 118), a position which some authors took to be that of a prisoner, since he often wears, like the foot soldiers, a loincloth wrapped round his body like shackles, is probably dictated by the manipulation of this batten-like rudder. The other ten vessels are those at the south-east corner of the outer gallery of the Bayon (Fig. 115) and the two exceptional ones (types 5 & 6) moved by paddlers likewise placed in two parallel rows (Figs 117 & 118). These paddlers, who may be seated or squatting (it is difficult to tell) are not protected by a rattan wattle screen like the oarsmen. Another difference is that they face the front of the vessel. The paddles lack handles and tillers, and their ends are pointed. The helmsman on these vessels is identical to those on the other vessels.

It is interesting to compare these Khmer vessels with the rival Cham vessels. The latter, in the two groups of bas-reliefs, only number 14, or half the number of Khmer boats. They are, like the Khmer vessels, more or less completely illustrated, and a dozen can be studied:

(a) their shape is not different from Khmer vessels;

(b) their decoration has the same themes. The most common is the Khmer type 2 (Fig. 114), that is, the single *makara* head on the prow and a plain stern. Six vessels have this decoration. We have illustrated one which can be seen in the Bayon in the naval encounter because of its forward-leaning sternpost (Fig. 119).

Three Cham vessels are close to the Khmer type 4. They are found at the Bayon, but outside the naval encounters, more to the west, and taking part in a kind of isolated attack on Khmer positions (Fig. 120); their occupants are getting ready to disembark, and further on, meet the Khmer warriors (Fig. 110). Coming after the great naval encounter, this scene may represent a final Cham attempt to seize the advantage after their naval defeat.

We have shown these vessels by a sketch because, except for the Khmer type 4, whose decoration they parallel, they are infinitely more carefully and richly carved.

We also illustrate one Cham vessel from the naval encounter shown at the Bayon (Fig. 121), because, in addition to the decoration of type 2, it carries a small covered

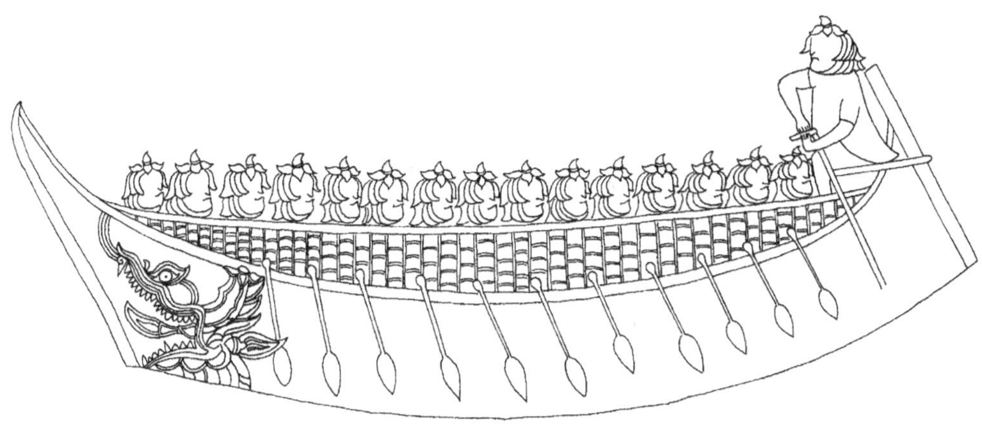

Fig. 119. Cham war vessel.
Bayon, ext. gal., S side, E wing, lower level. Dufour 22.

cabin at the prow, little different from that at the stern of the Khmer vessel of type 5 (Fig. 117).

All these vessels are propelled by oars; the oarsmen, protected by rattan screens, face the stern, as with the Khmer, except for three vessels depicted at Banteay Chmar which we have already discussed and whose oarsmen, probably to be able to flee more readily, all face the front.

The direction of the vessels is controlled by the steersman placed in the rear, who uses the same kind of large oar already observed on Khmer boats.

These similarities between the rival Cham and Khmer vessels seem to prove that they are not true copies of precise models.

Fig. 120. Cham war vessel.
Bayon, ext. gal., S side, E wing, lower level. Dufour 27.

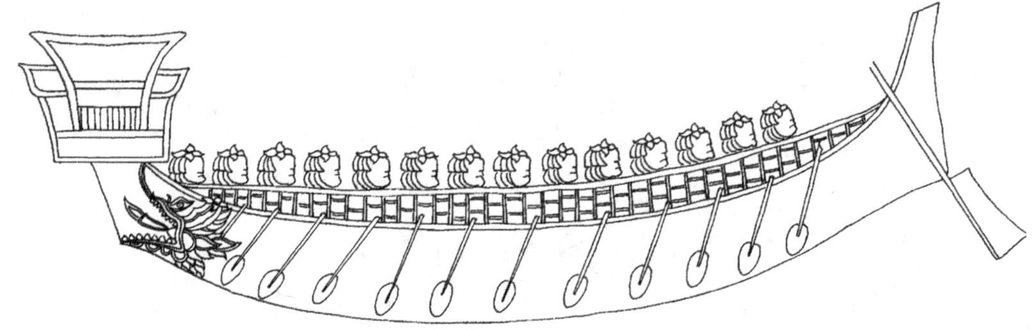

Having described the different vessels seen on the bas-reliefs, we now need to consider their likely dimensions, the materials used, and the manner of their construction.

A text dating from the Southern Qi (479-501), quoted by Pelliot in his article on 'Le Founan' gives the following details: 'They make boats eight or nine *chang* [in length]. They are five or six feet wide. The front and the rear are like the head or tail of a fish.'[6] Groslier[7] gives as corresponding to the Chinese measurements 24-25 m long, 1.5-1.8 m wide.

If one tries to get an idea of their size by counting the number of oarsmen or paddlers, or the number of oars or paddles, one runs into a serious difficulty: it is very rare that the two numbers correspond in any one vessel, Most of the time the numbers of oarsmen is larger than the number of paddles or oars that can be seen.

P. Paris[8] in his article on boats in Khmer bas-reliefs counts on average 13 oars on each side, supposing that at least one metre separates each oarsman, that makes 12 spaces of one metre, to which have to be added the front and rear ends of the boat. Paris calculates that one can estimate the length of the boat to be a minimum of 17 m. But it can be seen that in some examples (the boat located below type 5 in the naval encounter at the Bayon (Fig. 111) the sculptors, concerned about verisimilitude, perhaps, placed 23 oars in a space originally conceived for eight less, at the lowest estimate.

Taking this figure of 23 oars, the boats can reach 27 m, long, as proposed by Groslier in his transcription of the measurements of the Southern Qi texts.

For paddle-propelled boats, Paris indicates the same lack of certainty. The space between the paddlers can be reduced to 0.8 m. The flagship at the Bayon had 21 paddles (the most suggested), giving a length of 21 m.

Paris adds that the dugout canoes of contemporary Cambodia have 15 paddlers on each side and their length is between 20 and 21 m, which means it is possibly

---

[6] P. Pelliot, 'Le Founan' *BEFEO*, III, 1903, p. 261.

[7] G. Groslier, *Recherches...* op. cit., p. 111.

[8] P. Paris, 'Les bateaux des bas-reliefs khmers', *BEFEO*, XLI, 1941, pp. 335-61.

necessary to increase the dimensions proposed for the earlier vessels, especially taking into account the front and the rear.

At all events, apart from the vessels using paddles in the south-east corner carving, the two flagships propelled in this way, respectively at the Bayon and Banteay Chmar, seem to be at least one and a half times bigger than those propelled by oars.

Let us consider what might be the materials used for the construction of these vessels.

Zhou Daguan[9] informs us that 'the small vessels are built from a big tree which is hollowed out in the shape of a trough; it is softened by fire and widened by inserting pieces of wood; so these boats are wide in the centre and tapering at both ends.'

G. Groslier[10] notes the similarity between the vessels of this type in modern Cambodia, and proposed that the means of construction must have remained the same. He then listed a number of types of trees used today in the construction of these boasts: the *koki* (a hard wood resistant to water and to worms), the *khlong*, the *popel*, the *khnong*, and the *maysac*.

He added that all these trees reach great heights and that almost flawless dugout canoes can come from a 35 m bole. In addition, he said, there is virtually no need for caulking the vessels, but perhaps they were coated in shiny black varnish nearly always used for japanning hulls; this coating is produced from a resin of the *krul* tree, mixed with oleo-resins known by the generic term *chear-toek*.

It is possible and even probable that the carved figures on the prows and sterns were painted in bright colours, or gilded.

We think, then, following authors who have discussed the matter before us, that these boats were monoxylous, that is, made from one piece of timber. It is most unlikely that they were made of planks fitted together and caulked: the lines of the joints would have been shown by the sculptors, at least in a few samples. The only vessel which, in all the bas-reliefs, shows this construction detail (south gallery, east wing, Dufour 26) is of a completely different type. It is a kind of sea-going junk with high gunwales.

The boats we have just described are all full of warriors armed to the teeth (Figs 114 & 123). They are nearly all equipped with a lance and a round or long buckler. In a few rare cases, they have bows and arrows: this is, in particular, the case of the vessel below the flagship at the Bayon, which we mentioned on account of its large number of paddles (Fig. 111); there, in three rows, the warriors carry bows. There are also a few examples on a vessel at Banteay Chmar where the leader on the flagship also has one (Fig. 118).

The dress of the warriors varies. Among the Khmers it ranges from a short jacket together with a single loincloth wrapped in a roll around the hips, with the ends hanging

---

[9] Zhou, *Mémoires…* op. cit., p. 172.

[10] G. Groslier, *Recherches…* op. cit., p. 18.

loose in front, to just a loincloth, sometimes supplemented by another rolled around the torso, They never have a headpiece and their hair is cut and combed. Only the chief on the platform of the flagship has a cutlass (Fig. 118). The Cham, on the other hand, all wear the same dress we saw them with in the combats on land, together with their curious headdress.

The warriors, shown as one, two (Fig. 114) or even three rows (as with the bowmen at the Bayon), stand up between two rows of oarsmen in an area which could be called the gangway of the boat. They vary in number from fifteen to twenty.

On the two flagships, we have already noted that the commander stood on a raised platform. Paris[11] suggested comparing this platform to that on which the bowman stands on the dugout canoes engraved on bronze drums studied by Goloubew[12] (Fig. 122). The comparison is tempting. Paris adds that the 'objection that the superstructure, where the bowman is found, would make every monoxylon (or boat having the proportions of a dugout) unstable is not crucial, since a single-hulled dugout expanded by fire and water can be 1.8 m wide or 1.4 m in the waterline. Its cross-section is evidently a circular arc extended above the waterline by two tangential ends. This profile places the initial metacentre very high and it goes higher still when the boat dips... A vessel thus equipped and overloaded throughout its length by standing warriors on a central passage would not cease to be stable.'[13]

According to the rank of the warriors they transport, these vessels can also have honorific emblems; one often sees parasols on them. There may be only one or several. We have shown one above a person of high rank who is leading his warriors to a boarding on a Khmer vessel at the Bayon (Fig. 123). This person is bigger than the other warriors, which is a way of calling attention to him, here and in many other instances, on both the Khmer and Cham sides.

The boats can also carry standards at the prow and the stern, the form of which varies according to the nation the boat belongs to. When the standards comprise three vertical and diminishing bands, they are Khmer, and decorate the prow (Fig. 115). These cloth bands look rather like a flame of a candle being blown out. When they are Cham, they are also in three parts, but horizontal, in the Chinese fashion, without, though the pennants having jagged edges. They are decorated with florets, and are found at the ends of the boats (Fig. 120).

Lastly, we should say something about the tactics employed in these battles. It would seem that the aim was to seize the adversary's boats by invading them, killing their occupants, and throwing them overboard. At the Bayon in particular, there are several scenes of this kind, but one can see similar ones at Banteay Chmar. The boats are invaded and the Khmer warriors do their worst. The dead, mostly Cham, pile up in the water. Still at the Bayon, a Cham vessel is sent to the bottom while a Khmer vessel, in the thick of the fray, is harpooning a Cham boat using a technique which seems clear

---

[11] P. Paris, 'Les bateaux…', op. cit., p. 339.

[12] V. Goloubev, 'L'âge de bronze', op. cit., *BEFEO*, XXIX, p. 34, pl. XXVII, 1929.

[13] P. Paris, 'Les bateaux…', op. cit., p. 357.

Fig. 122. Magic boat. Bronze drum of Ngoc. Lu.
Figure reproduced from the drawing in pl. XXVII in the article by V. Goboulew, BEFEO,
1929, pp.1-16.

(Fig. 124): in front of the vessel, two men have succeeded in throwing two grappling hooks on the enemy's bows, tugging on the ropes attached to the hooks to pull the enemy vessel towards them and then invading it.

On this subject, at Banteay Chmar, in one of the boats, one can see two Khmers brandishing above their heads tools designed for the purpose of grappling (Fig. 112).

In all these scenes, it should be remembered, the furious nature of the combat is suggested by the large numbers of dead, especially Cham, found in the water. Moreover, at Banteay Chmar, the Cham, as we have said, beat a retreat by trying to free their boats from the fray.

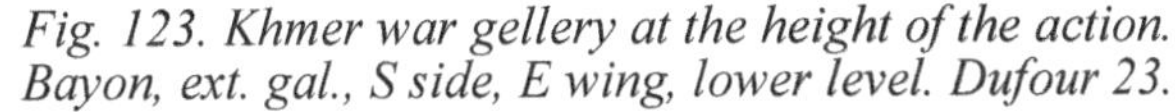

Fig. 123. Khmer war gellery at the height of the action.
Bayon, ext. gal., S side, E wing, lower level. Dufour 23.

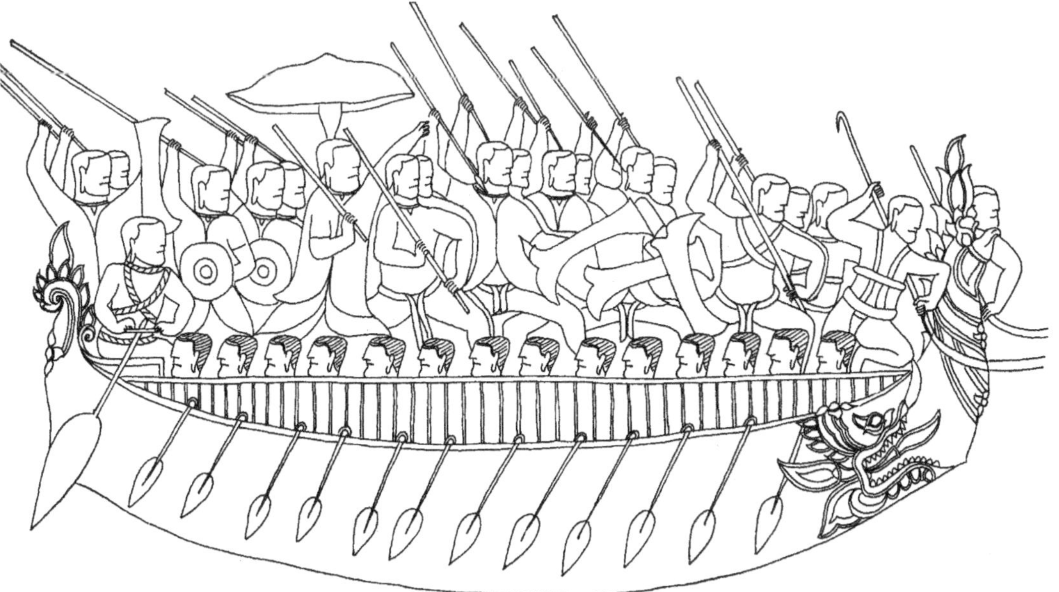

Fig. 124. Method of boarding enemy boats.
Bayon, ext. gal., S side, E wing, lower level. Dufour 22-23.

PART III

1. Military accessories

We mean by military accessories two things: one concerns military bands which mingle with the warriors; the other the bearers of parasols and insignia of different kinds surrounding the mounts of important persons in great numbers.

Military bands and musicians
There is one band in the 'historic' march past at Angkor Wat. It immediately precedes the bearers of what is traditionally called the sacred fire. A little before, other musicians accompany the litter of a non-military person who is given the title of High Priest, or Royal Sacrificer, his presence should cause no surprise since, as Quaritch Wales[1] has indicated, the Khmers, following the Indian example, considered war a sacrifice made to a god, under the auspices of the god.

The instruments themselves (Fig. 125) have, as the most important element, at the Bayon and Banteay Chmar as well, a heavy gong, a very large metallic disk, probably bronze, close to a metre in diameter. It is suspended by a ring from a horizontal bar carried by two men on their shoulders (Fig. 125A). The gong here has no particular decoration, and neither does the bar, the ends of which are slightly upturned. It is struck by a small person with two sticks with rounded and bent-back ends. Behind him can be seen a trumpet player (Fig. 125B) who, like all the others we shall see, holds his instrument aloft.

Mixed in with the other musicians, two other trumpeters can be seen (Fig. 125C) the instrument of one being more elaborate; the end part is like the opening of a shell.

Between the two trumpets are two conch shell blowers (Fig. 125D) who G. Groslier tells us 'were always used in royal ceremonies [and] used a shell coming from Chinese waters, having the anomaly of twisting from right to left, *khyang sing*'.[2]

Level with the two trumpeters (Fig. 125C) are two drummers. One of them (Fig. 125E) carries his instrument horizontally in front of his stomach; it is held up by a strap going round his neck, and the two drum heads are struck with two sticks. His neighbour (Fig. 125F) has a different type of drum, with only one drum head struck with the hand. The instrument hangs from his left shoulder by a graceful *nāga*-ended hoop, the rear fastening of which can be seen, as well as the top of the front fastening decorated with a *nāga*; the body of the drum with only a single drum head is long and well proportioned. Perhaps the musician holds the drum at his side by passing the left forearm though a cord not seen here and which would be tied to the body of the drum.

All of them only wear loincloths, some with pendant flaps, or 'breeches' held up by the loincloth. Their torsos are bare, and their hair is cut and combed.

Preceding the litter of the royal sacrificer, as noted, other musicians are ringing a

---

[1] H.G. Quaritch Wales, *Ancient South-East Asian Warfare*, op. cit., p. 85.
[2] G. Groslier, *Recherches...* op. cit., p. 128.

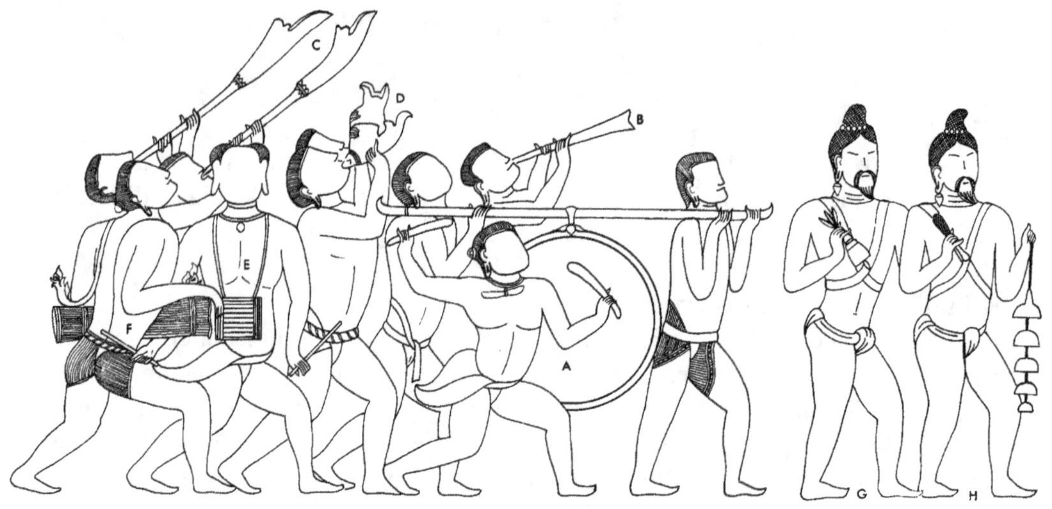

Fig. 125. Military band.
Angkor Wat, S gal., W wing, Coedès 549.

small bell with a handle, ending in a trident (Fig. 125G), many of which, Groslier informs us, have been found from the classic period.[3] They are, in this instance, ritual instruments.

Mixed in with these bell ringers are musicians who hold in their left hand a string of five bells suspended on a cord, which they strike with a small mallet wrapped in a plaited sheath, held in the right hand (Fig. 125H).

These musicians surrounding the Royal Sacrificer are pundits; their dress and coiffure are special.

All these instruments are either wind (conches and trumpets) or percussive (gongs, drums, and bells). They must have produced a shattering noise suitable to mark the rhythm of a rowdy army on the march, which the manifold bells on the elephants and horses must have made still noisier.

It is fairly certain that military bands were not limited to a single group, as is the case in the march past at Angkor Wat, but that, as at the Bayon and Banteay Chmar, one sees them all the time (Fig. 100), keeping time for the march or drowning out, with their racket, the shouts of the combatants, the roaring of the elephants and the neighing of the horses at the height of the battle.

At the Bayon and Banteay Chmar, the number of musicians attached to any one formation is variable. The essential element is, as noted, the gong, carried in the same manner as at Angkor Wat (Fig. 126A) and of similar size. Its surface is very often decorated with stylized leaf motifs and the outer edge is decorated with bands and

---

[3] G. Groslier, *Recherches... op. cit.,* p. 126.

142

beading. The bar from which it is hung is decorated with up-turned *nāga* heads at both ends which may or may not be stylized. In front of the gong, as at Angkor Wat, is a small person equipped with two sticks with rounded and bend-back ends, used to strike the gong.

Apart from the gong, there are generally, close to the gong carriers, up to three musicians playing instruments similar to those playing the trumpets at Angkor Wat (Fig. 126B, B1, B2); the form most frequently seen is in Fig. 126B2, but forms comparable to the other two are fairly frequently encountered.

All the bands also have one or several drums; some (Fig. 126C) are small in size, hung from a strap around the player's neck, and struck by the hands. Others, longer and well-proportioned (Fig. 126D) are hung from a strap passing over the musician's shoulder and are struck at one end only, again without using sticks.

As at Angkor Wat, there are conch shell players (Fig. 126E). Others play what seem to be both cymbals and castanets (Fig. 126F). Some hit with sticks a big bell hung at the neck by a string (Fig. 126G).

These last three musicians are very rarely seen at the Bayon and Banteay Chmar. The others are never met with all together. The essential element, as noted, is the gong which is always present. It may be joined by a drummer using one of the drums described, and up to three trumpeters.

The maximum number of persons in a band, including the two gong bearers, rarely exceeds seven or eight persons, and is most often closer to five or six: three with the gong, two trumpeters and on average one drummer, though the drummer is missing from the ensemble in Fig. 100.

Fig. 126. Military band.
Bayon, Banteay Chmar.

These musicians are dressed in the same fashion as the foot soldiers who are closely linked to them that is, in very different dress styles, with a propensity for the loincloth and the short vest. They are bare-headed at the outer gallery of the Bayon, but in the inner gallery they have the lotus headdress, also worn frequently by the foot soldiers in this gallery, as noted.

It is only the little gong striker who sometimes has a more elaborate headdress and loincloth slightly different from the foot soldiers and the other musicians (Figs 100 & 126).

Flag and emblem bearers

They are legion in the army, both on route marches and in combat, where broken or dangerously balanced emblems (Fig. 109) are always the sign of an imminent defeat of their bearers.

These bearers precede, surround and follow the mounts of important persons in the army, that is the warriors on elephants and the cavalrymen. With the exception of those who accompany the high-ranking cavalryman on horseback, in the outer gallery at the Bayon, that we have already discussed (Figs 127 & 103), a scene which is also found in the inner gallery (west side, north wing), and the Cham parasol bearers perched on

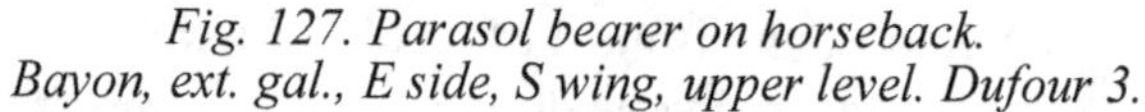

Fig. 127. Parasol bearer on horseback.
Bayon, ext. gal., E side, S wing, upper level. Dufour 3.

the elephants' rumps (Fig. 85), the bearers of honorific emblems only travel on foot. They cannot always be seen because the sculptors place them on the hidden flanks of the mounts they group around, or behind the foot soldiers who also closely encircle the mounts, for obvious reasons of clarity in the bas-relief itself. One mostly sees, especially at Angkor Wat, only a forest of shafts bearing various emblems forming a kind of backdrop and putting the army in relief.

These honorific emblems come in many forms. The most common, which can be seen everywhere on the bas-reliefs of all the monuments, are the parasols. Next come the standards which we shall see are much more varied at the Bayon and Banteay Chmar than at Angkor Wat. Then come the fans and the emblems in the form of effigies, mostly of the monkey Hanuman or the Garuḍa. To all these are to be added the unusual and inexplicable emblems that are only found at the Bayon and Banteay Chmar.

The parasols differ little from one monument to another (Fig. 128). They are all more or less the same and always seen in profile. They are rather shallow but the diameter is fairly big (probably 80 cm on average). The upper part is flat and decorated in the centre with an open lotus flower. The sides fall freely and are wavy; some of them seem scalloped (Fig. 128 A1) or doubled (Fig. 128 B1-3), which makes one think that some parasols were made of two thicknesses of material, not completely covering each other, and possibly of different colours.

Their construction seems fairly simple. They are placed at the top of bamboo shafts more or less depending on whether the parasol is meant for a warrior, an elephant or a cavalryman (inside any one group their height is also variable). The oiled material was fixed to a rod frame attached to the bamboo shaft by a series of rings (Fig. 128 A2 & 3). Sometimes the sculptor takes the trouble to let us glimpse the mechanism and in

Fig. 128. Parasols.
Angkor Wat, A: Bayon, Banteay Chmar, B.

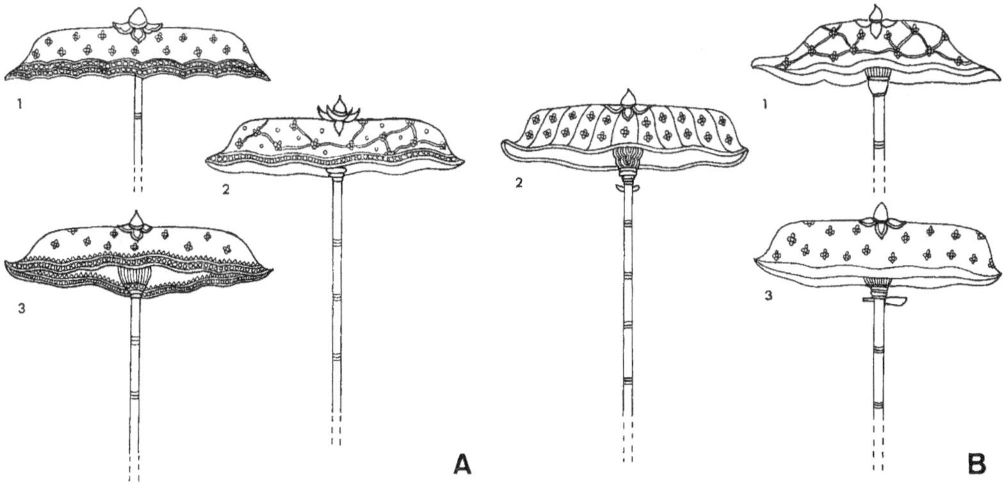

A

B

that way to see the rear underside of the parasol, but often the bamboo shaft stops at the front lower side of the material (Fig. 128 A1). At the Bayon and Banteay Chmar the sculptors often show the small pin which keeps the parasols open (Fig. 128 B2-3).

In addition to the lotus flower topping them, the open form of which can vary, the material is traditionally always strewn with florets, sometimes joined together by ribbon motifs (Fig. 128 A2, B1) or arranged in stripes probably corresponding to the gaps between the rods (Fig. 128 B2).

The edges, floating naturally or scalloped, are enhanced at Angkor Wat by a beaded selvedge (Fig. 128 A2), sometimes doubled (Fig. 128 A1) or decorated with a row of small leaves (Fig. 128 A3). At the Bayon and Banteay Chmar the edging is unadorned, but we have mentioned that the edges of the parasols were often doubled (in civilian use, a scarf is often tied to the top of the shaft; this is not usually found among the military). For their colour, Zhou Dagaun speaks of 'parasols in red taffeta'.[4] He also notes the 'white parasols set off in gold with gold handles'[5] of the ruler; white was his preserve. The golden handles were in fact 'wood covered with a thin piece of gold leaf without which a man could not have carried them'.[6]

The greater or lesser abundance of these insignia, according to the monuments, is perhaps linked to the nature of the scenes presented. At Angkor Wat the number of parasols surrounding the cavalrymen varies from three to six; for the elephants, it goes from six to sixteen. They complement the other insignia about which we shall speak. At the Bayon and Banteay Chmar, on the other hand, there are far fewer parasols (two to three) but this is offset by the abundance of standards and other honorific insignia we shall now consider.

At Angkor Wat, in the 'historic' march past, the standards seem to be like long pennants with a tapering end, attached to a long pole, which can be seen through the material. Only the end of the material is free and undulating (Fig. 129).

These pennants are not very wide and are decorated with a combination of standard themes: pearl-like rows of beading, florets in diverse forms, and leaf motifs. They almost always accompany the elephants, preceding them somewhat, and sometimes are mixed with other honorific insignia.

They can number between two and five around an elephant, but mostly come in twos or threes. Some groups of horsemen add to their parasols, the only insignia they usually have at Angkor Wat, a few of these pennants in groups of two to three.

We have said that bearers of insignia are never seen among the warriors. They are only seen at the 'historic' march past surrounding the holy fire and carrying in a very curious manner these long pennants which they amuse themselves with by balancing them in convoluted positions (Fig. 129); the pennants must have been very light. At Banteay Chmar only a few isolated pennants are seen among the parasols, whilst at the Bayon the standards are plentiful and have more varied shapes than at Angkor Wat; the pennant shape dominates, similar to the concept and form we have examined

---

[4] Zhou, *Mémoires…* op. cit., p. 148.

[5] idem., p. 176.

[6] G. Groslier, *Recherches…* op. cit., p. 83.

146

Fig. 129. Bearers of standards.
Angkor Wat, S gal., W wing, Coedès 550.

(Fig. 130C), or, on the contrary, they are more elaborate, ending in a kind of flag cut into three tapering bands, the central band being the longest (Fig. 130B), or else cut diagonally at the end with an added piece of tapering material (Fig. 130A), which lacks the flexibility of the ends of the Angkor Wat flames or the same form at the Bayon (Fig. 130C).

Their decoration, which makes one think of Chinese silks, often consists of scrolls of flowers and leaves covering the entire surface of the material, but it can be compartmentalized, each rectangle or each square being decorated with a flower in full bloom. The edges are always notched.

At the Bayon can be seen, in the east outer gallery in particular, another form of standard not found in the inner gallery. It consists of a band of material, on average twice as broad as the previous type and much shorter, decorated on the edge with tapering bands of cloth which seem to be added in most instances or, on the contrary, to be part of the very material of the standard (Fig. 130F, G). Three small pennants (Fig. 130D), often of trefoil shape, with notched edges (Fig. 130E-H), seem to be flags similar to the model in Fig. 130B, sewn on to the edge of the standard and sometimes extending the shaft (Fig. 130E-H).

Their vegetal decoration is the same as found in the preceding standards. The numerous combinations of floral motifs conceived by the sculptors makes them all original. We have only found one different from the mass because it combines a décor of lotus flowers with a small person difficult to identify (Fig. 130F).

Another honorific emblem is the fan. It is mostly used in civilian life. At the 'historic' march past at Angkor Wat, we have reproduced (Fig. 131) those which accompanied the generals, the commanders in the war, on their elephants and surrounded by parasols. We have not considered those surrounding the sovereign when he is still in his palace and the numerous fans accompanying the sacred flame and the Royal Sacrificer. The cavalrymen who have parasols have no fans. The most interesting are found near the person of King Paramaviṣṇuloka (Sūryavarman II) mounted on his elephant (Fig. 131B, C, E, H).

The others are seen around lesser military chiefs (Fig. 131A, F, G) in one of two examples, never more, while the king alone has eleven; the model of Fig. 131G is reserved for him only; this is closer to a fly-whisk than to a fan.

What strikes one in these fans is the variety of their shapes: oval, round, triangular, and tapering, and the wealth of decoration taking up the classic themes of Khmer ornamentation: beading, rows of foliage, lotus flowers, and florets. Like the parasols, the fans are attached to long bamboo poles.

At the Bayon and Banteay Chmar they are also found, in identical forms, but degenerated in design and décor, in religious ceremonies. None are found among the other insignia surrounding the long lines of warriors in the outer east gallery at the Bayon. On the other sides of this gallery we have found only a single example of a mount, an elephant in this instance (west side, north wing) surrounded not only by parasols and standards, but also by fans, belonging to types A, B, E, F, G, H at Angkor Wat, but similarly degenerate. This mount is that of a high-raking warrior (probably Jayavarman VII himself), whose dress we have already studied (Fig. 58E).

148

Fig. 130. Standards, Bayon.
Ext. gal., E side, S wing, Dufour 2 for sketch F.

149

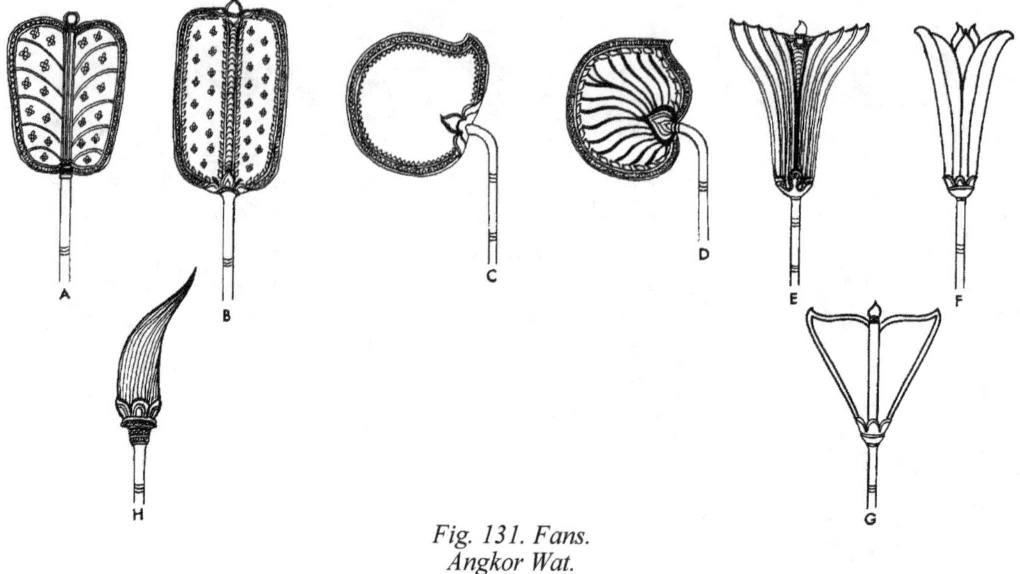

Fig. 131. Fans.
Angkor Wat.

In the inner gallery of the same monument there are also fans in a similar situation as the previous instance, around elephants taking part in mythological scenes; these are not relevant to our study.

To complete our consideration of honorific insignia, we must now discuss the standards. We understand by this term the small statuettes attached by one of their feet to a small base like a capital of a pillar, placed on a shaft.

In the 'historic' march past at Angkor Wat there are several preceding the warriors. Eight statuettes of Hanuman can be seen, two of Garuḍa, and a unique one showing Viṣṇu mounted on the Garuḍa, belonging to King Paramaviṣṇuloka.

In Thailand Bosselier[7] was able to study three bronze statuettes with similar characteristics to the models found on the bas-reliefs at Angkor Wat. They are attached to their base by only one leg; this base is like a lotus and notably is prolonged by a socket pierced at variable heights by two diametrically opposed holes, clearly intended to receive a pin to fix the statuette to the shaft. This led him to oppose the validity of the link G. Groslier made[8] between the representations on the bas-reliefs and two statuettes in the Phnom Penh museum, one representing a god, the other Viṣṇu on the Garuḍa. Their height of 12.5 cm could correspond to this use but the base of the first indicated a way of fixing the image with holes and rivets which seems inadequate for the top of a staff, and both have their feet on the base in passive postures.

---

[7] J. Bosselier, 'Note sur quelques bronzes khmers d'aspects insolites', *Artibus Asiae*, supplement: Felicitation volume for Prof. G.H. Luce, Ascona, 1966, pp. 30-36.
[8] G. Groslier, *Recherches*...op. cit., p. 83, fig.52.

150

The characteristic of these small statuettes used as standards is to appear vindictive, and all their attitudes are directed to this purpose: Hanuman (Fig. 132 A, B) is ready to leap on the enemy or brandishes his club; Garuḍa is preparing to fly off with a menacing eye and beak (Fig. 132C); when he is transporting Viṣṇu his attitude is unchanged, and the god holds his club in one of his four hands, the lower left hand (Fig. 132 D) ready to strike.

At the Bayon one can see many standards showing Hanuman alone, poorly executed. The attitude in which he is shown by the sculptors is the same as at Angkor Wat (Fig. 132A): his left foot is resting on the base, the other foot raised very high, arms in the air, and his face bearing a threatening countenance (Fig. 100). But very often in this attitude he is flanked by two small flame-shaped banners with serrated edges (on the front side) whose tips point in the same direction (Fig. 133A) or in the opposite direction (Fig. 133B). Hanuman can himself brandishes one of these small banners, whilst level with the base are found fringed streamers on each of his sides (Fig. 133C).

To all these honorific insignia must be added others only found at the Bayon and Banteay Chmar, which are difficult to identify. In the bas-reliefs of these monuments many elephants are preceded by standards showing lattice-work fixed on one or two shafts, ending in tiny pennants (Fig. 134 E, F).

Some authors saw in these a sort of protection against arrows used by warriors mounted on the elephants, but it is hard to see how they could have been of use in the tumult of battle. Moreover, the chain-mail, as shown, would not have impeded any lance or arrow. If they were to protect important combatants, they would also have obstructed their own aim. We propose no additional hypothesis to those already suggested, but merely indicate these forms and include them among the honorific insignia.

The same problem fairly often encountered with the insignia, is also observed in Fig. 134A, the lattice-work in which seems to turn on a triangle attached to the shaft by its tip: they are often seen in pairs at the Bayon, with the insignia of Fig. 134B, a kind of horizontal bar with projections, the shaft of which is sometimes decorated with a knotted scarf.

The insignia shown in Fig. 134C is only encountered at Banteay Chmar. It is almost the same as Fig. 134B but upside-down, if it were not for the lotus flower on the upper part. It is probably a very clumsy representation of a fringed parasol, some examples of which are found at the inner gallery of the Bayon; but this parasol—if it is one—seems extremely shallow. Its shaft is also often adorned with a scarf.

Lastly, the insignia shown in Fig. 134D is found at the Bayon: this takes the form of a small banner supported by a twisted hook, the shaft of which ends in a Śaivite trident.

This gives some idea of the enormous variety of honorific insignia accompanying the Khmer army in its journeys and combats. They probably had some sentimental value such as European armies formerly showed in connection with their numerous flags and banners, and to lose their standards, parasols or insignia during a battle would be considered particularly blameworthy and dishonorable. The losers in these

Fig. 132. Standards.
Angkor Wat, S gal., W wing, Coedès 533 for sketch
132C; Coedès 542 for sketch 132D.

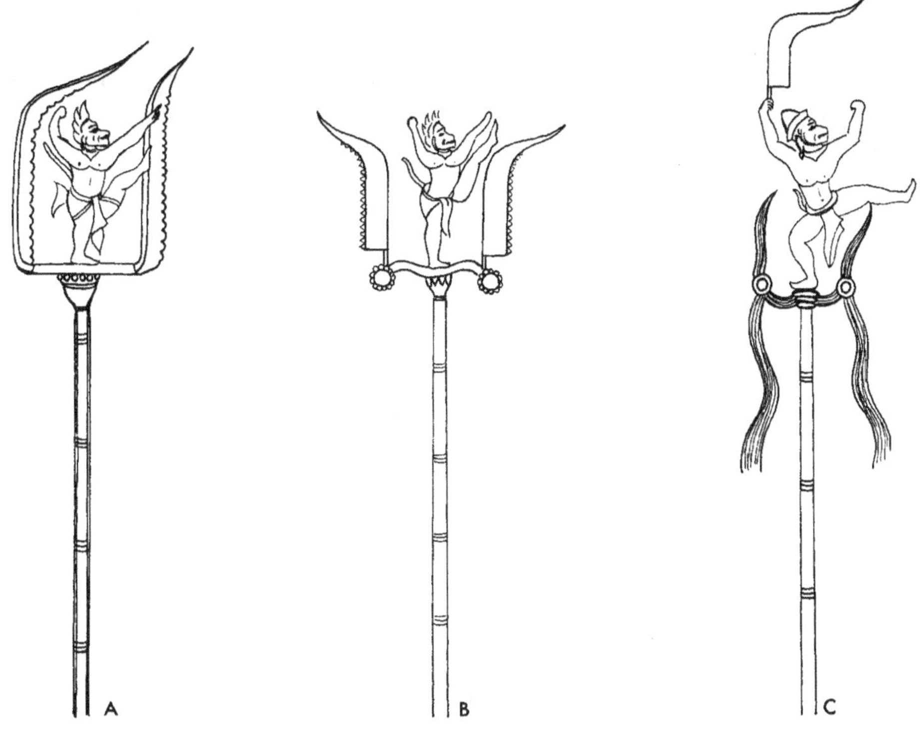

Fig. 133. Standards.
Bayon.

Fig. 134. Honorific insignia of uncertain identification.
Bayon, Banteay Chmar.

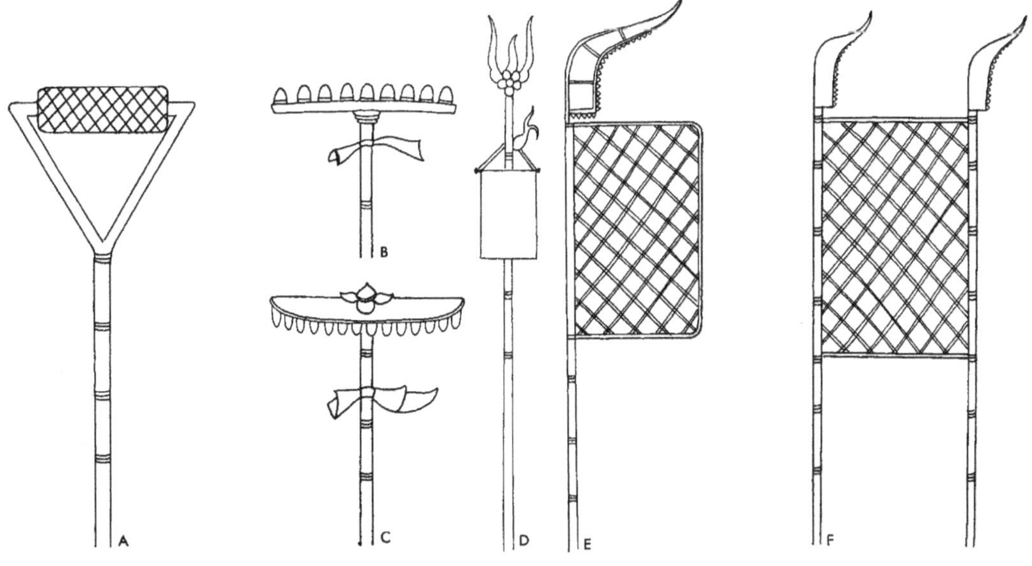

bas-reliefs, in this case the Cham, also had their insignia which were broken and trampled upon.

In all cases, the large number of insignia must have added much interest and colour to a motley army already remarkably diversified.

154

2. The 'commissariat'

At the Bayon and Banteay Chmar there are many bas-reliefs showing civilians, both men and women, alongside armed men on the march. This leads us to believe that there existed a kind of 'commissariat' in the Khmer army. The term is probably too exact; it suggests in our days a precisely defined organization aimed at supplying an army throughout a campaign, with victuals, weapons, and everything necessary to prolong the combat in the best conditions. This organization, very recent in European armies, certainly did not exist in the Khmer army; but the army did not go off trusting to luck when a campaign was decided upon, as we shall see.

The most suggestive groups of scenes for this are located on the south side of the outer gallery at the Bayon. There, on two of the lowest panels (Figs 135-6) one can observe, mixed in with the soldiers, a large number of men and women busy placing packs on the backs of several elephants accompanying carts drawn by buffaloes, and transporting all kinds of baskets, chests and various implements.

The narrative skill of the sculptors was well able to come to the fore here. The two levels of carvings are alive with picturesque details. On one of them (Fig. 135) two men hang behind to hunt game for the day with a bow, by climbing up trees, while another struggles to heat up his cooking pot beside two men drinking from an earthenware jar using straws; a little further on a woman is managing to carry her baby in her arms, a package on her shoulder, another on her head, and the lance of her husband. Still further on beside a mounted elephant, surrounded by marching foot soldiers, a whole family is assembled around its wagon: the father is pushing it from the rear and carries one of his children astride his shoulders, whom the mother protects from the sun with a parasol; another child pushes between the two wheels of the wagon what seem to be two sheep. On the other level (Fig. 136) there is the same atmosphere: a man is leading a young pig with a stick, while others cut to pieces a roe deer they have just killed. They chat, they point to each other with what seems the greatest good humour in the world.

We shall try to put some order in this pleasant confusion by placing alongside this key bas-relief other scenes taken from other galleries at the Bayon and Banteay Chmar.

Above all people had to feed themselves—though they did not pass up the chance of hunting, as we have seen—so they had to carry kitchen utensils and provisions; without any doubt. They had also to foresee bringing spare clothes and weapons.

How was all that carried? Apparently in many different ways. First of all, on the backs of elephants. We have earlier considered this animal at the height of battle; here, its activity is more peaceful. Its back is not bearing a howdah with an armed warrior or with a balista, but piles of bales and packets kept in position by oval wattles made of osier (willow shoots) secured by more or less faithfully carved straps (Figs 137-8). Mahouts are getting ready to guide them; a woman has positioned herself on the rump of one of them, sitting on a bale. Elephants so engaged can be found at Banteay Chmar

Fig. 137. Elephants laden with bales.
Bayon, ext. gal., E side, S wing, middle level. Dufour 6.

Fig. 138. Elephants laden with bales.
Bayon, ext. gal., E side, S wing, lower level. Dufour 6.

*Fig. 135. Scenes showing the 'commissariat'.
Bayon, ext.gal., E side, S wing, lower level. Dufour 6.*

Fig. 135 Detail. Scenes showing the 'commissariat'.
Above – detail of left half of relief
Below – detail of right half of relief

Fig. 136. Scenes showing the 'commissariat'.
Bayon, ext. gal., E side, S wing, middle level. Dufour 6.

Fig. 136 Detail. Scenes showing the 'commissariat'.
Above – detail of left half of relief
Below – detail of right half of relief

(Fig. 139), surrounded by foot soldiers marching five abreast; but in this example it is hard to fathom how the bales, looking like goat skin containers, do not fall off, since no way of tying them is shown.

Another way of transporting provisions, in carts, appears in many of the bas-reliefs. G. Groslier has described them at length.[1] When examining the war chariots we adapted the sketch he provided to illustrate the similarity of the two vehicles (Fig. 140). We shall not therefore describe them; their construction, the way of tethering the draught animals being the same as those we detailed for the chariots, as Figs 141 and 142 show.

There are only two differences between the two vehicles: the carts always have a simple osier roof (Fig. 142), or, on the contrary, a complicated design with upturned ends forming a canopy (Fig. 141); at the level of the axle of the wheels, outside them, is 'a horizontal bar which is slightly concave, assuming the shape of a runner of a sledge' (as Groslier has it), which, in an often marshy land, had the advantage of reducing the sinking of the wheels in the mud and facilitating the freeing of the cart. He stresses, with reason, the remarkable suitability of this vehicle for travelling conditions in the country, noting that the harnessed cattle are exactly in front of the wheels. He adds that this advantage is 'invaluable in the bush. The driver, often going over ground covered with weeds or water, can see where his animal goes and can, if it goes over a stump or falls into a hole, avoid the wheel hitting the obstacle. In the savannahs, where grasses

---

[1] G. Groslier, *Recherches…*, op. cit., pp. 96-98.

Fig. 139. Scenes showing the 'commissariat' mixed with foot soldiers.
Banteay Chmar, N gal., E wing. Beylié 77.

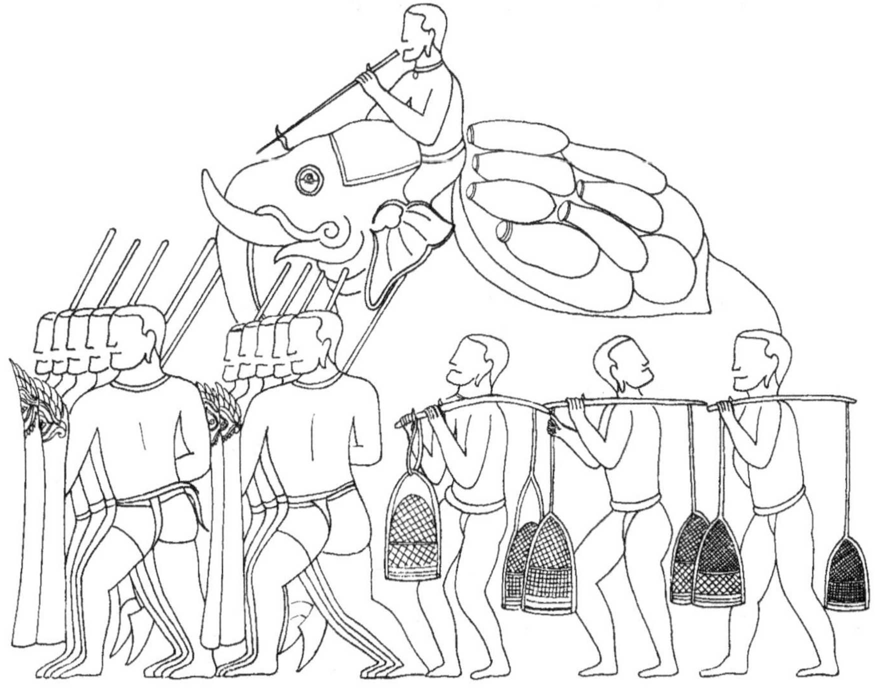

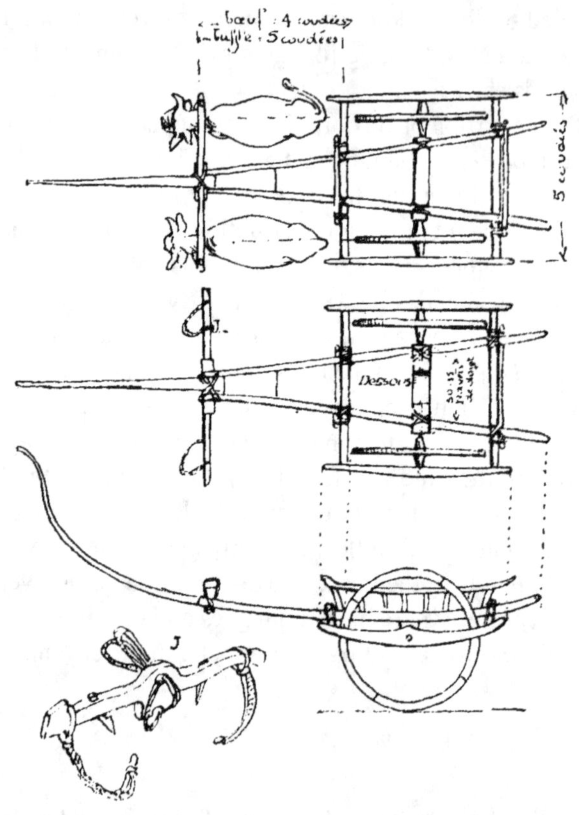

Fig. 140. Schema of a contemporary cart.
Fig. taken from G. Groslier, Recherches sur les Cambodgiens, *fig. 61, p. 98.*

Fig. 141. Cart being fitted out.
Bayon inner gal., N side, E wing, lower level. Dufour 118.

Fig. 142. Cart fitted out.
Bayon, ext. gal., E side, S wing, lower level. Dufour 6.

can reach 1.5 m high, the oxen prepare the path for the wheel by pushing the grass to one side, and avoiding any braking action.' This cart, so well adapted to the country and of such simple and cheap construction, since only wood is employed, is still used in Cambodia, as we have indicated, with the same dimensions, since, as Groslier remarked, the deep furrows in the paving stones of the carriage gateways at Banteay Chmar and Angkor Wat have the same spacing between them as contemporary carts.

Hump-backed oxen, harnessed in various ways, pull the carts, like the horses at Angkor Wat in Fig. 141, or, more simply, as in Fig. 142 where only the bridle bit is shown. The way of attaching the yoke is generally poorly indicated. The oxen often have a bell on a cord around the neck. The reins are held by a driver who stands on the cart's bars to goad the oxen that seem to labour so much that, very often (Fig. 135) they have to be helped by having the vehicle pushed from the rear.

The various bales and packets can be carried by men using the wooden shoulder yoke, a means of porterage still used and very frequently portrayed. In most instances it is straight and rests on the shoulder of the bearer who balances his two loads, hung from the ends by straps, or placed on a tray, as in the case with the cooking implements balancing the bales at the end of one of the yokes shown in Fig. 143. But most often (Figs 139-143) typical osier baskets were suspended by a series of straps holding them firmly in position; they are cylindrical and closed with a cover at the rounded top end. Some skill was probably required to carry packets in this manner without dropping them; at the Bayon, as the end of one of the levels of bas-reliefs we were discussing (Fig. 135), a woman is helping a man to secure his loads.

Sometimes the shoulder yoke bends (Fig. 144) and its ends turn up, and it is given what appears to be gourds as a load. This type, poorly rendered, is mostly seen in the

Fig. 143. Porters carrying loads.
Bayon, ext. gal., E side, S wing, middle level. Dufour 6.

bas-reliefs of the inner gallery at the Bayon, which, moreover, provide some charming scenes in the same vein as those already noted in the outer east gallery, but more clumsily rendered: we have reproduced the outline of the father loaded down with his children accompanied by his wife carrying on her shoulder a folded parasol (Fig. 144).

When the load was too heavy to be balanced and carried in this way, two men took charge of it. Each end of the yoke was placed on one of their shoulders; in this way, with the aid of straps, they could carry heavy quadrangular chests with short feet, richly decorated with foliated scrolls, as can be seen at the Bayon in the bas-relief of the outer gallery (Fig. 143).

Fig. 144. Porterage.
Bayon, inner gal., N side, E wing, upper level. Dufour 110.

Fig. 145. Various kinds of porterage.
Bayon.

Precious objects were also carried on platforms that were sometimes moulded, placed on two shafts with decorated upturned ends, borne on the shoulders of at least four men, surrounded by parasols (Fig. 144). In our sketch, the objects being carried were concealed from view by a curious miniature roofed shelter, like the upper part of a cart.

That is not the end of the way things were carried. The women, as noted, took part, balancing on their heads what seem to us heavy (Fig. 145A) or at least cumbersome loads (Fig. 145B).

The soldiers, too, armed or not, often carry on their shoulders the traditional Khmer bundle still used today (Fig. 145C, D). So necessary articles for the subsistence of the army on the march was assured by these diverse forms of transport.

The overnight stops took on the appearance of those frequently illustrated scenes throughout the bas-reliefs of preparing food (Fig. 146) and from which, strangely, women are excluded. The cooking utensils have been taken out and the men are getting ready to cook in pots, on curious Khmer grates, rice, freshly killed pork, and brochettes of meat placed on skewers over a big fire.

Perhaps, after the meal, the camp, which is never shown in the bas-reliefs, resounds with jousts and bare-fisted fights between some of the warriors wanting to show off their prowess in throwing the lance or their strength in the presence of their comrades in arms (Fig. 147).

Perhaps too, while the foot sloggers were amusing themselves, their stomachs filled, the head of the army gathered together his chief advisors to decide the course of the following day's activity (Fig. 148).
This is only an attempt as reconstituting, by means of scenes scattered though the bas-reliefs, what might have been army life apart from marches and battles. We shall

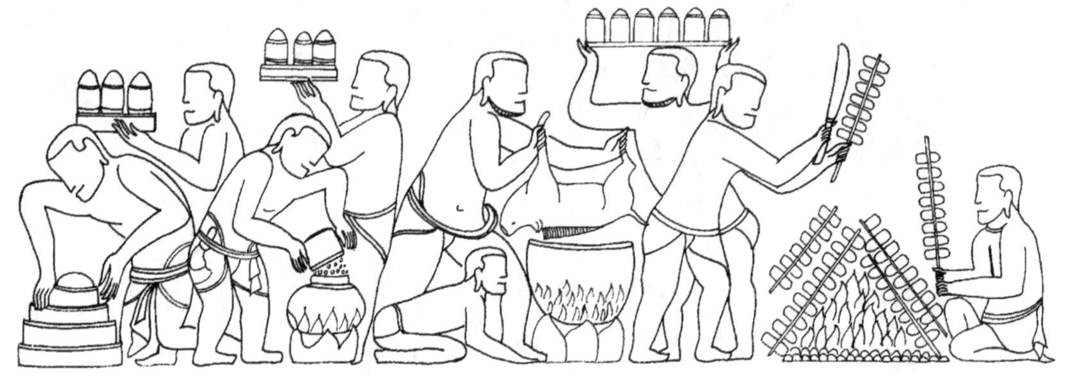

Fig. 146. Preparing food.
Bayon, ext. gal., S side, E wing, lower level. Dufour 29.

perhaps be accused of 'requisitioning' for military purposes scenes which have nothing to do with them: so be it.

Concerning the commissariat, we believe that, exactly like feudal European armies and even modern ones, there was no strict organization of this service in the Khmer army. On the contrary, everyone looked after himself: the chiefs called on their domestics, lesser beings sometimes took with them their entire family in a cart,

Fig. 147. Friendly fights among soldiers.
Bayon, ext. gal., S side wing, lower level. Dufour 26.

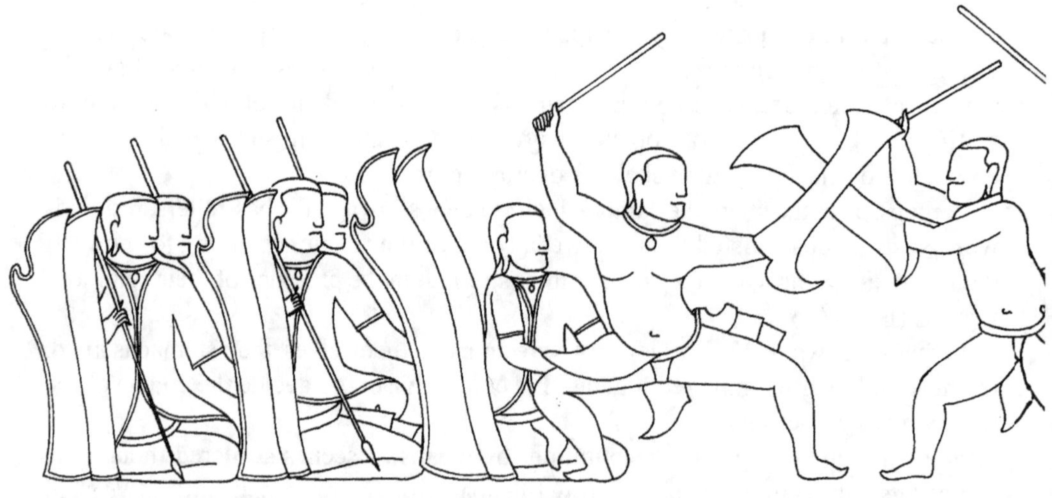

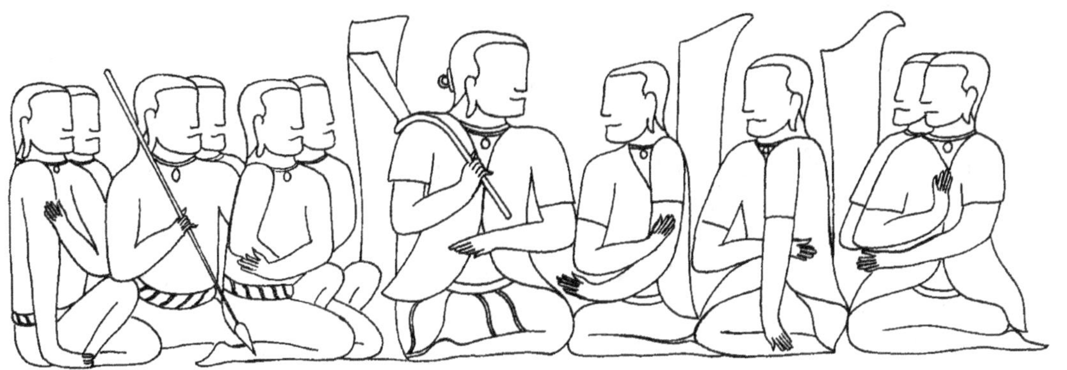

Fig. 148. Discussions among warriors.
Bayon, ext. gal., S side, E wing. Dufour 26, 27.

or what was recovered from the hunt or strokes of good luck; hence the picturesque nature of some scenes we have observed.

There are others just as good for local colour. These illustrate in several instances the inclusion of upper class women in the train of the army; it can be reasonably assumed that they were the wives or concubines of the military chiefs.

163

3. Camp followers

The scenes showing the camp followers do not only appear at the Bayon and Banteay Chmar, and chronologically we must first speak of those at Angkor Wat.

At the western end of the 'historical' march past, one can observe a collection of vehicles transporting upper class women, plentifully surrounded by their domestics. Do these vehicles form part of the march past proper? It is difficult to say: but the existence, in the other two monuments, of similar scenes, as we have said, which appear to us to be part and parcel of a route march, makes us believe those at Angkor Wat could represent the retinue of ladies who followed Sūryavarman II's army on military campaigns.

Fig. 149 shows one of two types of vehicles portrayed. Zhou Daguan[1] gave us in the thirteenth century a description of vehicles which is very close to this type: 'Their palanquins are built of one piece of wood which is bent in the middle and raised at the two ends. It is adorned with flower motifs and covered with gold and silver… At about one foot from each end a hook is inserted and a large piece of material folded several times is attached to the two hooks with ropes. One places oneself inside this cloth and two men carry the palanquin.'

---

[1] Zhou, *Mémoires…* op. cit., p. 172.

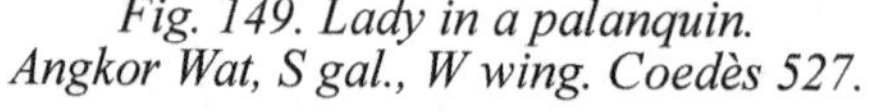

Fig. 149. Lady in a palanquin.
Angkor Wat, S gal., W wing. Coedès 527.

On the model of Fig. 149 the elegant curving of the shaft can be seen, with its splendid upturned ends forming many-headed *nāga* issuing from *makara* heads; decorative rings and carved hooks supported the hammock cloth covered with florets and with beaded selvedges. The whole ensemble exudes the most refined luxury. The richly attired lady seated inside is protected from the sun's rays by a roof such as appears in all representations of this type of palanquin. Built probably of light materials, it had two slopes and was supported at the point where the shaft bends by several men who were additional to those carrying the palanquin proper. There is exuberant decoration on this example; the slopes of the roof seem to comprise three distinct elements with their bases terminating in uplifted *nāga* heads. The roof ridge has decorative projections and the slopes have a décor of florets in squares and an ornamental central strip; small statues enliven this décor.

One would like to think that most of this decoration was carved in wood, but G. Groslier notes[2] his discovery of 'two splendid hooks and hammock rings' now in the Phnom Penh museum. They are made of bronze and, he says, are very heavy, which makes one think that this kind of vehicle was extremely heavy to transport. This discovery by Groslier is not exceptional and since then many bronze hammock hooks and rings have been found. At least eight to ten bearers of the Angkor Wat palanquin can be distinguished. Their precise number is quire difficult to determine as they are

---

[2] G. Groslier, *Recherches…* op. cit., p. 101.

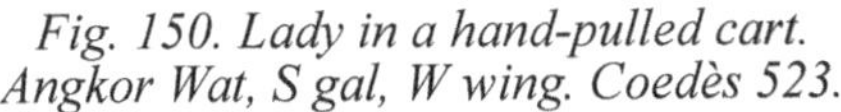

Fig. 150. Lady in a hand-pulled cart.
Angkor Wat, S gal, W wing. Coedès 523.

mixed in with a crowd of servants, parasol bearers, and fan holders accompanying the noble ladies.

These ladies could also be seated in another kind of vehicle (Fig. 150), this time on wheels, which has something of the simple cart and chariot about it. The cart is exemplified in the roof rising from the cart rails, the top forming a canopy; the chariot is equipped with wheels without the side runners which the carts have.

The richly attired lady sat on the front edge of the vehicle, her legs under her or dangling down. She was surrounded by parasol or fan bearers, and her ladies-in-waiting carried bottles and precious chests, ready to serve her.

The vehicle was not yoked to oxen but drawn and pushed by men. There were several women in their train and they form an elegant and colourful group.

At the Bayon scenes of this nature are more numerous and this time without any doubt are intermingled with troops on the march. This is apparent in Fig. 151, where two women carried in palanquins are followed by foot soldiers and preceded by the entire army on the march. This appears in part of the upper level of the east outer gallery, south wing, located immediately above the two levels which were considered when dealing with the commissariat.

Similar examples could be found in the inner gallery; however, the example we have cited in the outer gallery is the only one there, and also the best to be found in the monument.

Fig. 152A illustrates a type of palanquin found in the inner gallery, and is similar in its conception to that in Angkor Wat which we have studied. Its decoration is less rich; the ends of the shaft are transformed into stylized *nāga* heads, and the hammock is secured on one side by a ring and on the other by a hook similarly bent. The roof above the palanquin is again upheld by men, and is decorated with lotus flowers, florets, and stylized *nāga*. This somewhat simplified décor is characteristic of the bas-reliefs of the inner gallery. In some examples in this gallery the roof is replaced by a simple parasol.

The lady being carried has a lotus flower in her hand and her silhouette seems to stand out on a curtain falling at half its height, but it is not possible to see how it was held in place. It is difficult to distinguish between the porters, mixed up as they are with servants carrying parasols and fans. The clumsiness of the carvings in this gallery reduces the female attendants traditionally accompanying the ladies to tiny characters appearing below the hammock, who we have not shown.

The palanquin in Fig. 152B, an enlargement of the types of palanquins in Fig. 151, is closer to that of Angkor Wat with its richer decoration and the minute details of the host of servants of all kinds who accompanied the travels of one of these ladies. The bearers of honorific insignia are very numerous, as are maidservants, and to all these one must add the musicians of a band, some of whom we have shown in Fig. 152 A for ease of illustration. This band would not have the same tone as the military bands we have considered. It was designed to produce harmonious music and delight the ears of the noble ladies being transported. Two guitar-like instruments can be seen

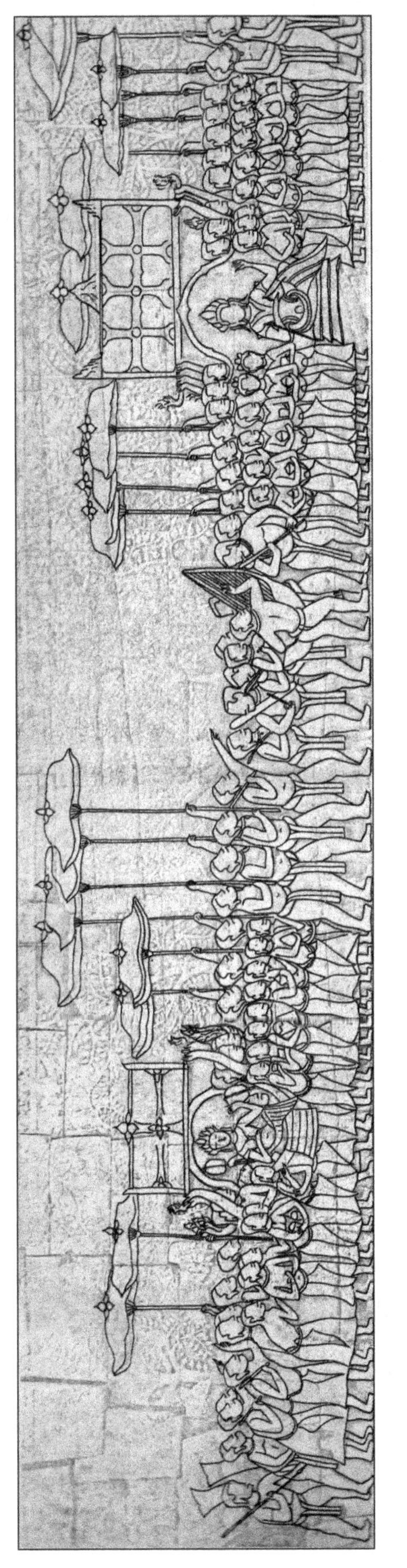

Fig. 151. Ladies in pa'anquins among the persons on the march in the army. Bayon, ext. gal., E side, S wing, upper level. Dufour 6.

Fig. 151. Detail. Above – detail of left half of relief
Below – detail of right half of relief

Fig. 152. Ladies in palanquins and their attendants.
Bayon, ext. gal., E side, S wing, upper level. Dufour 6.

(Fig. 152 A1, B1), fixed to a bamboo with a sound box formed of two hollow gourds placed at its ends (like a *viṇā*), a kind of violin with a short bow (Fig. 152 A2) with strings placed over a large tube, and a harp (Fig. 152 B2) with a long handle ending in a curved sound box; these are the only stringed instruments seen, as opposed to the wind and percussion instruments of the military bands.

All these details gradually bring to life a rather surprising atmosphere of refinement in the train of this army. At the Bayon hand-pulled carts can be found similar to those at Angkor Wat, though less elegant. The model in Fig. 153 is taken from the inner gallery, the only place they appear, and it is one of the rare examples with someone

Fig. 153. Lady in a hand-propelled cart.
Bayon, inner gal., E side, N wing, lower level. Dufour 124.

inside this type of vehicle in the Bayon. Other identical carts, also pulled by men, in action or not, are empty and appear to be connected with the omnipresence of a god. This emphasizes the fact that this is a vehicle for display, reserved for the gods and persons of noble birth.

The vehicle we discussed when considering chariots (Fig. 31), seen front-on in a bas-relief at the north-west corner pavilion at Angkor Wat, occupied by a god and given a roof, must be, in spite of being pulled by horses, a vehicle of this type.

In our example here, it is still pulled and pushed by men; the lady is seated at the edge, legs tucked beneath her. She is holding a lotus flower in her hand; her servants are close by; a parasol protects her from the sun's rays. This vehicle immediately follows a march past of foot soldiers under arms.

At Banteay Chmar, still among the camp followers, are found palanquins similar to those already considered at the inner gallery of the Bayon, and hand-propelled carts, but, beyond these, other vehicles having the same purpose, but not found in the other monuments.

Fig. 154. Lady in a litter.
Banteay Chmar, N gal., E wing, upper level. Beylié 74.

They comprise, firstly, litters. Four examples are found, one after the other, integrated into the army on the march, in the north gallery, east wing (Fig. 154).

G. Groslier[3] compares them to vehicles which still existed in his time in the stores of the royal palace in Phnom Penh, and which were used at the end of the nineteenth century for the journeys of the queen mother and princesses of the blood. He supplies a photograph (pl. VIIA) and notes that between the examples found in the bas-reliefs and that which he was able to photograph, only the way of attaching the shafts was different. He describes the vehicles in the bas-reliefs thus:

'A small platform mounted on shafts formed the base. The two big rosettes, probably of metal, provided sockets at right angles into which the shafts were inserted. A small triangular roof held up by four columns covered the passenger who was also hidden from view by curtains tucked into the curtain loops.'

The poor quality of the photographs available prevents us from drawing very precisely the decorative details of this vehicle, but they seem very rich: the ends of the shafts are decorated in raised *nāga* heads, the balustrade is carved, the base is decorated with telamons (perhaps geese, *haṃsa*), the roof is ornamented.

Of course, as always, the vehicle is shown from the side, which stops us from observing here its right side; only the outline of the porters on that side can be seen. They number eight in all (two for each end of the litter). The lady, kneeling and richly attired, holds a lotus flower in her hand. The number of parasol and fan bearers

---

[3] G. Groslier, *Recherches…* op. cit., p. 103.

Fig. 155. Special type of litter.
Banteay Chmar, W gal., E wing, upper level. Beylié 76.

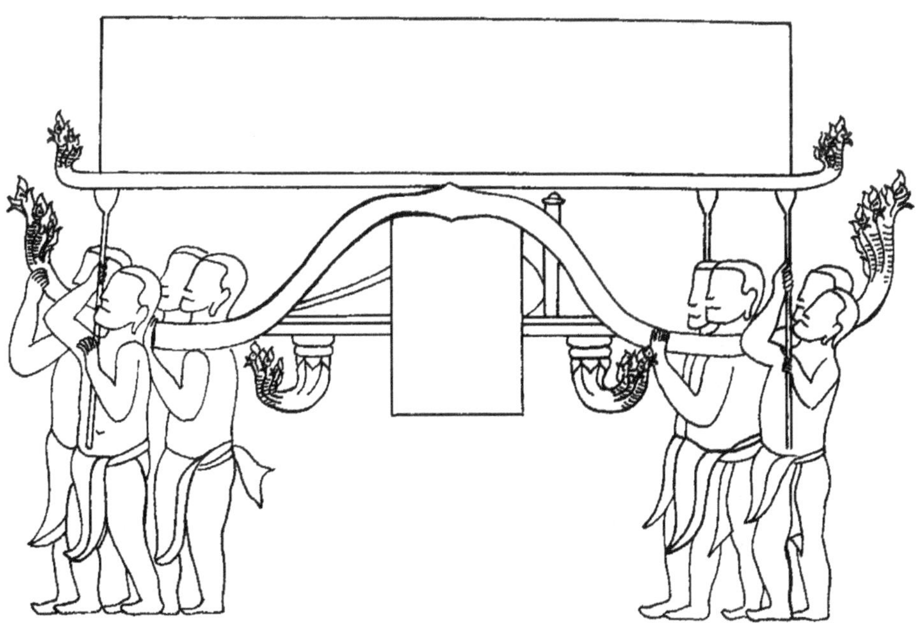

surrounding her litter, her numerous servants (we have shown only a few) attest to her high social rank.

Closely following these four litters is another of a different conception (Fig. 155). There is only one example, in poor condition, but apparently complete, but in any case too difficult to consider because of the poor quality of the photographs.

This litter, represented as ever side on, is only comprehensible if it is taken to be a platform resting on four upturned feet in the shape of *nāga* heads.

The platform is attached to two parallel shafts (only one can be seen), exactly similar to the palanquins already described, and borne by at least four pairs of men. The platform itself seems to be supplied with a cushion and a back rest of which the sides can be seen, but the person inside cannot be seen because of a lowered curtain.

To this is added what appears to be a dais covering the whole, and upheld by four shaft bearers. Apart from the end of the bottom of the dais, in the form of *nāga*, it is impossible to distinguish any decoration on the surface.

The different honorific insignia surrounding the litter indicate the high rank of the occupant, who may be a man or a woman. Small persons move around the litter, whom we have not shown; they carry bent sticks shaped at one end like a walking cane. They may be clowns. We consider this vehicle here because, like the others, it is followed by armed foot soldiers and elephants harnessed for war.

There exists at Banteay Chmar, in the west gallery, south wing, another vehicle carried by men (Fig. 156). This is unique. It is a kind of chair, that is, a platform with

Fig. 156. Open sedan chair.
Banteay Chmar, W gal., S wing. Beylié 30.

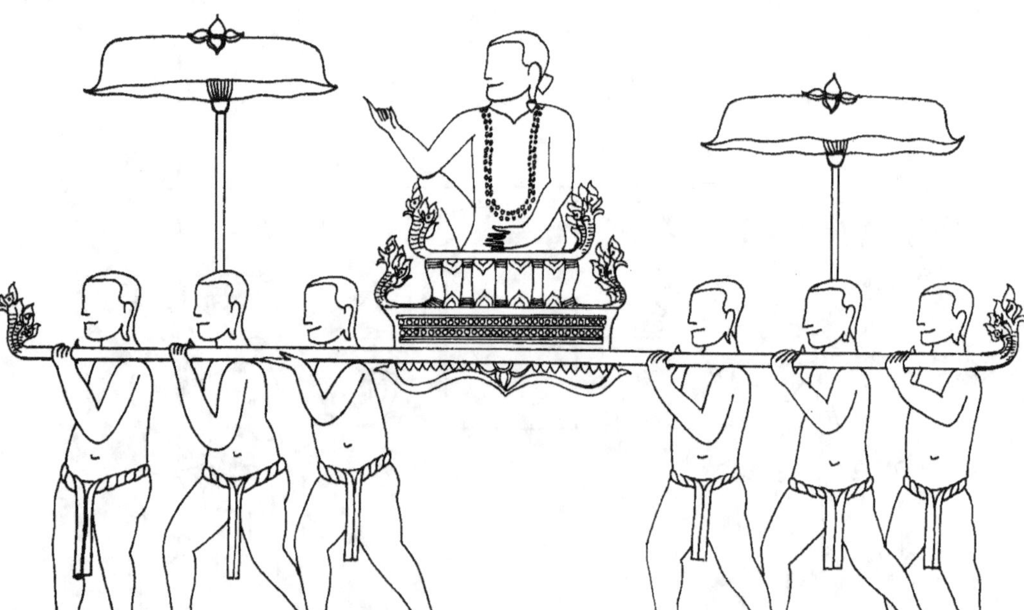

a balustrade, the side view and decoration of which resemble the howdahs of some elephants we have studied. It is upheld by a pair of shafts with the end in raised *nāga* heads, and borne aloft by twelve men, only half of whose feet can be seen. Under the chair are the bent silhouettes (not shown in the sketch) possibly of bearers of honorific insignia.

A man with a long necklace, probably a sign of his religious rank, is seated on the chair in the manner of those warriors mounted on elephants—he is seated on his left leg, the right is flexed. It is the only example we know, in the three monuments, of someone in a chair. Usually, as we have seen (Fig. 144), this vehicle transports precious or ritual objects. This train is preceded and followed by palanquins transporting ladies, followed by an army on the march.

Lastly we shall consider what seems to us a type of 'vehicle' capable of transporting women as with palanquins, litters, or hand-drawn carts, and who for various reasons wanted to follow the movements of the army. These are elephants carrying on their backs the curious howdahs equipped with a roof similar to those on the carts (Fig. 157). They are only found in several places at Banteay Chmar and they are always closely linked to the crowd of foot soldiers. The possible occupants of these shelters cannot be seen, but the presence, as in Fig. 157, of a woman seated on the rump of the elephant next to such a shelter leads one to suppose that it is being used to transport a noblewoman. This presence though is unusual, and for the most part, these curious

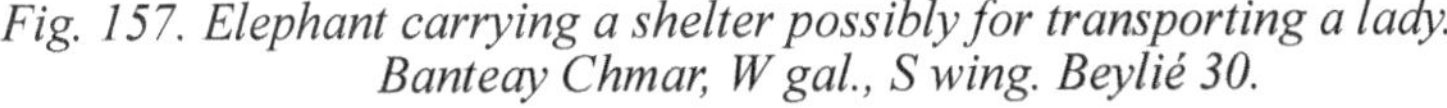

Fig. 157. Elephant carrying a shelter possibly for transporting a lady.
Banteay Chmar, W gal., S wing. Beylié 30.

howdahs only show a piece of rich cloth (Fig. 158) while preserving their mystery—are they a special form of transport of an upper class lady, are they carrying precious objects? We do not know.

Here we shall conclude listing the vehicles which probably carried ladies wishing to follow the army. The foot soldiers seem to have waged war and had their families follow them, so great is the number of women next to them in some bas-reliefs. If this were so, why should the chiefs not be followed by their wives or concubines? The texts sometimes make allusions to this, and perhaps the bas-reliefs confirm the fact.

Fig. 158. Shelters carried on elephants' backs, of uncertain use.
Banteay Chmar, N gal., E wing, Beylié 74, in particular.

Conclusion

From this study of the arms and organization of the Khmer army in the twelfth and thirteenth centuries, what can we deduce? The image of an army of its period and also its country.

This polity, at this time, as we have seen, made use of the most basic weapons, essentially lances, bows and arrows, and bucklers, sometimes in tandem with breastplates. It was only at the end of the period that the first 'war machines' appeared—and it is a very imposing term to use for the balistae with imprecise operating mechanisms which we saw on the bas-reliefs of the Bayon and Banteay Chmar. But the fact that these 'machines' were probably not native inventions proved that the Khmer desired to provide their army with the latest novelties in weaponry by borrowing them, as necessary, if they thought them useful, from their neighbours.

This army was also adequate for its country, the centre of which, the king's capital, and therefore of the army, was a plain allowing *a priori* for easy movement, but the soil was clayey or sandy in which it was easy to get stuck, and traversed by numerous streams and lakes which overflowed in the rainy season, transforming the land into a swamp. It was necessary that an army did not have to fear getting bogged down or floundering.

The Indian texts, which the Khmer certainly knew, proclaimed that an ideal army comprised four corps: the infantry, the cavalry, the elephants, and the chariots. Should they have had all four because the Indians said they were useful? Clearly no. The Khmer have always been selective in the lessons to be learnt from what they derived from the sub-continent.

There was no problem in having an infantry: the country had plenty of able-bodied men, and mercenaries could swell their ranks. The acquisition of a cavalry raised many more problems: horses had to be imported, perhaps from India—like those of the embassy of the king of Funan, Fan Zhan, received as a gift from the court of the Muruṇḍas around AD 230-240, most likely from China via Vietnam. This difficulty must always have acted as a restraint on the development of this corps. This is felt most acutely in the bas-reliefs of the Bayon and Banteay Chmar. As for the formation of an elephant corps, there were far fewer constraints, since the animals were available locally. There remained the problem of the chariots, since their existence assumed a certain type of vehicle and swift horses which the country could not supply. This last difficulty was not negligible, but the first was in our view insoluble. It required people to acquire swift vehicles in a country where one can only travel slowly because, as we have said, conditions on the ground were not conducive to speed, and also, perhaps, because Khmer never like to be hurried.

The chariots were abandoned, as we think we have demonstrated, and the army was built around a solid corps of elephants, surrounded by foot soldiers used from birth to march without fatigue and on whom reliance to win battles was placed, more, we believe, than on the elephants or the cavalry, which, as we have said was reduced to insignificance by the beginning of the thirteenth century, even if during the twelfth century it had been more important.

The army we have studied and described was thus composed according to Khmer criteria and not following an Indian model.

To this organization, reflected in its troops, the Khmer army added colour, which we can only imagine—in the clothes made from flowered and embroidered textiles, in the refined harnesses of the elephants, in the shimmering multitude of parasols, standards, and insignia. To this were added the sound which the troops, certainly loquacious, could well have done without; but as we have seen each elephant had at least five bells to which were added the deafening chords, marked by the boom-ing gong, of military bands throughout a route march. What a din that must have made! Enough to impress, and instil fear in the most valiant army. But perhaps this din caused less fear in the adversary than reassurance among its own ranks, helping them to overcome their own fears. We need to remember the role of some European military bands playing in the middle of battles, in the not too distant past. Colourful and noisy, this army was also extremely picturesque: think of the carts drawn by oxen followed by entire families, the yoke bearers and elephants tottering under the weight of their bales, not forgetting the camp followers of this army in richly decorated litters and palanquins transporting luxuriously dressed ladies surrounded by their female attendants and sometimes their string orchestras.

We are therefore most grateful to the Khmer sculptors for allowing us to bring to life again, through the interminable enclosing walls of their temples, these lively scenes which, for many centuries yet, we trust, will remind people that in the twelfth and thirteenth centuries in Cambodia one went to wage war with one's family, lance on one's shoulder, and buckler in hand, in an atmosphere of a village fair, and that the heavy elephants, which they tried to protect on all sides, were above all present to impress the enemy much more than deciding the outcome of the battles which were won or lost by the foot soldier

Bibliography

1. Photographic documents

de Beylie, Général, photographs of the bas-reliefs of Banteay Chmar (1913) deposited in the photographic collection of the Musée Guimet.

Coedes, G., *Le temple d'Angkor Vat*, 3 partie : *La galerie des bas-reliefs*, Paris, 1932, in folio.

Dufour, H. and G. Carpeaux, *Le Bàyon d'Angkor Thom. Bas-reliefs*, Paris, 1913, in folio.

It is necessary to add the new photographic documents of the Musée Guimet and those which were kindly lent to us by Mr Jean Boisselier.

2. Ancient texts

Coedes, G., 'Etudes cambodgiennes'.

    XI: 'La stèle de Pālhāl', *BEFEO*, XIII,6, 1913, pp. 27-36.

    XXIV: 'Nouvelles données chronologiques et génealogiques sur la dynastie de Mahīdharapura', *BEFEO*, XXIX, 1929, pp. 297-330.

Kangke, B. P., *The Kauṭilya Arthaśāstra*, 3 vols.

    Part I: *A critical edition with a glossary*, 1960;

    Part II: *An English translation with critical and explanatory notes*, 1963

    Part III: *A study*, 1965, Bombay, 1960-1965.

Kautilya, *L'Arthaśāstra* (extracts), Paris (Marcel Rivière), 1971.

Ma Touan-Lin [Ma Duanlin], 'Ethnographie des peuples étrangers à la Chine, II', *Méridionaux,* translation by Hervey de Saint Denys, Genève, 1876-1883.

Pelliot, P., 'Textes des Ts'i Méridionaux dans l'article *Le Fou nan*', *BEFEO*, III, 1903, pp. 248-303.

Tcheou Ta-Kouan [Zhou Daguan], 'Mémoires sur les coutumes du Cambodge', (XIIIe siècle), translation by P. Pelliot, *BEFEO*, 1902, p. 123-77, and a new version with an unfinished commentary, Paris (Maisonneuve), 1951 (Oeuvres posthumes, vol. III) (page references given are those of the 1902 edition).

3. General studies

Auboyer, J., *La vie quotidienne dans l'Inde ancienne*, Paris (Hachette), 1961.

Boisselier, J., *La statuaire khmere et son evolution*, EFEO (Saigon), 1955, vol. XXXVII, 2 vols

—*Le Cambodge* (Manuel d'archeologie d'Extrême Orient, vol. 1), Paris (A. and J. Picard), 1966.

Coedes, G., 'Les bas-reliefs d'Angkor Vat', BCAI, p. 170, Paris, 1911.

—'Etude des bas-reliefs décoratifs', in H. Dufour, *Le Bàyon d'Angkor Thom*, Paris, 1913.

—'Etudes cambodgiennes, XXIV, Nouvelles données chronologiques et généalogiques sur la dynastie de Mahīdharapura', *BEFEO*, XXIX, 1929, pp. 297-330.

—'Etudes cambodgiennes, XXVIII, Quelques suggestions sur la méthode à suivre pour interpreter les bas-reliefs de Banteay Chmar et de la galerie extérieure du Bàyon', *BEFEO*, XXXII, 1932, pp. 71-81.

—*Pour mieux comprendre Angkor*, Paris (A. Maisonneuve), 2nd ed, 1947.

—and J. Boisselier, 'La date d'exécution des deux bas-reliefs tardifs d'Angkor Vat', *Journal*

Asiatique, 1962, pp. 235-43, and with J. Boisselier, 'Note sur les bas-reliefs tardifs d'Angkor Vat', pp. 244-8.

—*Les Etats hindouisés d'Indochine et d'Indonésie*, Paris (de Boccard), 1964.

Commaille, J., *Guide aux ruines d'Angkor*, Paris, 1912.

—*Description archéologique du temple dans Le Bàyon d'Angkor Thom de H. Dufour*, Paris, 1913.

Dumarçay, J. and B-P. Groslier, *Le Bàyon. Histoire archeologique du temple*, vol. I, *Atlas et notice des planches*; vol. II, *Atlas et notice des planches et inscriptions du Bàyon* by B-P. Groslier; *mémoires archéologiques*, III, 1 and III, 2, EFEO, Paris, 1967-1973.

Filliozat, J., 'Le symbolisme du monument du Phom Bàkheng', *BEFEO*, XLIV, 2, 1954, pp. 527-54.

—'Le temple de Hari dans le Harivarṣa', *Arts Asiatiques*, VIII, 3, 1961, pp. 195-202.

Giteau, M., *Histoire d'Angkor*, Paris, 1974.

Glaize, M., *Les monuments du groupe d'Angkor*, Paris (A. Maisonneuve), 3rd ed., 1963.

Groslier, B-P., *Indochine, carrefour des arts*, Paris (Albin Michel), 1960.

Groslier, G., 'Banteay Chmar, ville ancienne du Cambodge', *L'Illustration*, 3 April, 1937.

Nafilyan, G., 'Angkor Vat. Description graphique du temple', (with Alex Turletti, Mey Than, Dy Proeung and Vong Von), *Mémoire archeologique, IV*, EFEO, Paris (A. Maisonneuve), 1969.

Nguyen Phuc Long, 'Les nouvelles recherches archéologiques au Vietnam', *Arts Asiatiques*, XXXI, 1975.

Parmentier, H., 'Les bas-reliefs de Banteay Chmar', *BEFEO*, X, 1910, pp. 205-22.

Renou, L. *Anthologie sanskrite*, Paris (Payot), 1947 and 1961.

4. Works dealing with the study of arms and armies

Bezacier, L. 'L'art dans les constructions militaires annamites', *Le Bulletin des amis du vieux Hue*, 28· 4, October-December 1941, pp. 323-49.

Boisselier, J., 'Note sur quelques bronzes khmers d'aspect insolite', *Artibus Asiae*, supplement. (Felicitation volume for Prof. G.H. Luce), Ascona, 1966, pp. 30-36.

Dikshitar, R., *War in ancient India*, Calcutta, Bombay, Madras, London (MacMillan & Co. Limited), 1944.

Goloubew, V., 'L'âge du bronze au Tonkin et dans le Nord Annam', *BEFEO*, XXIX, 1929, p. 146.

Groslier, G., *Recherches sur les Cambodgiens d'apres les textes el les monuments depuis les premiers siecles de notre ère*, Paris, 1921.

Jacques, C., 'Supplement au tome VIII des inscriptions du Cambodge', *BEFEO*, LVIII, 1971, pp. 179-95.

Lefebvre des Noëttes, Commandant, *L'attelage. Le cheval de selle à travers les âges*, Paris, (A. Picard), 1931, 2 vol.

Mus, P., 'Les balistes du Bàyon', *BEFEO*, XXIX, 1929, pp. 331-41.

Paris, P., ' Les bateaux des bas-reliefs khmers', *BEFEO*, XLI, 1941, pp. 335-61.

Quaritch Wales, H.G., *Ancient South-East Asian Warfare*, London (B. Quaritch Ltd.), 1952.

Sahai, S., *Les institutions politiques el l'organisation administrative du Cambodge ancien (VIᵉ-XIIIᵉ siècle)*, EFEO, Paris, 1970 (L'organisation militaire, p. 134-7).

Index